Patronage Pedigree and Power
In Later Medieval England

Patronage
Pedigree and Power
In Later Medieval England

Edited by Charles Ross

Alan Sutton
Rowman & Littlefield
1979

Alan Sutton Publishing Limited
17a Brunswick Road
Gloucester GL1 1HG

Rowman & Littlefield
Totowa, N.J.

First published in Great Britain in 1979 by Alan Sutton
First published in the U.S.A. in 1979 by Rowman & Littlefield,
Totowa N.J.

ISBN 0 904387 37 2 Alan Sutton
ISBN 0-8476-6205-5 Rowman & Littlefield

British Library Cataloguing in Publication Data
Patronage, pedigree and power in later medieval England.
    1. Great Britain-History-Richard II, 1377-1399-Congresses
    2. Great Britain-History-Lancaster and York, 1399-1485-Congresses
    I. Ross, Charles, b. 1924
    942.04   DA235
    ISBN 0-904387-37-2

Typesetting and origination by
Alan Sutton publishing Limited

Set in Stempel Garamond 11/12.5

Printed in Great Britain
by Redwood Burn Limited
Trowbridge & Esher

Contents

		Page
Abbreviations	. . . .	6
Introduction	. . . .	8

R.A. Griffiths
1 The Sense of Dynasty in the Reign of Henry VI 13

A.J. Pollard
2 The Richmondshire Community of Gentry
during the Wars of the Roses 37

Michael Hicks
3 The Changing Role of the Wydevilles in Yorkist
Politics to 1483 60

Carole Rawcliffe
4 Baronial Councils in the Later Middle Ages 87

Margaret Condon
5 Ruling Elites in the Reign of Henry VII 109

K.R. Dockray
6 Japan and England during the fifteenth century:
The Onin War and the Wars of the Roses 143

Alison Allan
7 Yorkist Propaganda: Pedigree, prophecy and the
'British History' in the Reign of Edward IV 171

Anne Curry
8 The First English Standing Army? Military
Organization in Lancastrian Normandy,
1420-1450. 193

Index 215

List of Abbreviations

BL	British Library
BIHR	*Bulletin of the Institute of Historical Research*
CCR	*Calendar of Close Rolls* (HMSO)
CP	(G.E.Cokayne), *The Complete Peerage* (new edition, ed. V.H. Gibbs and others, 13 vols., 1910-59)
CPR	*Calendar of Patent Rolls* (HMSO)
CS	Camden Society Publications
DNB	*Dictionary of National Biography*
EcHR	*Economic History Review*
EHR	*English Historical Review*
NYRO	North Yorkshire Record Office
PRO**	Public Record Office, London
R	
RP	*Rotuli Parliamentorum* (Record Commission, vols., 1832)
SS	Surtees Society Publications
VCH	*Victoria History of the Counties of England*
YAJ	*Yorkshire Archaeological Journal*

** The following classes of documents in the Public Record Office are designated by abbreviations:

(Chancery): C 1, Early Chancery Proceedings; C 43, Placita in Cancellaria, Rolls Chapel Series; C 49, Parliamentary and Council Proceedings; C 81, C 82, Warrants for the Great Seal,

Series I and II; C 136, Chancery Inquisitions Post Mortem, Series I, Richard II; C 142, Chancery Inquisitions Post Mortem, Series II, Henry VII-Charles II; C 237, Tower and Rolls Chapel Series, Bails on Special Pardons; C244, Tower and Rolls Chapel Series, Corpus cum Causa; C 255, Tower and Rolls Chapel Series, Miscellaneous Files and Writs.

(Chester, Palatinate of): Ches 1, Warrants, etc.

(Common Pleas): CP 40, De Banco Rolls.

(Duchy of Lancaster): DL 3, Depositions and Examinations, Series I; DL 5, Entry Books of Decrees and Orders; DL 12, Warrants; DL 42, Miscellaneous Books.

(Exchequer): E 34, Privy Seal for Loans; E 36, Treasury of Receipt, Miscellaneous Books; E 40, Ancient Deeds, Series A; E 101, King's Remembrancer, Various Accounts; E 143, K.R., Extents and Inquisitions; E 159, K.R., Memoranda Rolls; E 163, K.R., Miscellanea; E 175, K.R., Parliamentary and Council Proceedings; E 208, K.R., Brevia Baronibus; E 315, Augmentations Office, Miscellaneous Books; E 326, Ancient Deeds, Series B; E 401, Receipt Rolls; E 404, Writs and Warrants for Issue; E 405, Rolls and Books of Receipts and Issues.

(King's Bench): KB 9, Ancient Indictments; KB 27, Coram Rege Rolls; KB 29, Controlment Rolls.

(Prerogative Court of Canterbury): PROB 11, Registered Copy Wills.

(Special Collections): SC 1, Ancient Correspondence; SC 6, Ministers' and Receivers' Accounts; SC 8, Ancient Petitions; SC 11, Rentals and Surveys, Rolls; SC 12, Rentals and Surveys, Portfolios.

(Star Chamber, Court of): Stac 1, Proceedings, Henry VII.

(State Papers): SP 1, Domestic and Foreign State Papers, Henry VIII, General Series.

Introduction

This volume is the outcome of a Symposium on the history of late-medieval England held in the University of Bristol in July 1978. Many of those who took part were former students of history in this University. Others were invited out of friendship and common historical interests. A main aim was to produce an informal and friendly gathering in which some of the younger scholars would have the opportunity to read and discuss papers of their own.

No specific theme was suggested to the contributors. Nevertheless, as the title suggests, certain significant themes emerged naturally and independently. Perhaps the convergence of interests may be partly explained by the fact that all of us were, either directly or indirectly (even unto the third generation), pupils of the late K.B. McFarlane, whose teaching and writing inspired 'the only school that fifteenth-century historiography has had'.[1] Yet the interests of students currently working in this field have not stood still since McFarlane himself provided the first decisive switch of attention away from constitutional and administrative history towards a study of the roles of the crown and the aristocracy, and the interaction of the two, in late-medieval politics and society. His inquiries into the history of the nobility have now been extended. There is, for example, an increasing awareness of the importance of the gentry at all levels of political and social activity,[2] although, perhaps, it has been concerned with upward rather than downward social mobility. This particular extension of interest stands out very clearly in Dr. Pollard's anatomy of the influential gentry community in Richmondshire, North Yorkshire. It is also unmistakably reflected in the increasingly important role of the gentry in the counsels and councils both of the higher aristocracy (as Dr. Rawcliffe shows) and of the king himself (as demonstrated by Miss Condon).

The pre-occupation in several of these papers with 'pedigree' reflects another emphatic interest of the current generation of scholars in this field. It mirrors, no less, a major concern of the ruling classes of late-medieval England themselves. To inherit an accepted, or better still, an ancient pedigree was a natural mark of gentility. Those less fortunate had, in an age of social aspiration, to acquire gentility through marriage, especially to a gentle-born heiress, or by procuring for themselves that other mark of gentle status, an inheritance in land. At the highest political level, descent from a king raised its own special considerations. It is no coincidence that this period saw the emergence for the first time, round about the middle of the century, of the concept of 'princes of the blood royal'. Dr. Griffiths shows how problems raised by descent from Edward III cluttered the corridors of power during the reign of Henry VI (as indeed they continued to do later), to a degree which historians have not hitherto appreciated. Dynastic considerations, he suggests, may be a more important factor in the origins of the Wars of the Roses than is generally allowed. Connections with the crown — in this case through marriage — were no less important in the next reign. The special importance attached to ancient pedigree — real or imagined — in an age of dynastic uncertainty is most clearly set forth in Miss Allan's paper, which provides us with a glimpse into a curious world of genealogical paranoia. To buttress a legitimist claim to a usurped throne, the Yorkists were not above tracing their descent from the Creation, the Kings of Israel, the ancient Welsh princes, or St. Louis of France.

In the last analysis, however, except where dynastic changes were concerned, patronage mattered more than pedigree. Properly used, it was the cement of what McFarlane called (in terms of the ruling classes) 'a hard, mercenary and shamelessly acquisitive society'. Improperly used, as kings so various as

Richard II, Henry VI, Edward IV (posthumously) and Richard III (who had little room for manoeuvre) were to discover, it could be political dynamite. Dr. Hicks's discussion of the Wydevilles brings this much to the fore, and in the process presents Edward IV in an even more unfavourable and unstatesmanlike light than other recent studies have suggested. His indulgence to his grasping queen and her family, and the active assistance he gave to their self-interested projects enabled them to establish 'a regional hegemony and a powerful and committed retinue, thus becoming more than a court party', with serious consequences for the future of his dynasty. It was their personal influence upon the king, and thereby upon his distribution of patronage, which provided the key to their sucess. Miss Condon's learned inquiry into the ruling elites of Henry VII's England spells out the same lesson (although in reverse, so to speak). For Henry VII was indulgent to no one, save his mother and his uncle, Bedford. Even his close friends and loyal supporters were liable to fines and punishments, if the king saw financial or political advantage therein. Yet it was still those who had the king's ear who possessed the advantage. Edmund Dudley (Miss Condon tells us) 'used his title of King's Councillor as proudly as any peerage', because to be a nobleman no longer meant automatic access to the shining fountain of royal patronage. Competing aspirants for the king's grace and favour showered fees, annuities and sinecures on William Hastings under Edward IV, Richard Ratcliffe under Richard III, or Reginald Bray under Henry VII. The price was thought well worth paying to a man 'about the king' who could arrange to bring a private petition to the king's personal notice, and, perhaps, if the petitioner were lucky, incline his royal grace to look upon it with favour.

This lesson of prudent pragmatism was not ignored at other levels of the social hierarchy. Dr. Rawcliffe is able to assert with conviction that to be the councillor of a great nobleman was *ipso facto* to become a 'man of worship', 'to be courted by the ambitious and preferred above others in such matters as local elections to parliament'. The rank of councillor to the duke of Buckingham, the wealthiest of all English magnates, 'bestowed a tremendous social cachet, which in turn brought additional fees, patrons and opportunities for social advancement'. Even far from the centre of government, in North Yorkshire, to attract a lord's patronage was regarded as no less important. Tightly connected by marriage and descent, independently minded, bitterly resentful of outside interference in their affairs, the 'county' community of Richmondshire gentry, as Dr. Pollard shows, nevertheless fluttered like eager moths around the great candle-flame of patronage stemming from the Lord of Middleham, be he Salisbury, Warwick, Richard of Gloucester, or Gloucester-become-king as Richard III.

Two papers in this volume stand apart from all this concern with English domestic affairs, and do not fit into any titular formula. In discussing the comparisons and contrasts between England and Japan in the later middle ages, Mr. Dockray modestly makes no great methodological claims, merely (he suggests) an identification of some remarkable similarities in the evolution of two societies a whole world apart geographically but not dissimilar economically and socially. The contrasts are no less interesting. If England lacked the splendid succession of concubines and catamites so prominent in Japan (rather mutedly presented in Mr. Dockray's *written* text), at least she was spared the bloodshed, starvation and mass popular suffering which occurred during the Onin War. As the distinguished Welsh scholar, the late Professor R.T. Jenkins, once observed, the English civil war had its advantages: 'One beauty of the war: the people who were killed were the people who were responsible. A very wholesome war; very few wars affected the common man less'.

Finally, Miss Curry's valuable inquiry into military organization in Lancastrian Normandy provides us with a welcome return to a subject somewhat neglected of recent years. Fine studies of other aspects of the Hundred Years War have come from scholars like K. Fowler, C.T. Allmand, M.G.A. Vale, and J.W. Sherborne, but, as Miss Curry observes, 'Except in the work of R.A. Newhall, the army has not been the subject of an independent and specialized study'.

12

Perhaps one day we may hope for the grand English approach
to the wars already achieved for France by M.P. Contamine in
his monumental *Guerre, Etat et Société à la Fin du Moyen Age.*
All participants in the Symposium would wish to thank the
University of Bristol for the financial assistance needed
to make it possible, and the contributors to the volume
are no less in the debt of the publisher, Alan Sutton, and his
staff for their courteous and speedy cooperation. On a
personal note, I am most grateful to Mr. P.W. Hammond,
who has prepared the index.

University of Bristol, 1979.   Charles Ross.

* * * * * * *

1   DeLloyd J. Guth, 'Fifteenth-Century England: Recent Scholarship and Future
    Directions', *British Studies Monitor*, vii (1977), 16.

2   McFarlane himself was, of course, aware of the significance of this theme, but 'the
    rise of the gentry' becomes a much more conspicous affair under the Yorkist and
    the early Tudor kings, whose reigns have attracted much more attention from
    scholars in recent years. McFarlane's major preoccupations lay rather in the
    fourteenth century and the Lancastrian phase of the fifteenth.

The Sense of Dynasty in the Reign of Henry VI

R.A. Griffiths
Reader in Medieval History
University College, Swansea.

The importance of dynastic title and royal pedigree in the later years of Henry VI's reign is expressed unequivocally by the early-Tudor chronicler, Polydore Vergil, in his *English History*. Richard, duke of York (he wrote under the year 1452)

> aspired to the soveraintie, trusting to that title, whereby, as we have before described in the life of king Richard the second, thinheritance of the kingdome was to descend unto the house of Yorke. . . .

And later in his chronicle he referred to the year 1455,

> . . . when those two, that is to say, king Henry, who derived his pedigree from the house of Lancaster, and Richard duke of Yorke, who conveied himselfe by his mothers side from Lyonnell, sonne to Edwarde the Thirde, contended mutually for the kingdome. . . . But the source of all this stirre rose (as we have before shewed) from Richard duke of Yorke; for he had conceaved an outrageous lust of principalitie, and never ceassed to devise with himselfe howe and by what meanes he might compasse it; . . .[1]

In brief, Polydore Vergil's judgement (and in this he was followed closely by Edward Hall and other sixteenth-century writers, Richard Grafton among them) was that Richard of York had coveted the kingdom of England since at least the early-1450s, resting his title on descent from Edward III's second surviving son, Lionel of Clarence.[2]

In striking contrast are the opinions of two twentieth-century historians, writing quite recently about the same question. According to Mortimer Levine,

The Wars of the Roses did not originate out of any dynastic rivalry. . . . Whatever the secret ambition of Richard of York, . . . no dynastic issue was involved at St. Albans [1455].

And even more recently, Charles Ross has concluded:

The dynastic issue was not clearly raised until the return of Duke Richard of York from Ireland in the autumn of 1460.[3]

To put it equally shortly, Professors Levine and Ross are at one in denying that the dynastic issue had any significant part to play in precipitating civil strife in England during the 1450s. In other respects, however, their views diverge a mite. According to Professor Ross, the dynastic issue was 'not clearly raised' before 1460, though he does not deny that it may have been present, lurking in some men's minds. Professor Levine, more firmly, doubts that the issue was at all relevant to the early violence and battles of the 'Wars of the Roses' before 1455, though even he does not dispute that the matter could have occupied Richard of York's own mind.

The certainty of Polydore Vergil presumably arose from his determination to demonstrate that Henry VII and his Tudor successors united the two ultimately warring houses of Lancaster and York; in the process he simplified the issues prominent in the early stages of the civil wars so that the struggle to which they gave rise appeared to be a contest between Lancaster, who was determined to keep the throne, and York, who was bent on seizing it. The dynastic issue was reduced in Vergil's mind to an uncomplicated rivalry between the two. It is this simplification that is the historical distortion, not the chronicler's assertion that the dynastic issue was prominent well before 1460.

The views of Professors Levine and Ross probably arise from their conviction that we should shed the supposedly propagandist veil cast by Tudor historians about the origins of the 'Wars of the Roses', and accordingly relegate the dynastic issue (amongst other things) to a more discreet corner of the picture. That, too, distorts a true appreciation of late-Lancastrian politics. This paper attempts to re-assess the place of this dynastic issue in Henry VI's reign and, thereby, its relevance to the forthcoming civil war. The issue should be placed in a perspective rather different from that adopted by Polydore Vergil, Mortimer Levine and Charles Ross, both extending the chronological basis of the discussion (i.e., both before and after 1450), and by raising it beyond the confines of what all three writers believed they were observing, namely, a simple and direct confrontation, sooner or later, between Henry VI and Richard of York. In this connection it is worth re-examining contemporaries' conscious awareness of the importance of royal lineage and of the need to maintain and protect it, both for reasons of stability and because God-given qualities ought of themselves to be preserved — until, of course, events showed that what God had given he could also take away.[4] How conscious of lineage were contemporaries; how pre-occupied were they with dynasty; how strong a sense of dynasty had they? It may be suggested that the king and his ministers, the nobility, and even lesser folk, were far more conscious than is usually recognised of this wider 'sense of dynasty', and that it is this awareness which accounts for many of their political actions after Henry VI came of age in 1436-37. If this is so, then the dynastic issue should be brought back to the centre of the stage whenever the origins of the 'Wars of the Roses' are portrayed.

The dynastic stability, strength and cohesion of the house of Lancaster were a matter of permanent concern to many after 1399. It is worth recalling that, even in 1461, the Lancastrians had occupied the English throne for a shorter period of time (sixty-two years) than other Western dynasties had theirs since the twelfth century — in Aragon and Castile, France and Scotland, as well as England herself.

The succession to the English throne had been formally vested in the house of Lancaster by Henry IV's declaration of February 1404, as amended by statute two years later.[5] The crown would henceforth pass to the king's eldest son, Prince Henry, and to his heirs general; should they fail, then it would go to each of Henry IV's other sons in turn and their respective heirs general. The Lancastrian succession to the French throne was acknowledged by King Charles VI in the treaty of Troyes in May 1420.[6] It was vested in Henry V as Charles's adopted son and his heirs, that is, in the same line as the English throne, though Henry V's brothers and their heirs were not specifically mentioned in the treaty. The Lancastrian family met the dynastic challenge quite adequately at first: Henry V had a son, though he succeeded to both thrones at the dangerously early age of nine months; and Henry VI himself had a son, though of course he, Prince Edward, had no opportunity of succeeding to either.

Nevertheless, the Lancastrian succession to the English and French thrones was acutely vulnerable throughout almost the entire life of the dynasty. In the first place, it was an usurping dynasty, which inevitably meant that it would have its rivals: whether actual rebels who would attempt to overturn the usurpers (and there were plenty of those up to 1415), or potential challengers (most notably the line of Lionel of Clarence, which was senior in one important respect to that of Henry VI's own father, John of Gaunt).[7] Thus, an unequivocal and assured line of succession beyond the immediate heir was unusually vital to the Lancastrians, especially if the next heir or the king himself was a child (which was the situation after 1421).

No serious dynastic problem arose during Henry V's reign, even though he did not marry until 1420, when he was thirty-three (which was rather old by contemporary standard).[8] He had three apparently healthy brothers, Thomas, John and Humphrey, and then a son in 1421 when the king himself was still only thirty-four. After Henry V's unexpected death in 1422, leaving a nine-month-old heir, the dynastic importance of Henry's surviving brothers, John and Humphrey, became suddenly more immediate, though the succession to both thrones was not in dispute. The position of these brothers would be vitally significant if the child-king died before reaching adulthood, or before he married, or before he produced children. They were important in practical terms in ensuring the stability of the Lancastrian regime during the inevitably long minority ahead, when the government must needs be entrusted to others in place of the king. And they were important, too, in the task of maintaining the French inheritance of the young king, and completing its conquest; during Henry VI's minority these tasks had perforce to be someone else's practical responsibility.

The fate of Henry VI's three uncles demonstrates how vulnerable, dynastically speaking, the house of Lancaster was in reality. The eldest, Thomas, duke of Clarence, was killed at the battle of Baugé in March 1421 in the course of one of those reckless sorties for which he was renowned; although he had married, he left no legitimate or illegitimate heir.[9] The second brother, John, duke of Bedford, married Anne, sister of the duke of Burgundy, in 1423, but he left no legitimate heir either. He had, it is true, an illegitimate daughter Marie and a bastard son Richard; but although the son was legitimated in 1434, when it was doubtless evident that John was unlikely to father any more children, Richard strangely enjoyed no significance dynastically or personally as his father's heir.[10] Duke John's sense of dynasty goes some way towards explaining his rapid marriage in April 1433 after Anne of Burgundy died. The wedding to Jacquetta of Luxemburg was arranged within three months and in such haste that he was prepared to brave the angry disapproval of his brother-in-law, the duke of Burgundy, and manfully overcome his undoubted grief. When John died in September 1435 he still had no legitimate heir.[11] And the king was still unmarried and had no children of his own.

The third uncle, Humphrey, duke of Gloucester, married Jacqueline of Hainault early in 1423; then, in 1428, he discarded her in favour of Eleanor Cobham, an English lady who was one of Jacqueline's ladies-in-waiting and had been the duke's mistress for some time past. Despite his somewhat eccentric marital record, Humphrey had no legitimate heir — only an illegitimate daughter whose name, Antigone, he culled from classical reading, and a bastard son Arthur who owed his name to mediaeval romance.[12] Thus, after 1422, the heir to the

English throne had been John of Lancaster and his heirs general, followed by Humphrey and his heirs general. By 1435 the dynastic prospect had deteriorated alarmingly: John was dead and had left no legitimate heir; Henry VI, at the age of fourteen, was unmarried and childless; and even Duke Humphrey, now aged forty-four, had little likelihood of fathering the legitimate heir that had hitherto eluded him and his two wives — and this contemporaries realised when, from 1440 onwards, steps were taken formally to arrange the disposal of his property in the event of his death.[13]

The personality and political attitudes of Humphrey and his second wife, Eleanor, intensified contemporaries' concern for the succession, even while Humphrey still lived. It was fully apparent after 1435 that should Henry VI die, Humphrey would succeed to both thrones and Eleanor Cobham would become queen (for no previous English king had not made his wife queen). But (and this intensified the current concern) there was no further heir of the immediate Lancastrian family available and no likelihood of one in the direct line until Henry VI married. Then, too, Humphrey had acquired a formidable list of enemies over the past twenty years. For these two reasons, therefore, the prospect of Humphrey succeeding the young Henry VI probably played a decisive part in the scandal that enveloped his wife in 1441. Eleanor Cobham's eagerness to engage in astrology and magic, partly to discover whether the Gloucesters would ever reach the throne, partly even to hasten their sitting on it, seems to have been skilfully exploited by the duke's enemies. Humphrey was seriously discredited (though he remained the Lancastrian heir), his wife was exiled and (what is more to the dynastic point) their marriage was annulled so that she should never be queen nor produce a king.[14] The scandal of 1441 highlighted the fragile dynastic hold which the Lancastrians had on the English (let alone the French) throne, regardless of whether Humphrey himself was personally acceptable or not in certain influential quarters.

In these circumstances there was an imperative need to

fortify the Lancastrian house dynastically. Accordingly, discussions were soon being held to arrange a marriage for the young king — first in 1438 when Henry VI was seventeen, but especially after Humphrey had lost much of his political influence by the beginning of 1440. Eventually, an agreement was reached with the French in 1444 that he should marry Margaret of Anjou. It was demonstrably a slow process, either because suitable brides were in short supply in western Europe, or, more likely, because conflicting political counsels at home postponed a final decision.[15] Even with Henry married or about to be married, it was almost as urgent to fortify the dynasty less directly, though up to the point where the next heir could be indicated. This was a sensitive and delicate matter in view of the existence of a potential challenger of distinguished lineage, York, and the imprecision of the rules then governing the inheritance of the crown; certainly, there was no unequivocal law of succession to guide the thoughts of contemporaries beyond Henry VI and Duke Humphrey.[16]

Urgency was made more urgent by the surprising fertility of Richard of York and his stout-bodied wife, Cecily Neville. Starting with a daughter, Anne, in 1439 and a son, Henry, in 1441, in the thirteen years between 1439 and 1452 they produced eight sons and three daughters — not to speak of an after-thought, Ursula, in 1455.[17] A comparison with this prolific progeny would underline the extreme poverty of the Lancastrian family and increase the dynastic threat from Lionel of Clarence's line.

It was natural that Henry VI and his advisers should turn cautiously, yet unmistakeably, to the wider royal family of Lancastrian blood in order to secure dynastic support. The possibilities on the male side were reasonably encouraging. The Beauforts had been born illegitimately to John of Gaunt, Henry IV's father, and John, Henry and Thomas were therefore Henry's half-brothers and Joan Beaufort his half-sister. They had been legitimated in 1397 but specifically debarred from the royal succession in February 1407, after Henry IV in parliament had vested the crown in his squad of sons — of whom there then seemed an adequate supply. There was room for doubt about the validity of this act of exclusion, and it may even have been regretted by Henry VI in later years; there was also the possibility that it could be overturned by the letters patent which had established it, though that would admittedly have been provocative.[18] Among the Beauforts, the family's senior heir was Margaret, the daughter born in May 1443 to John, duke of Somerset, who himself died one year later.[19]

Secondly, the Holands were descended from Henry IV's full sister, Elizabeth, whose family in Henry VI's reign was represented by John Holand, duke of Exeter, until his death in August 1447, and then by his son Henry, who was seventeen when his father died.[20] In addition there may be added the Staffords, who, although not of the Lancastrian family itself, were descended from John of Gaunt's youngest brother, Thomas of Woodstock. Earls of Stafford since 1351, in 1444 Humphrey Stafford became duke of Buckingham.[21] To regard Lionel of Clarence's descendants, now represented by Richard of York, in the same light would have been to admit implicitly that Duke Richard had a better claim than the Lancastrians themselves to the English throne. It would have been tantamount to proclaiming themselves usurpers.

There are indeed indications that in the 1440s Henry VI and his advisers chose to ignore the duke of York as a possible heir to the throne. Instead, they seem to have espoused the Beaufort, Holand and Stafford families. Without openly preferring one, Henry advanced all three, though ultimately with perhaps some preference for the Beauforts. After all, Henry Beaufort, the cardinal-bishop of Winchester, still had formidable influence at court and in the council in the early-1440s, and his protégé, Suffolk, enjoyed the same later in the decade.[22] Marriages and noble creations were the two principal means employed by the king to achieve his design — and both lay at the heart of any sense of dynasty.

On 28 August 1443 the king's cousin, John Beaufort, earl of Somerset and grandson of John of Gaunt, was created duke, with precedence above the duke of Norfolk, in acknowledgement of his blood relationship to Henry VI.[23] A few months later, in January 1444, John Holand, earl of Huntingdon, was created duke of Exeter specifically (as the patent has it) because of his proximity of blood to the king; at the same time, he was given precedence over all other dukes save York.[24] (In August 1447, John was succeeded by his son, Henry Holand.) In September 1444 Humphrey Stafford was created a duke, only a few months after John Beaufort, duke of Somerset, died, leaving an one-year-old heiress. In May 1447 the new duke of Buckingham was given precedence over all who might in the future be created dukes, unless they were of the king's own blood; and this occurred only three months after the death of the king's heir, Humphrey of Gloucester. Buckingham, incidentally, was already married to Anne, the daughter of Joan Beaufort and the earl of Westmorland.[25] Humphrey Stafford, then, was created duke and given this special precedence specifically because he was close in blood to the king, and these steps were taken immediately after the impoverishment of the Lancastrian house by sudden death.

In March 1448 Edmund Beaufort was created duke of Somerset; he was the younger brother of the late duke and had already, during 1442-43, been raised in quick succession to the dignities of earl and marquess of Dorset; he was also, of course, uncle of the senior Beaufort heir, the five-year-old Margaret (I).[26] It is not without significance that Edmund's own daughter, also called Margaret (II), had married none other than the duke of Buckingham's son and heir in 1444.[27] When she was barely seven years old, the Beaufort heiress, Margaret (I), was married to John de la Pole, son and heir of the king's chief minister, Suffolk, early in 1450. Some at the time detected dynastic significance in this match as a possible route by which the de la Poles might reach the throne.[28] That suspicion in itself reflects the dynastic importance which contemporaries were coming to attach to the Beaufort family among Lancastrian relatives.

Margaret Beaufort (I) was a much-married lady. Her marriage to John de la Pole was annulled in February 1453 and soon after March 1453 she married the king's eldest half-brother, Edmund Tudor, who had been raised to the peerage in the previous November as earl of Richmond, one of the late duke of Bedford's titles.[29] Though Edmund could not conceivably have had a claim to the throne himself, this marriage would undoubtedly fortify the royal family and give it greater cohesion. Indeed, this may have been the very reason for the annulment of the de la Pole match. The apparent proof of this particular pudding, of course, lies in the accession of Henry VII, the son of Edmund and Margaret. Perhaps, as S.B. Chrimes speculated, this eventuality was perceived as a possibility by the childless Henry VI at the time the marriage was arranged; after all, in March 1453 it is just possible that it was not yet apparent that Queen Margaret was pregnant for the first time in her eight years of married life.[30] One may wonder, further, whether there is not an echo of this perception of Henry VI's in Shakespeare's *Henry VI, Part Three*, act IV, in the scene, there dated to 1471, in which the king is made to meet the young Henry Tudor and predict his accession to the throne:

> Come hither, England's hope.
> If secret powers
> Suggest but truth to my divining thoughts,
> This pretty lad will prove our country's bliss.
> His looks are full of peaceful majesty,
> His head by nature framed to wear a crown,
> His hand to wield a sceptre, and himself
> Likely in time to bless a regal throne.

Edmund Tudor died in November 1456. Margaret Beaufort (I)'s third (though by no means her last) marriage reflects how her dynastic attractions continued into the late-1450s. By 1459 she had married Henry Stafford, the second son of Humphrey, duke of Buckingham. This was a seemingly obscure union, but it should be remembered that Henry Stafford's elder brother, the earl of Stafford, had recently died in 1458, and that the new heir to the dukedom, the late earl's son, was still only eight and the old duke in his late-fifties.[31] The two family links between the Beauforts and the Staffords helped to buttress the Lancastrian dynasty, ensured unmistakeably that the Staffords would resist the pretensions of the duke of York, and pointed towards Beaufort blood as perhaps the best possible means of fortifying the Lancastrian line. May not this conclusion be echoed, not in *Henry VI*, Part One, act II (the scene in the Temple Garden where red and white roses are plucked by opposing factions), but rather in Part One, act IV, where King Henry is portrayed choosing the red rose in preference to the white, for a red rose is likely to have been a Beaufort emblem by this time?[32] If this is so, and if contemporaries' dynastic preoccupation was as strong as it appears, then one may restore some sense of contemporary reality to the concept of 'The Wars of the Roses', of which Professor Chrimes has sought to deprive it.[33]

Before examining the duke of York's reaction to these Lancastrian designs, it is worth considering a few indirect reflections of the importance which King Henry attached to his dynasty's lineal security.

During 1445-46 negotiations were underway between York and King Charles VII of France for the marriage of York's three-year-old son, Edward, to a French princess. Charles offered his fourth daughter, Madeleine (who was all of one-and-a-half), even though his second daughter, Jeanne, was still unmarried. Understandably, York preferred Jeanne's hand, as he explained in a letter to the French king in June 1445. The environment in which the negotiations were taking place changed dramatically when the Dauphin Louis's wife, Margaret of Scotland, died in August 1445. By December, York had withdrawn his request for Jeanne's hand and had accepted Madeleine's. But he was too late. The French king's concern was now focussed on his still childless and recently widowed eldest son and heir, Louis, and nothing further is heard of the proposed Yorkist match. Rather did Charles VII's eyes light on one of the duke of Buckingham's daughters (and his two eldest daughters were still unbetrothed in 1445) as perhaps as close and suitable a link as was possible with a

Lancastrian royal family which Margaret of Anjou had recently joined.[35] The creation of Buckingham as a duke little more than a year earlier may have been read as a dynastic signal by Charles VII in 1445. This may, indeed, be the reason why the negotiations with York were broken off, rather than because, after two years of open discussion, Henry VI intervened to prevent a Valois marriage with the house of York (which was Miss Scofield's view).[36] A Stafford match would have seemed the best possibility to Charles VII in 1445: Margaret Beaufort (I) was barely three years old, and the daughter of Edmund Beaufort, the new earl of Somerset, was already married to Buckingham's own son and heir. Charles VII's plan eventually fell through only because the Dauphin had other ideas — much to his father's annoyance.

The second indirect piece of evidence is provided by the researches of T.B. Pugh.[37] He has noted that the largest sum by far known to have been paid by a nobleman in late-mediaeval England to purchase a husband for his daughter was the 6,500 marks which York agreed to pay as dowry in August 1445. The contract allowed his eldest daughter, Anne, to marry the son and heir of John Holand, who had been created duke of Exeter the previous year. Aside from the Beauforts, the Holands were Henry VI's nearest male kinsmen in England, and the fat price may have been dictated (as Mr. Pugh has suggested) by the prospect of a Holand succeeding to the throne of England.[38]

A third indication arises from the greater appreciation of the parlous dynastic situation of the Lancastrian royal family after the duke of Bedford died in 1435 — perhaps even as soon as it became apparent that he was unlikely to sire legitimate children. This appreciation was certainly strong by 1440, when it was clear that none could be expected from Duke Humphrey either. The consequent need to buttress the Lancastrian line dynastically is accordingly reflected in the buoyant business of pedigree production. Pedigrees from Adam and Eve or Noah especially proliferated during Henry VI's reign, and not solely to stress the king's unique dual descent in the royal lines of England and France.[39] Some of these seem to have been manufactured for domestic dynastic purposes, though they are sometimes difficult to date. There are several still surviving today from the 1430s or '40s which pointedly exclude all reference to the line of Lionel of Clarence, and at least one incorporates the Staffords and the Beauforts, as well as the Holands, and can be dated precisely to 1444.[40]

There is no reason to doubt that Richard of York's sense of dynasty was as strongly developed as the king's, and he could be relied on to react in a predictable fashion once he became aware of the Lancastrian manoeuvres. There is ample testimony that he was so aware by 1450. By that year, there was a welter of suspicion, rumour and accusation abroad that the king should be deposed in York's favour, and some of the evidence at least implicated his servants and councillors.[41] Even if these were not coherent treason plots or formal counter-claims directed at the Lancastrian house, they graphically reflect the uncertainty that existed about the succession to the throne, the confusion that reigned about whose was the better and more senior descent, and the nervous appreciation by some of Lancastrian intentions to secure the present dynasty. Others were also aware of the significance of events, for Cade's rebels, in their demand that the king should recall the greater nobility to his counsels, placed special emphasis on York's 'trew blode of [the] realme'.[42] When the duke returned to England from Ireland in September 1450, he professed himself to be concerned about the possibility of his own attainder, whereby his blood would be corrupted and his lineage dishonoured — which at a stroke would have undermined his dynastic pretensions and that, surely, was a likely step for the Lancastrians to take?[43] In this context, it is easy to appreciate why, when Thomas Yonge, the M.P. for Bristol and one of York's councillors, proposed in the 1451 parliament that the duke should be formally declared heir apparent to the Lancastrian throne, the outspoken member was treated harshly and peremptorily.[44]

The onset of Henry VI's serious illness in August 1453 gave the question of an heir greater immediacy and to the antagonisms it had already aroused greater bitterness.[45] The birth of a son, Prince Edward, in October 1453 might ordinarily be expected to have taken the heat out of the dynastic discussion. But, coinciding as it did with the king's illness, it simply thrust to the fore the question of who should govern the realm during the king's incapacity while his heir was a minor — or, if the king should die, during the inevitable, long minority. In these changed circumstances, dynastic security became of overriding importance. Whatever provisions were made for the realm's governance, they were almost bound to have implications for the succession.

Queen Margaret of Anjou's wish was that she should become regent, and that would certainly have averted a crisis in government. But such a French fashion had been unacceptable in the past, and the memory of 1422 was still green in England.[46] Rather was a protectorate preferred, with England ruled by a protector and defender of the realm, aided by a council. In 1422, the next heir to the throne, John of Bedford, had been nominated as protector, unless he were in France in which case the second acknowledged heir, Duke Humphrey, should serve. They had been designated by Henry V to have charge of both realms, and no one challenged their prominence as the baby king's successive heirs. The argument in 1422 had rather revolved around their powers in England, nothing more.[47] Nor is it irrelevant to note what happened thirty years later in 1483. On that occasion, Edward IV supposedly nominated his adult heir (that is, after the two young princes who found themselves in the Tower), Richard of Gloucester, as protector and defender of the realm, and he was accepted as such.[48]

Thus, the choice of protector in 1453-54 would be of the utmost significance, not only in assigning the practical powers of government, but as an indication of who the ultimate Lancastrian heir should be in circumstances where it was unclear who he was by right. This explains the lengthy and bitter argument that took place in the winter of 1453-54, contrasted with the smoother passage of events in 1422 and 1483, and the vigour of the queen in forwarding her own demand for the regency. It explains, too, Richard of York's devotion to the memory of Duke Humphrey and his part in the campaign to rehabilitate his reputation.[49] It accounts equally for the imprisonment of Edmund Beaufort, duke of Somerset, late in 1453.[50] And it has some bearing on the rising of the Holand duke of Exeter in the north of England round about Christmas 1453, with its indications that, with so much at stake dynastically, he at least felt that the protectorate should be his.[51]

The similarity between the situation in 1453-54 and that of 1422 is, in fact, only superficial and does not extend beyond the need felt on both occasions to provide effective government. In 1453-54 the king was alive and adult, though incapacitated; England was therefore faced with the possibility of a helpless monarch (or, if he should die, a child king) under the influence of the queen. There is also a sharp contrast to be drawn between the personality of the two queens: between Katherine of Valois, who was a passive figure in English politics, and Margaret of Anjou, a more combative individual.[52] But above all, the experience of the previous decade made the conditions of the 1450s markedly different from those of the 1420s. The attempts to sustain a Lancastrian house, dynastically vulnerable in an uncertain legal situation, had made York's future highly problematical. Hence, perhaps, the rumours that were disseminated at this time that Prince Edward was not, in fact, King Henry's son.[53] It should be said that there is no evidence that Edward of Lancaster was regarded by anyone in authority — least of all by the delighted king — as other than Henry VI's own offspring.[54] But the rumours may well express the disappointment (even the fear) felt by some at this decisive reinforcement of the Lancastrian line.

After the question of the regency had been disposed of, York was appointed protector in March 1454 in preference to both Somerset and Exeter. The decision was taken by the lords present as a body, partly on the basis of who was most competent. By 1454 there was considerable resentment at the advancement of the Beauforts in terms of their power, wealth and influence. There were also serious doubts about their past record, particularly in France.[55] They had been, moreover, too closely associated with the reprehensible actions of Suffolk and others, while Exeter was known to be a violent man of limited intelligence ('fierce and cruel', as one contemporary described him).[56]

The choice of York would also have the critical advantage of averting a yet starker polarisation of faction and the further victimisation of his line. Unity, not division; efficiency, not inefficiency and corruption; sound reputation, not failure — these were the considerations that weighed with the lords. And credit must go to them as a body for their choice; it postponed a violent clash. But the implications of the protectorate were potentially just as disastrous.

York may be pardoned for thinking (or choosing to think) that his nomination as protector was a sign of aristocratic favour towards the dynastic possibilities of his line. This belief may have led him incidentally to appeal to James II of Scotland for aid in winning the English crown (or so King James said).[57] A second implication arises out of his dismissal from the protectorship in February 1456. The long-term prospect was thenceforward one of a king increasingly incapable of exerting authority himself and dominated by his queen, or of the minority of a Lancastrian prince guided by his strong-willed mother. Thus, after York surrendered the protectorship, there would be slim chance of his ever again being a peaceful choice as protector or, therefore, as England's heir. The comparison with 1483 is striking.[58] The surprising thing is that civil war did not come sooner than 1459.

The fighting at Blore Heath and Ludford Bridge in the autumn of 1459 put the final stop to York's hope of a renewed protectorate and, thereby, of the ultimate accession of his line to the English throne as the acknowledged heirs of Lancaster. Unless he were prepared to accept this situation, his only alternative was to take the throne for himself — almost as an act of self-protection and to do justice to his lineage. This raises the question of the motives of the duke of York and his closest supporters in the months prior to the invasions from Calais and Ireland in 1460.

On 16 March 1460 Warwick and York conferred in Ireland about how best the return to England should be contrived.[59] One may safely assume that they discussed when and how it should happen, and what would follow it. The best available opinion at present is that the actions of Warwick, Salisbury and the earl of March were the previously agreed plan — largely, perhaps, because it actually happened, and also because they appear to have been dismayed when York attempted to do something different.[60] But an alternative scenario can be presented. The meeting in Ireland on 16 March 1460 almost certainly agreed plans for the invasion of England, with the Yorkist lords in Calais bearing the main burden of responsibility — and with good reason. Invasion from there was geographically and logistically easier than from distant Ireland; there were indications of support from Kent, Surrey and Sussex; and Calais was much nearer the capital which the Lancastrians had deserted and whose sympathy the Yorkists regarded as crucial. It was perhaps of decisive importance that there was a force of men available in the fortress-town.[61] By contrast, the journey from Ireland was longer and hazardous at the best of times; by 1460, the Lancastrians had established a formidable centre of power in the midlands. York, moreover, had no experienced army of any size with him in Ireland that could be easily transported to the mainland. In any case, the distance from London and from sympathetic opinion in the south-east was a major discouragement, while York's personal estates were scattered and not necessarily reliable for his present purpose.[62] Thus, the Yorkist lords landed from Calais in the south-east of England on 26 June.

York followed them at an interval, after the next stage in the invasion had been achieved; he landed near Chester round about 8 September.[63] By then news of the achievement of this next stage had presumably reached him — it certainly had time to do so. But what he heard may not have been entirely in accord with the original plan. After two or three days in London, the Yorkist lords had marched northwards against the king. For the first time (apart from at St. Albans in 1455), Henry was involved in an overt military engagement: in 1459 it was the queen who precipitated the skirmish at Blore Heath, and at Ludford the Yorkist forces had fallen back before the king himself. Now a battle was actually fought (and presumably anticipated), and the death of the king must have been acknowledged as at least a possibility. At Northampton on 10 July, the Lancastrians were defeated and the duke of Buckingham was killed, Henry VI was captured, but the queen and the prince were safely in the north.[64] Was this eventuality foreseen as a possibility on 16 March? It could hardly have been planned that way.

The discussions between Warwick and York in Ireland may also have envisaged an early meeting of parliament to deal with the situation, and one was summoned only a fortnight after the earl of Warwick returned to London with the captive Henry VI.[65] It was to assemble at Westminster on 7 October, and York's landing in Wales was well timed for it. One wonders what was its purpose. Was it, in fact, to arrange the deposition of Henry VI after the example of 1399? Certainly no one mentioned the possibility of nominating York as a protector before he arrived in the capital. Was it also its purpose, in accordance with the plan of 16 March, to acclaim York as king by true dynastic right, for, as York reminded the lords in parliament, 'though right rest for a time and be put in silence, yet it does not rot nor shall it perish'.[66] All one can say in this connection is that immediately after York landed near Chester on or about 8 September, he acted as rightful king; he progressed in a leisurely and dignified manner through the English shires bordering Wales; he disdained the use of Henry's regnal year from 13 September at the latest; he used Lionel of Clarence's arms and a banner with the royal arms of England; and he had his sword held upright before him.[67] It would be a logical conclusion of this behaviour for him to walk into the parliament chamber on 10 October and expect acclamation.[68] The circumstances in which Richard of York found himself in the autumn of 1460 may not have been quite those that were anticipated when the plans were laid in Ireland. Unforeseen obstacles had been placed in his path. For one thing, King Henry was still alive, and accordingly anyone claiming the throne and demanding acclamation would be taking awesome steps. Secondly, the freedom of the queen and the prince was an insurmountable hindrance to any seizure of the throne. The deposition of the king and the disinheriting of his son could hardly be made effective so long as Queen Margaret was at liberty with Prince Edward. If eventually the example of the treaty of Troyes (1420) was followed in order to reach a compromise between York and Henry VI — whereby the latter would remain king until his death, though his son and heir would be disinherited — one lesson of the arrangement made at Troyes was just as obvious. So long as the Dauphin had remained at large, his ultimate recovery of his rights and realm was a possibility — in his case triumphantly realised in 1450.[69]

For these reasons, the Yorkist lords drew back from the consequences of the battle of Northampton, leaving York, who had openly declared his hand, utterly exposed. Merely to capture the king can hardly have been the plan in 1460, if only because it had not worked in 1455; it would certainly not work so long as the queen and the prince were free. Despite the embarrassment which even York's closest associates showed in parliament on 10 October, and despite the strenuous efforts after the battle to make Henry's household thoroughly Yorkist in its personnel, it is difficult to conclude other than that the original plan had been to depose (even to kill) King Henry VI.[70] It is small wonder that Richard of York refused to greet the king, installed himself in the royal palace, and insisted that the crown was his.

Notes

1. Sir H. Ellis (ed.), *Three books of Polydore Vergil's English History* (Camden Soc., XXIX, 1844), pp. 86, 93-94. The quotations are from a translation, made towards the end of Henry VIII's reign, of Vergil's Latin chronicle.
2. E. Hall, *The union of the two noble families of Lancaster and York* (London, 1550; repr. 1970), f. 80*v*; R. Grafton, *A Chronicle at large* . . . (London, 1569; repr. 1809), p.646. A son William, born in 1336, died in childhood; Lionel was born in 1338.
3. M. Levine, *Tudor dynastic problems, 1460-1571* (London, 1973), p.15; C. Ross, *The Wars of the Roses* (London, 1976), p.43.
4. This point is well made by J.R. Lander, *Conflict and stability in fifteenth-century England* (3rd. ed., London, 1977), pp.12, 184.
5. *Rotuli Parliamentorum* (6 vols., London, 1767), III, 525, 574-76; 7 Henry VI c. 2 in *Statutes of the realm*, II (Record commission, 1806), 151, and reprinted in S.B. Chrimes and A.L. Brown (eds.), *Select documents of English constitutional history, 1307-1485* (London, 1961), pp.225-26. This line of succession seems to have been explicitly accepted even earlier, at councils held shortly before Christmas 1403.
6. T. Rymer (ed.), *Foedera, conventiones, literae* . . . (The Hague, 1739-45), IV, iii, 179-80, partially reprinted in modernised English in A.R. Myers (ed.), *English historical documents*, IV, *1307-1485* (London, 1969), pp.225-26. Significantly, the succession to the French throne was not restricted in the treaty to the heirs of Henry V's body.
7. Lionel's descendants were the heirs general (as opposed to the heirs male) of Edward III.
8. No English monarch had married so late in life since Richard I (in 1191) and none would do so again until Mary Tudor (1554).
9. *C.P.*, III, 258-60. For his illegitimate son, John, see S. Lee (ed.), *The dictionary of national biography* (63 vols., London, 1885-1900), LVI, 159.
10. E.C. Williams, *My lord of Bedford* (London, 1963), pp. 247, 275; *C.P.*, II, 70-72. His first wife seems to have died in childbed.
11. Williams, *Bedford*, pp.222-24. There were also pressing diplomatic reasons for the Luxemburg match.
12. K.H. Vickers, *Humphrey, duke of Gloucester* (London, 1907), pp.127-28, 165, 205 (though the exact date of neither marriage is known). For his children, see *ibid.*, pp. 335-36; and for his books, *ibid.*, pp. 426-38, and *Duke Humfrey and English humanism in the fifteenth century: catalogue of an exhibition* . . . (Oxford, 1970).
13. E.g. *C.P.R., 1436-41*, pp. 401, 444. These steps were taken even before Humphrey was humiliated by the trial of his wife in July 1441 (for which see below no. 14).
14. R.A. Griffiths, 'The trial of Eleanor Cobham: an episode in the fall of Duke Humphrey of Gloucester', *Bulletin of the John Rylands Library*, LI (1969), 381-99 (p. 394 for the annulment).
15. M.E. Christie, *Henry VI* (London, 1922), pp. 135-36; J. Ferguson, *English Diplomacy, 1422-1461* (Oxford, 1972), pp. 26-27, 114-15. Moreover, changed

circumstances abroad, over which the English government had no control, played a part in frustrating the German and Armagnac negotiations of 1438 and 1442 respectively.

16. S.B. Chrimes, *English constitutional ideas in the fifteenth century* (Cambridge, 1936), pp. 9-13, 62-64.
17. C.L. Scofield, *The Life and reign of Edward the fourth* (2 vols., London, 1923), I, 1-3. It is not without significance that in 1441 Richard and Cecily gave their first-born son a name favoured above all others by the house of Lancaster (but not by the Mortimers or Nevilles) since the thirteenth century.
18. *C.P.R., 1396-99*, p. 86 (fully printed in *Foedera*, III, iv, 126); *C.P.R., 1405-8*, p. 284. See the comment in J.L. Kirby, *Henry IV of England* (London, 1970), pp. 209-10. The words *excepta dignitate regali* were squeezed between the lines of the 1407 confirmation of the act of legitimation of 1397.
19. *C.P.*, XII, i, 48.
20. *Ibid.*, V, 211-12.
21. C. Rawcliffe, *The Staffords, earls of Stafford and dukes of Buckingham, 1394-1521* (Cambridge, 1978); below p. 21.
22. C.L. Kingsford, *Prejudice and promise in fifteenth-century England* (London, 1925), pp. 153ff.
23. N.H. Nicolas (ed.), *Proceedings and ordinances of the privy council of England*, V (Record commission, 1835), 252-53; *C.P.*, XII, i, 47. The decision to create him duke had been taken as early as 30 March 1443.
24. *Reports from the Lords committees touching the dignity of a peer of the realm*, V (London, 1829), 241-42, 248; *C.P.*, V, 208.
25. *Ibid.*, II, 388-89; *Dignity reports*, V, 243, 257-58.
26. *Ibid.*, pp. 238, 240-41, 258-59; *C.P.*, XII, i, 50-51. Henceforward, the daughter of John, duke of Somerset will be referred to as Margaret Beaufort (I), and Duke Edmund's as Margaret Beaufort (II).
27. *Ibid.*, II, 389; Rawcliffe, *Staffords*, p. 21 n. 45.
28. R.A. Griffiths, 'Duke Richard of York's intentions in 1450 and the origins of the Wars of the Roses', *Journal of mediaeval history*, I (1975), 193-94; *C.P.*, XII, i, 449-50.
29. The marriage had certainly taken place before 1455: *ibid.*, X, 826. The royal earldom conferred on Edmund Tudor is significant, especially in view of the simultaneous elevation of his younger brother, Jasper, to the earldom of Pembroke, one of Humphrey of Gloucester's titles. R.S. Thomas, 'The political career, estates and "connection" of Jasper Tudor, earl of Pembroke and duke of Bedford (d. 1495)' (unpublished University of Wales Ph.D. thesis, 1971), pp. 32-36, establishes beyond doubt that both earls were created on 6 November 1452.
30. S.B. Chrimes, *Henry VII* (London, 1972), p. 13. Prince Edward was born on 13 October 1453. There is no record of an earlier miscarriage by Queen Margaret.
31. Thomas, 'Jasper Tudor', p. 141; Rawcliffe, *Staffords*, p. 21 n.45.
32. For the association of a red rose with the Beauforts as descendants of the house of Lancaster, see J.R. Planche, 'On the badges of the house of Lancaster', *Journal of the British Archaeological Association*, VI (1851), 378-83; B. Seward, *The symbolic rose* (New York, 1960), p. 56 n.2. A red rose also appears at the head of

a pedigree of Henry VI originally composed *c.* 1429-38: A. Wall (ed.), *Handbook to the Maude Roll* (Auckland, N.Z., 1919). A rose (but not the double Tudor rose) also figures on Margaret Beaufort's tomb in Westminster Abbey: R.F. Scott, 'On the contracts for the tomb of Lady Margaret Beaufort', *Archaeologia*, LXVI (1914-15), facing p. 365.

33. S.B. Chrimes, *Lancastrians, Yorkists and Henry VII* (2nd. ed., London, 1966), pp. xii-xiv. See Ross, *Wars of the roses,* pp. 12-15, for a less sceptical view of the implications of the roses symbol.

34. J. Stevenson (ed.), *Letters and papers illustrative of the wars of the English in France* (2 vols. in 3, Rolls Series, 1861-64), I, 79-86, 160-63, 168-70; *Catalogue of . . . the well-known collection of . . . the late W. Westley Manning, esq.* (Sotheby & Co., 24-25 January 1955), p. 45, which is also noticed (but misdated to 1456) in *Historical Manuscripts Commission,* Report IX, part 2 (1884), p. 410.

35. Rawcliffe, *Staffords,* p. 21; G. du Fresne de Beaucourt, *Histoire de Charles VII* (6 vols., Paris, 1881-91), V, 135-37.

36 Scofield, *Edward the fourth,* I, 9-11.

37. T.B. Pugh, 'The magnates, knights and gentry', in S.B. Chrimes, C.D. Ross and R.A. Griffiths (eds.), *Fifteenth-century England: studies in politics and society, 1399-1509* (Manchester, 1972), p. 118 n.11.

38. The marriage is not inconsistent with York's concern for the dynastic rights of his own line.

39. Among many that may be cited, see Bodleian Library, Madgalen Latin MS. 248 (from Adam); B.L., Additional MS. 18,002 (from Noah).

40. E.g., *ibid.* (dateable to 1438-41); Bodleian Library, Marshall MS. 135 (*c.* 1427-41); Bodleian roll 10 (*c.* 1427-41); Wall, *Handbook to the Maude Roll* (from Noah, *c.* 1429-38). B.L., Add. MS. 27,342 can be dated between May and September 1444. Many of these genealogies and pedigrees were later amended to include York's descent.

41. Griffiths, *Journal of Mediaeval History,* I (1975), 191-94.

42. From John Stowe's memoranda in J. Gairdner (ed.), *Three fifteenth-century chronicles* (Camden Soc., new series, XXVIII, 1880), p. 94, partially reprinted in modernised English in B. Wilkinson, *Constitutional history of England in the fifteenth century (1399-1485)* (London, 1964), p. 84, and Myers, *E.H.D.,* IV, 267.

43. See York's first letter to Henry VI, in Griffiths, *Journal of Mediaeval History,* I(1975), 203.

44. Latin annals, in Stevenson, *Letters and papers,* II, ii, [770], translated in Wilkinson, *Constitutional history,* p. 114; *Rot. Parl.,* V, 137. Yonge was sent to the Tower and parliament dissolved towards the end of May 1451. See J.C. Wedgwood, *History of parliament: biographies of the members of the commons house, 1439-1509* (London, 1936), pp. 981-82; *idem, ibid., Register* (London, 1938), p. 147. That part of 'Gregory's Chronicle' which is considered to have been composed about 1451 refers interestingly to York as 'Rycharde Plantagenet' under the year 1448-49: J. Gairdner (ed.), *The historical collections of a citizen of London in the fifteenth century* (Camden Soc., new series, XVII, 1876), p. 189; C.L. Kingsford, *English historical literature in the fifteenth century* (Oxford, 1913), pp. 96-98; J.A.F. Thomson, 'The continuation of

"Gregory's Chronicle" — a possible author?', *The British Museum Quarterly*, XXXVI (1971-72), 92-93.

45. R.L. Storey, *The end of the house of Lancaster* (London, 1966), p. 136.

46. *P.L.*, II, 297; J.S. Roskell, 'The office and dignity of protector of England', *English Historical Review*, LXVIII (1953), 205ff.

47. *Ibid.;* S.B. Chrimes, 'The pretensions of the duke of Gloucester in 1422', *ibid.*, XLV (1930), 101-3.

48. Ellis, *Polydore Vergil*, p. 173; J. Gairdner (ed.), *Memorials of King Henry the seventh* (Rolls Series, 1858), p. 28 (Bernard André's chronicle); J. Gairdner, *History of the life and reign of Richard the third* (2nd. ed., London, 1898), pp. 44, 55. Notice, too, that according to Edward Hall, it was recommended in parliament on 31 October 1460 that York should be proclaimed heir apparent and protector at one and the same time: Hall, *Union of Lancaster and York*, f. 98, reprinted from the 1809 edition in Chrimes and Brown, *Select documents*, pp. 318-19.

49. *Rot. Parl.*, V, 335 (1455); J.S. Davies (ed.), *An English chronicle . . .* (Camden Soc., LXIV, 1856), p. 88 (1460).

50. *P.L.*, II, 290-92; Storey, *End of Lancaster*, p. 138.

51. R.A. Griffiths, 'Local rivalries and national politics: the Percies, the Nevilles and the duke of Exeter, 1452-1455', *Speculum*, XLIII (1968), 606ff.

52. There is no satisfactory biography of either queen, but see R.A. Griffiths, 'Queen Katherine of Valois and a missing statute of the realm', *The Law Quarterly Review*, XCIII (1977), 248-58, and J.J. Bagley, *Margaret of Anjou, queen of England* (London, n.d. [1948]).

53. Davies, *English chronicle*, p. 79.

54. *P.L.*, III, 13 (9 January 1455).

55. The hostility to Duke Edmund was expressed most pointedly by York in 1452 and by the duke of Norfolk in 1453: Sir H. Ellis (ed.), *Original letters illustrative of English history*, series I, i (1825), 11-13; *P.L.*, II, 290-92. But it was evidently much more widely felt: Storey, *End of Lancaster*, pp. 137-38.

56. See the assessment in Griffiths, *Speculum*, XLIII (1968), 628.

57. Stevenson, *Letters and papers*, I, 324-25 (before 28 June 1456); for a comment, see R. Nicholson, *Scotland: the later middle ages* (Edinburgh, 1974), p. 394. About this time (*c.* 1455-58), genealogies displaying York's descent from Lionel of Clarence began to appear, incorporating emphasis on the death of the royalist earl of Northumberland and the duke of Somerset at St. Albans (1455); York's circle may have encouraged their dissemination. See, e.g., B.L., Harleian roll T. 12; All Souls College, Oxford, MS. 40; Queen's College, Oxford, MS. 168. (These references were made available to me by Miss A. Allan.)

58. P.M. Kendall, *Richard III* (London, 1955), pp. 153ff. It was Richard of Gloucester's awareness of the implications of a regime in which the young Edward V would be dominated by the queen and her Woodville relatives that convinced him that he should seize the throne.

59. Scofield, *Edward the fourth*, I, 59. A.H. Thomas and I.D. Thornley (eds.), *The Great Chronicle of London* (London, 1936), p, 192, says that Warwick met York 'to have his Counsayll how they shulde Entir in to this land'; compare W. and E.L.C.P. Hardy (eds.), *Recueil des croniques et anchiennes istories . . . par Jehan de Waurin*, V (Rolls Series, 1891), 287.

60. For an account of the events of July-October 1460, based on contemporary chronicles, see J.R. Lander, *The wars of the roses* (London, 1965), pp. 102-15. Compare Storey, *End of Lancaster*, p. 188.

61. For the importance of Calais in these years, see G.L. Harriss, 'The struggle for Calais: an aspect of the rivalry between Lancaster and York', *English Historical Review*, LXXV (1960), 30-53.

62. J.T. Rosenthal, 'The estates and finances of Richard, duke of York (1411-1460)', in W.M. Bowsky (ed.), *Studies in mediaeval and renaissance history*, II (1965), 194-96.

63. Scofield, *Edward the fourth*, I, 101.

64. *Ibid.*, pp. 76-89.

65. F.M. Powicke and E.B. Fryde (eds.), *Handbook of British Chronology* (2nd. ed., London, 1961), p. 532.

66. *Rot. Parl.*, V, 378, reprinted in modernised English in Myers, *E.H.D.*, IV, 418.

67. K.B. McFarlane, 'The wars of the roses', *Proceedings of the British Academy*, L (1964), 93 and n.1, 2; *Great Chronicle of London*, p. 192.

68. H.T. Riley (ed.), *Registrum abbatiae Johannis Whethamstede*, I (Rolls Series, 1872), 376-78, translated in Myers, *E.H.D.*, IV, 283-84; Waurin, *Croniques*, V, 310-18.

69. Myers, *E.H.D.*, IV, 415-19. For the treaty of Troyes, see above p. 16.

70. According to Davies, *English chronicle*, p. 100, he had already arranged that his coronation should take place on 1 November. Many of Henry's household servants were swiftly replaced with dependable Yorkists after the battle of Northampton; they were led by Sir Walter Scull, treasurer of the household: Powicke and Fryde, *Handbook of British chronology*, p. 79.

The Richmondshire Community of Gentry During the Wars of the Roses

A.J. Pollard
Senior Lecturer in History
Teesside Polytechnic

In April 1486, when Henry VII was making his first and politically critical visit to the city of York, 'the folk of the north', according to Polydore Vergil, 'savage and more eager than others for upheaval', were reported to be gathering together a little beyond Middleham.[1] This paper is about those savages and the neighbourhood of Middleham from which they came. In one respect the topic is intensely local: it is a study of the community of gentry in that part of north-west Yorkshire made up of the wapentakes of Gilling East and West, Hang East and West, and Hallikeld which formed the feudal Honour of Richmond and the nucleus of the Archdeaconry of Richmondshire (see Map 1). Richmondshire as it was known then, and still is known, was the jungle in which Vergil's savages lived. But Vergil had heard correctly of their reputation for rebelliousness. In the thirty years before Henry VII's visit to York their rebellions had several times shaken the throne of England. The people of Richmondshire had an importance in national politics out of all proportion to their wealth and location. This national importance seems to me to justify a close examination of the social and political structure of the community of this remote corner of England.

Before moving into this analysis it is worth reminding ourselves of some of the occasions on which the people of Richmondshire rose in rebellion. Especially noticeable is their involvement in the events of 1469-71. According to Warkworth, Robin of Redesdale was Sir William Conyers. It has become customary on the strength of W.A.J. Archbald's article in the *Dictionary of National Biography* to argue that it

TABLE 1

PEDIGREE OF CONYERS OF HORNBY

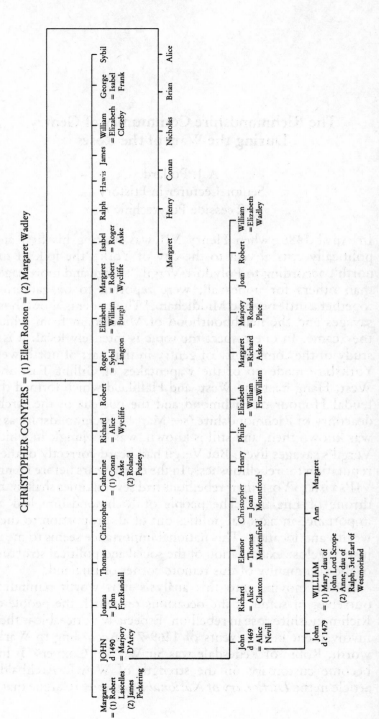

MAP 1

RICHMONDSHIRE: PHYSICAL FEATURES AND WAPENTAKES

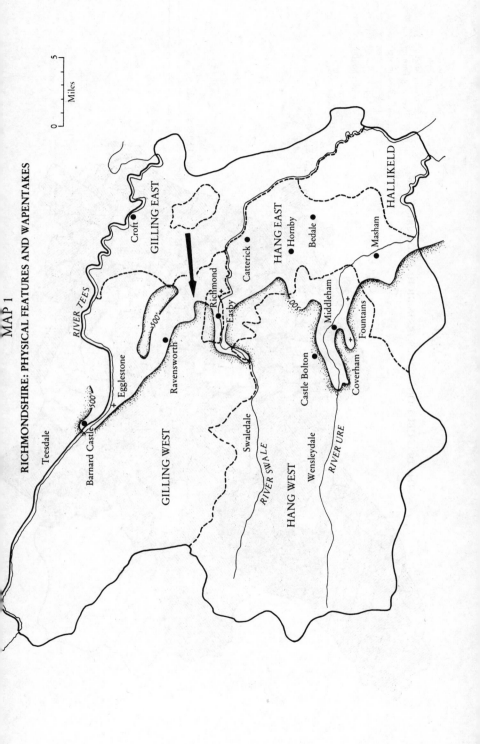

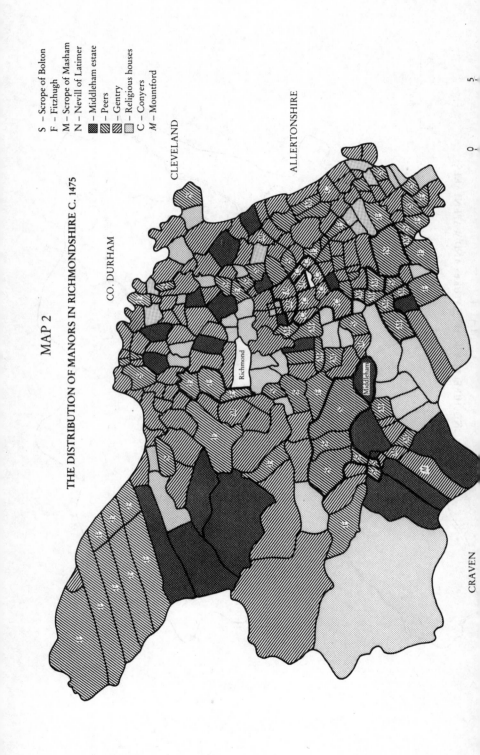

MAP 2

THE DISTRIBUTION OF MANORS IN RICHMONDSHIRE C. 1475

S – Scrope of Bolton
F – Fitzhugh
M – Scrope of Masham
N – Nevill of Latimer
– Middleham estate
– Peers
– Gentry
– Religious houses
C – Conyers
M – Mountford

CO. DURHAM

CLEVELAND

ALLERTONSHIRE

Richmond

Middleham

CRAVEN

0   5

was in fact Sir John Conyers and not his brother. He based his case on information in the *Chronicle of the Lincolnshire Rebellion* that Sir John submitted to Edward IV at York in March 1470. But as we shall see it is clear in the text that this relates to a rising then and not nine months earlier.[2] It seems, therefore, that there is no reason not to take Warkworth at face value and identify Robin of Redesdale as Sir William Conyers of Marske in Swaledale. With Sir William Conyers in this rising were John Conyers, his nephew and son and heir of Sir John, Sir Henry Nevill, son and heir of Lord Latimer and a Richard Nicholson of Hornby, the Conyers seat, all of whom were killed on the winning side at the battle of Edgecote.[3] There can be little doubt that the leadership of Robin of Redesdale's rising in the summer of 1469 was drawn from the Richmondshire gentry. In the spring of 1470 they were in arms again. The *Chronicle of the Lincolnshire Rebellion* tells the story:

'In this season (12 March, just after the defeat of the rebels at Loosecoat field) the king, understonding that the commocion in moving people in Richmondshire by the stirring of the lorde Scrope and othere, sent by the saide Duc (Clarence) and erle (Warwick) there for that cause with many lettres, his highness sent into Northomberland and Westmoreland to arredre certain filaship to afilowed uppon theym if they had com forwarde and to Markes Montague, with his felaship to have countred theym in theire faces; *thay* (Scrope etc) understanding and havyng tithinges also (of) the kinges victorie, and, as divers gentilmen of that felaship said, thinkyng, by the maner of the saide erle of Warrewike writing sent thidre in his own name oonly to arreise the people, that theire stirring shulde be ayenst the king, and fering his spedy comyng unto their parties with his oost, left theire gadering and satt still.'[4]

In a later passage the author refers to Warwick's hopes of,

oute of Yorkshire to (have) assembled so gret a puyssaunce that thay might have be able to have fought with the kinges highnes in plein felde.[5]

But, finally, when the king was at York between 22 and 26 March, there com to the king the Lorde Scrope, Sir John Conyers, young Hilyard of Holdernes and others which had laboured specially provoced and stirred the people in their parties to have (made) commocion ayeinst the king, wherein they frely submitted them to the kinges grace and mercy . . . and also of ther fre willes, unconstreyned and undesired, they clerely confessed that so to make commocions they were specially laboured and desired by the said duc and erle.'[6]

Nowhere else are our sources so specific in identifying the participants in these northern risings as the gentry and people of Richmondshire. Nevertheless it is clear that it was they who were in arms again four months later. In July and August, as Sir John Paston reported, 'ther be many ffolkes uppe in the northe' under the leadership of Lord FitzHugh.[7] In fact, as the lists of pardons in the patent rolls show, there were at least twenty of the gentry of Richmondshire, including two more of the irrepressible Conyers family, who were suspected of coming out with FitzHugh and drew Edward IV north, so allowing Warwick to land unopposed in the south.[8] And finally, after Edward IV's dramatic return to England in the spring of 1471 and his victories at Barnet and Tewkesbury, there was, according to the *Arrivall*, a last forlorn rising in the north which quickly collapsed on hearing of the Lancastrian defeat and that Edward was marching north, and because they did not have 'any of Warwick's or Nevill's blood unto whom they might have rested, as they had done afor'.[9]

This is not to imply that the gentry and people of Richmondshire were the only ones to be so rebellious between 1469 and 1471, even in the north. Of course people from other parts of Yorkshire and Cumbria participated. But nevertheless Richmondshire was the nucleus of the northern rebellions. The reason for this, as Edward IV knew and as the author of the 'official' Chronicle of the Lincolnshire rebellion knew, was that Richmondshire, dominated by his lordship of Middleham, was the engine room of Warwick's political power. That political power was stoked by the gentry of Richmondshire. Thus, an analysis of the community of Richmondshire is of some significance in explaining why not only Warwick, but also his successor Richard of Gloucester, were able to wield such power in Yorkist England. Such an analysis draws on collections of family papers, some published, some unpublished;[10] wills proved in the probate court of the diocese of York, mostly those published by Canon Raine in *Testamenta Eboracensia;* the register of the Archdeaconry, published by A.H. Thompson some years ago;[11] and ancillary public records. There are no private letters. It is particularly interesting that the correspondence of the Plumpton family, who lived only just south of Richmondshire, is of very little use for this study. All the relevant sources are in the last resort concerned with property. This obviously makes the analysis one-sided. But on the other hand it does reflect the fundamental shared interest of the gentry, for it was the possession, protection and extension of property which bound them together as a social group.

How many landowners were there in Richmondshire and what authority and wealth did they possess? As the basis of the answer to this first question I have adopted the controversial procedure of counting manors. It is a severely limited method. The ownership of manors was not the same as the ownership of land. The pattern of landownership was in fact much more complex. Gentry families owned the odd tenement and a few shillings of rent in widely scattered communities. Rarely did a lord of a manor own all the land in it. In most villages there were several different landowners besides the lord. In Brompton-on-Swale, for instance, where the Abbey of St. Agatha's Easby held the manor, land was additionally owned by Lord Scrope of Bolton, William Burgh, Richard Conyers, Thomas Metcalfe, Thomas Swaldale and Richard Brian.[12] Such holdings were often parcels of land which changed hands through marriage settlements, provision for younger children and endowments for charity. But in a rough and ready way this complexity cancelled itself out. As a rule of thumb the more manors he owned, the more land a gentleman possessed — wherever it was. Moreover the calculation is based on the *Victoria County History of the North Riding* which, though comprehensive, is not entirely reliable.[13] Nevertheless in the

absence of relevant tax returns there is no other way of
reaching an overall view of the pattern of landowning and
authority in the district.

Eight peers held land in Richmondshire. The largest
property owner was the lord of Middleham. He owned some
twenty-seven manors, including grants to him from the
Honour of Richmond, as well as parks and great stretches of
forest. The total yield was almost £1,000 p.a.[14] His local
authority was enhanced by the grant of the castle of Richmond, knights' fees, and castleward from the Honour of
Richmond. Next to the Nevills came Scrope of Bolton and
FitzHugh with some two dozen manors each, the former
based in Teesdale, the latter in Wensleydale. Their estates were
worth well over £500 p.a.[15] Scrope of Masham held eleven
manors concentrated in the southern corner of the district.
The other peers had much smaller estates. Nevill of Latimer, at
Snape and Well, had lands worth £100 and over;[16] Lovell at
Bedale and nearby had about the same.[17] Both of these,
especially Lovell, had holdings elsewhere, as did Greystoke
(two in Richmondshire) and the earl of Westmorland (one in
Richmondshire). The Percies did not have any property in the
district. There were two gentry families whose holdings and
wealth nearly matched Scrope of Masham. Pre-eminent were
the Conyers of Hornby who held the equivalent of eight
manors in Richmondshire, and others in neighbouring
Allertonshire. The Mountfords of Hackforth also held the
equivalent of nearly eight manors. There were at least ten other
gentry families, either with holdings concentrated in Richmondshire, or more widely spread in neighbouring districts —
FitzRandall, Ingleby, Lascelles, Laton, Markenfield,
Metham, Norton, Pigot, Saltmarsh, Strangways and Wandesford — whose holdings were worth approximately £200 a
year. A late fifteenth-century valor of the Wandesford
estates, for instance, shows an income of £185 from rents in 23
separate places.[18] All these gentry had greater wealth locally
than either Nevill of Latimer or Lovell. One then comes to the
great bulk of the local squirearchy with one or two manors,
and property worth anything from £20 to £100 p.a. There were

some forty-eight families in this category. Typical of them were William Burgh of Brough, near Catterick, lord of the manor of Brough, with lands there and elsewhere,[19] and Richard Clervaux of Croft-on-Tees, lord of East Cowton, owner of most of Croft and with lands in six other places,[20] both of whom enjoyed incomes of £50 p.a. or more. The manorial squirearchy by no means exhausts the gentry for beneath them in the social hierarchy existed all those styled merely gentlemen, lords of no manors but possessing lands producing at least £10 clear income a year, about whom Garter King of Arms admitted in 1530 that:

> those not vile born or rebels might be admitted to be ennobled to have arms having lands and possessions of free tenure to the yearly value of ten pounds sterling'.[21]

This was the grey area which merged into that of the yeomanry. How many there were of this status in Richmondshire we have no way of knowing. Only occasionally are their names thrown up by our sources. One such family was that of Stockdale. William Stockdale of Richmondshire, yeoman, was a commissioner for taking the oath against maintenance in 1434 and Thomas Stockdale, retained for life, by Richard Nevill earl of Salisbury in 1421, was for nineteen years his attorney at the Exchequer. A member of the next generation of the family, John Stockdale, gentleman, was a Yorkshire elector in 1467 and, styled yeoman, took out a pardon after FitzHugh's revolt in 1470.[22] Another 'service' family, as it were, was that of Weltden, of whom Christopher and John were successively feodaries and under-stewards of the lords of Middleham, who married into the local gentry families and eventually established themselves at Colburn.[23] Others in this social group were submanorial gentry such as the Colvilles, Lockwoods, Swaldales and Vincents and prosperous townsmen like William Clerionet of Richmond, Thomas Otter of Middleham and John Thomson of Bedale. But these are but a few names from amongst what must have been a large number of 'mere' gentlemen.

There is one other important category of landowner to be

considered, namely the church. Fifteen religious houses owned the equivalent of thirty six manors and a dozen granges in the district.[24] The biggest was Jervaulx with at least eight manors and as many granges which produced the greater part of its £235 net annual income at the dissolution.[25] The next largest were St Mary's York, Fountains, Coverham and St Agatha's Easby. Of these only Easby was principally a Richmondshire house and it enjoyed a net income of £112 at the dissolution.[26] Although there were many religious houses, most of them were small. In terms of manorial holdings they owned only 20% of Richmondshire. This certainly represents an underestimate of the clerical wealth in the district. For one, in the case of religious houses especially, the counting of manors conceals the extent to which in almost every community one or more of the local houses owned a few shillings of rent.[27] Secondly our figures do not include ecclesiastical livings especially the very valuable Archdeaconry of Richmondshire and Prebend of Masham worth something of the order of £300 per annum between them in the late fifteenth century.[28] And after 1475 there was a spate of chantry foundations in Richmondshire which transferred more wealth from lay to clerical hands.[29] But even making allowance for this it is hard to equate this picture of Richmondshire with Dr Schofield's calculation that in 1515 almost *two-thirds* of the assessed taxable wealth in the North Riding was clerical.[30] Allowing for the rough and ready basis of the estimates of wealth and landholding, it seems to be the case that in Richmondshire there was a greater concentration of wealth and property in lay hands than elsewhere in the North Riding. The impression that the district was densely populated by gentry seems to be confirmed by comparison with calculations for other parts of England based on taxation returns. One is, of course, not comparing like with like. In taxation returns, men were taxed, and therefore listed, on the basis of their principal holding. Several of our gentry in Richmondshire would therefore be taxed elsewhere. On the other hand taxation returns were by no means comprehensive. There were, however, approximately fifty gentry families with incomes of £20 and over who were resident in Richmondshire. This compares, for instance, with the fifty-four, a handful of whom were esquires of ancient blood but slender means, who were assessed in the whole of Lincolnshire, one of the richest counties of England, for the income tax of 1436.[31] This is an imprecise and impressionistic analysis. But nevertheless the general conclusion that there were many gentry as well as three powerful noble families in Richmondshire in the fifteenth century seems to be inescapable. Here then, in sheer numbers and collective wealth, lies the first of the characteristics of the Nevill political strength drawn from Richmondshire. The second lies in the social cohesion of the landowning class in Richmondshire.

Of all the social institutions and customs which bound the gentry together, marriage was the most important.[32] Constant intermarriage between the families tied them into a close-knit kinship group. Marriage was, of course, a business transaction. But besides being a property deal, marriage was also a means of social preservation or advancement. Through their marriage alliances one with another the gentry families constantly reaffirmed and strengthened their social positions, while for individual families marriage offered one way into the group and one way of advancement in the pecking order within it.

There was a marked tendency for the children of Richmondshire gentry to marry the children of other Richmond shire gentry. Elder sons had a greater propensity to marry outside the district. Three generations of eldest sons of the Clervaux, for instance, married daughters of Lumley of county Durham, Vavasour of Haslewood in the West Riding, and Hussey of Sleeford, Lincs. On the other hand five generations of eldest sons of Burgh in the fifteenth century all married into North Riding families, four of which — Aske, Lascelles, Conyers and Metcalfe — were Richmondshire neighbours.[33] Younger sons and daughters usually followed the pattern of the Burgh heirs. William Burgh III, who died in 1492, had daughters who married sons of Catterick, Saltmarsh and Weltden and a sister who married his neighbour Alan Fulthorpe.[34] Daughters of Sir James Strangways married sons of Aske, Clervaux and Ingleby. Richard Clervaux's younger children married, in addition to Strangways, children of Aske, FitzHenry, Laton and Conyers of Wynyard, county Durham.[35] And in fact the husband in the last case, William Conyers, was the nephew of Sir John. The Conyers family itself it perhaps the best example of this intermarrying, if only because it was the most prolific (See Table 1). Christopher, who died in c. 1465, had 24 children by two marriages. Four of his younger sons married daughters of Wycliffe, Frank, Cleseby and Langton of Wynyard. His daughters married sons of Aske (two of them), Burgh, Lascelles, FitzRandall, Pickering, Pudsey (two again) and Wycliffe. Sir John Conyers in the next generation could only manage twelve children, but amongst their marriages were alliances with Aske, Claxton (of Claxton, Co. Durham), FitzWilliam of Sprotburgh in the West Riding, Markenfield, Mountford and Place. The Conyers are also the finest example of a family advancing itself through marriage. Heiresses which came the way of this grasping family were Elizabeth Cleseby which set up Sir John's brother William at Marske in Swaledale and Sybil Langton which set up his brother Roger at Wynyard. Other marriages brought noble blood into the Conyers veins. Sir John was married to one of the joint heiresses of Lord Darcy, his own eldest son was matched with one of the heiresses of William Nevill, Lord Fauconberg, and his grandson and eventual heir William was married to Mary, daughter of John, fifth lord Scrope of Bolton.[36] In fact the occasional marriage between the less substantial gentry families and the lesser peerage, such as that between Agnes daughter of Henry, fourth lord Scrope of Bolton and Sir Christopher Boynton of Sadbury,[37] shows that there was no rigid barrier between gentry and peerage.

One could continue to catalogue examples of intermarriage, but it would be merely repetitious to do so. The fact is that in the later fifteenth century a member of the gentry of Richmondshire could count practically all the gentry of the district amongst his cousins. This kinship inevitably drew them together, not necessarily always amicably, as a group with common interests. Most important of these was the protection of titles to land. Thus it is that they were constantly associating themselves one with another as feoffees in land settlements or as executors of wills, and calling upon each other to witness these transactions. A typical enfeoffment is that organised by John Wandesford to ease the passage of his property to his son. Initially he placed it in the hands of William Burgh, James Strangways, Christopher Conyers and Randolph Pigot. On 4 April 1463 they passed their charge to a younger group of Thomas Mountford, John Pigot and Richard Pigot.[38] Strangways and both Christopher and Sir John Conyers, as dominant landowners, were frequently employed as feoffees, by gentry families such as the Wandesfords and Inglebies and by the peerage as represented, for example, by Lord Latimer in 1469.[39] Local lawyers, especially Sir Robert Danby and Richard Pigot were much in demand, both in enfeoffments and to execute wills. Danby was an executor of the will of William Burgh in 1465 as well as of Richard Nevill, earl of Salisbury. Pigot was an executor for Burgh and Thomas Witham in 1475.[40]

The witnessing of deeds was another important function carried out on one another's behalf by these gentry. At a time when titles were often uncertain and there was no system of registration the evidence of witnesses, especially witnesses of substance, could be crucial. On 11 January 1465, for instance, Sir James Strangways, an aged Christopher Conyers, Christopher Boynton, Thomas Surtees of Dinsdale in county Durham and Roger Vincent travelled to Croft to witness the final sealing of deeds and exchange of contracts which completed a complex exchange of property between Richard Clervaux and John, lord Scrope in Croft, Stapleton and Cleasby.[41] On 12 March 1476 Roger Aske, William Burgh and Thomas Mountford went down to York to witness the sealing of deeds which completed an exchange of property in Hipswell between Alan Fulthorpe and the abbey of St Mary's.[42] And on 12 June 1482, Sir James Strangways, jnr, Sir John Conyers, Thomas Mountford, Richard Clervaux and Roger Aske gathered at Brough Hall to witness the taking of a hundred-year lease of the mills of Richmond from Mount Grace Priory by William Burgh.[43]

These same gentry also helped out in the arbitration and settlement of disputes. The frequency with which this occurred suggests that as a group they found it speedier and less expensive to settle such differences amongst themselves rather than go through the due processes of the law. In 1463, for example, Richard Clervaux called upon his friends and neighbours to resolve a dispute with Thomas Fitton of Cawarden in Cheshire over a rent of £5 which Fitton claimed out of East Cowton from the time when his ancestor had sold the estate to the Clervaux family in the early fourteenth century. Sir James Strangways and John Nedeham, a justice of Common Pleas, agreed to arbitrate. Clervaux apparently accepted their recommendation that he should buy Fitton out for £53. 13s. 8d. Accordingly at Croft on 15 June Fitton ceremoniously quit his claim to the rent in the presence of Strangways, Sir John Conyers, Thomas Mountford, John Catterick and John Killinghall. The party then travelled over to Strangways' residence of Harlsey castle where the agreement was finally sealed and contracts for the payment were exchanged.[44] In August 1477 the Archdeacon of Richmondshire turned as a matter of course to the local gentry to decide in a dispute over the right of presentation to the living of Bedale and he commissioned Roger Aske, William Burgh, Thomas Frank, Alan Fulthorpe, Thomas Mountford, John Wycliffe and John Thomson of Bedale to make enquiry and recommendation.[45] Two of these men, Burgh and Mountford, with the lawyers Sir Guy Fairfax and Richard Pigot, were at the same time engaged in settling a quarrel between the Abbeys of St Mary's York and St Agatha's Easby over their boundaries and the possession of moorland in Hudswell upon which they made judgement on 10 March 1478.[46] Burgh and Mountford were kept fairly busy at this time, for a month later they appear to have been at Middleham when they were appointed by Richard, duke of Gloucester, with Frank again and William Pudsey, the late Rector of Croft, to act as guarantors of an arbitration which Gloucester had given in a quarrel which had blown up over several issues between Richard Clervaux and Roland Place in the parish of Croft where they both resided. And in fact two years later the guarantors had to deal with a fresh dispute between the parties.[47]

Through marriage, through the network of mutual co-operation with which they handled property, and through their other mutual interests, the landowning class of Richmondshire formed a community of their own. It was almost as introspective as it was close-knit. There seems to have been a low level of involvement with gentry from neighbouring districts. A certain amount of reciprocity existed with the gentry of south Durham, Cleveland and Allertonshire, stimulated by the property interests of the Conyers and Strangways families in particular. Conyers penetration of the area of Stokesley, for instance, seems to have flowed from their possession of the advowson of Rudby parish.[48] But there was very little reciprocity with the gentry of Craven and the Honour of Knaresbrough to the south. The Plumpton papers provide a useful correlation here. Plumpton marriages in their turn only exceptionally involved Richmondshire families. Trustees and witnesses in Plumpton deeds were drawn mostly from that circle of families — Babthorpes, Beckwiths, Gascoignes, Hamertons, Vavasours — associated with that part of the West Riding.[49] Some families like the Inglebies and Pigots had feet in both camps. And, as one would expect, lawyers like Robert Danby and Richard Pigot enjoyed the confidence of clients from both districts. One cannot, obviously, talk of these circles as county communities. Yorkshire was the county, but it was so large and administratively complex that it was almost impossible for there to have been a fully developed notion of the body of the whole shire. Moreover it was only in the early fifteenth century itself that election of representatives to parliament became the responsibility of the gentry themselves.[50] Much of the feeling of belonging to a community of gentry thus seems to have been absorbed within these 'counties' within the county, whose boundaries were determined not administratively, but partly geographically, partly historically and partly politically.

52

The political element is of great importance. Throughout England, we need no reminding, any sense of community as gentry was overlain by the vertical bonds of lordship and bastard feudalism. It is no accident that the gentry communities of northern and western Yorkshire, especially those of Richmondshire and Knaresborough, coincided with the zones of influence of the Nevill and Percy families. The Plumpton letters show quite vividly how Sir William Plumpton in the 1470s was bound to the Percy interest. When the earl of Northumberland took away the deputyship of Constable, Steward and Forester of Knaresborough and granted it to William Gascoigne, try as he might, Plumpton found no other lord who would help him. And when Northumberland also proved less than willing to promote his ambition of becoming a J.P. and he turned to Lord Hastings, Hastings refused to intervene and accused Plumpton of trying to set up a conflict between the two lords. 'Sir, I took that as a watchword for medling betwixt lords' wrote Godfrey Green who had received the snub on his master's behalf.[51] Exactly the same went for the Nevill interest in Richmondshire. The gentry there came within the Middleham zone of influence. At the same time these ties of lordship also helped bind the community more closely together. Several of the gentry were mesne tenants of the lordship of Middleham. Many more were mesne tenants of the Honour of Richmond, whose local prestige and authority the lords of Middleham possessed. The annual rendering of a peppercorn or rose in rent had more than a symbolic meaning. The employment they offered, the hospitality they made available and the patronage they commanded, especially when they were in favour at court, enabled the lords of Middleham to make themselves the focus of local landowning society. Lordship, therefore, was not just an alternative pattern of association; it provided itself another of the means by which the sense of community was reinforced.[52]

It does not follow that all the gentry of Richmondshire were ardent followers of Salisbury, then Warwick, then Gloucester. Before 1460 the Percies and their allies found some friends like Richard Clervaux in their rival's camp.[53] And other families —

the Lascelles and Nortons, for instance — seem to have stayed quietly in the background during these turmultuous years. But after 1461 until 1485 when Warwick and Gloucester were unassailable in the north there were powerful inducements for the ambitous, the importunate or the needy to turn to the 'Godfather' at Middleham. The best placed of the Richmond-shire gentry were those dozen or so who managed to become retainers or office-holders of the lords of Middleham, some of whom received exceptionally generous fees. Successive lords retained different men, but certain families seem to have had a special relationship with the lord of Middleham. One was the Metcalfe family, the number of whom receiving fees grew from just one under Salisbury to nine under Warwick.[54] But the Metcalfes in terms of the gentry community were a fairly insignificant family. Far more important were the Conyers. It seems to have been a tradition that the head of the family took the office of Steward of the lordship and of the rights of the Honour of Richmond possessed by the Nevills and Glou-cester.[55] It appears to be the case that they used this position to place as many of their (admittedly numerous) relations as possible on the payroll. Sir John, whose authority in the district under Warwick seems to have been all embracing, would appear to have been the man who smoothed the tran-sition from the last of the Nevills to his erstwhile enemy, even before Gloucester married his heiress. One of Gloucester's first acts on gaining possession of the lordship was to confirm Sir John's position with the inducement of an increase in his fee from £13. 6s. 8d. to £20. Between 1471 and 1474 the following immediate relations of Sir John were retained:

> his brothers Richard and William, whose contracts were renewed in December 1471 and January 1472 respectively, and likewise his brother-in-law John Robinson (n.d.),
> his grandson and heir, John (n.d.),
> his second son Richard in December 1471,
> his brother Roger in September 1473,
> his brothers-in-law William Burgh (Oct, 1471), Roland Pudsey (Oct, 1471) and Robert Wycliffe (Oct, 1473),

his son-in-law Thomas Markenfield (Dec, 1471),
his nephew Lionel Claxton (n.d.),
and his wife's half-brother, Thomas Tunstall, the younger brother
of Sir Richard Tunstall, retained in November 1471 with the huge
fee of £33. 6s. 8d.[56]

One cannot help wondering whether Richard of Gloucester's
early retainers at Middleham were chosen by Conyers rather
than by him.

Others of the Richmondshire gentry who are not known to
have been actually retained or given office were active in the
service of the lord of Middleham or looked to him for assistance. William Burgh II, who died in 1465, was a prominent
activist in the service of both the earl of Salisbury and the earl
of Warwick, but he does not appear to have received any fee
from either of them.[57] Thomas Mountford, on the other hand,
had been retained by Warwick but was apparently dropped by
Richard of Gloucester. He was, however, one of those Richmondshire men richly rewarded by Richard after 1483, which
suggests that he gave his active support to the usurper.[58] Other
Richmondshire men who are not known to have been retainers
or office holders — James Strangways, jnr, Ralph FitzRandall,
Randolph Pigot and William Ingleby — were knighted by
Gloucester on his Scottish campaigns in 1481 and 1482.[59] But
perhaps the most instructive example of an unretained fol-
lower and well-willer of the lords of Middleham is provided
by Richard Clervaux. Clervaux in 1459-61 was one of the
minority in the district who stayed loyal to Henry VI and
benefitted by it. But after Edward's usurpation he wasted little
time in making up for his misjudgement. It would appear that
over the winter of 1462-3 he was summoned to join the royal
forces besieging the northern castles, for on 17 January 1463
he secured a royal licence exempting him from all royal service
and allowing him to abide at his own place at his ease. The
licence, given under the signet at Middleham, was granted
because, as the king wrote,

'we been enformed by our ryght trusty entirely biloved cosyn of
Warrewyke that ye be vexed with such infirmite and diseease that

ye ne be of any power to laboure withoute grete jeopardies, we of our grace especial in concideracion of your sayde impotencie and at thinstance of our sayde cosyn have pardonned you . . . '[60]

That a recent opponent, who just two years earlier had been enjoying the office of under-steward of his lordship and the revenues of one of his manors granted by his enemies, could thus successfully approach Warwick for favours, shows clearly enough that the earl saw himself, and was accepted by others, as the natural leader of all the gentry of the district. It is no surprise to find that after the Readeption Clervaux found it prudent to buy a general pardon, but he was soon drawn into Gloucester's net. It was Gloucester's constable of Barnard Castle and newcomer to the local scene, Richard Ratcliffe, whom he made the steward of his court at East Cowton in or before 1476. It was to Gloucester that he and his neighbour Roland Place turned to resolve their dispute in 1478.[61] And on 26 September 1483, in gratitude for certain recent but unspecified services rendered by both Richard and his son Marmaduke, Clervaux, who had already been granted by the king the offices of steward and receiver of the lordship of Manfield during the minority of John FitzHenry (his grandson), was additionally granted the whole revenue of the lordship without account. And almost a year later, Richard, the king's servant, was granted a tun of wine from the customs at Hull.[62] Never a retainer, sometimes an opponent, Clervaux perhaps best respresents the level-headed and calculating political relationship between the gentry of Richmondshire and the lords of Middleham. Loyalty was not unquestioning. They might look elsewhere if they could; they usually accepted quite pragmatically the local political situation as it was; and they were quick to take advantage of any opportunities that came their way.

The last is clearly demonstrated in their relationship with Richard of Gloucester. Many of the gentry were not averse to basking in the all too brief sunshine of Richard III's reign. This is not the place to go into the use made by Richard of gentry drawn from his Middleham connection in the usurpation and defence of the throne. But his rich gifts to some of these friends are worthy of note. Sir John Conyers was made Knight of the Garter, was granted an annuity of 200 marks from the issues of Yorkshire and granted the manors of Aldebrough and Catterick from the lordship of Middleham. His brother Richard perhaps received the similar grant of South Cowton at the same time, as well as an additional annuity of £26. 13s. 4d. from Barnard Castle until he should have better provision. Thomas Markenfield, sheriff of Yorkshire in 1484, had his annuity from Middleham increased from £10 to 100 marks. Thomas Mountford was granted an annuity of £10 from the lordship of Rochester and appointed steward of Windsor Castle with a fee of £30.[63] And so one could continue. For the gentry of Richmondshire, loyalty to the lord of Middleham in his rebellions and treasons which went unpunished in 1469-71, paid handsome dividends after 1483. For a few the sudden loss of all this in August 1485 did prove too great and they joined Lords Lovell and Scrope in raising rebellion against the new regime in 1486 and 1487.[64] These were Vergil's savages. But the majority were in fact civilized and quickly adjusted to the new circumstances. The Conyers family, for whom Sir Richard was in the party which assembled at Robin Hood's Stone to welcome Henry VII to York in April 1486, Markenfield, Mountford and Richard Clervaux, knighted in 1487, quickly adapted. Sir John Conyers' heir, William, who succeeded his grandfather in 1490, was raised to the peerage in 1509 and slipped into the role played over the last century by the Nevills.[65] And the community of gentry of Richmondshire continued to arrange marriages, settle estates and exploit their property as they had always done, while the heady days of Warwick the Kingmaker and Richard III soon became but distant memories.

Notes

1. The 'Anglica Historia' of Polydore Vergil, ed D.Hay (CS, 1950), p. 11.
2. J.Warkworth, A Chronicle of the First Thirteen Years of the Reign of King Edward the Fourth, ed. J.O. Halliwell (CS, 1839), p. 6; 'The Chronicle of the Rebellion in Lincolnshire, 1470', Camden Miscellany, I (CS, 1847), p. 17; DNB, XVI, p. 1319.
3. CP, VII, p. 481; Wills and Inventories from the Archdeaconry of Richmond, ed. J. Raine (SS, 1853), pp. 5-6.
4. Camden Miscellany, I, p. 12.
5. Ibid, p. 16.
6. Ibid, p. 17.
7. PL, V (1904), p. 80.
8. CPR, 1467-77, pp. 215-16. For a fuller discussion of the involvement of the Richmondshire gentry in this rising see my 'Lord FitzHugh's Rising in 1470', forthcoming in BIHR.
9. Historie of the Arrivall of King Edward IV, ed. J.Bruce (CS, 1838) pp. 31-2.
10. Especially the Clervaux Cartulary belonging to Mr.W.D.Chaytor and the Lawson of Brough Papers deposited in the North Yorkshire County Record Office.
11. A.H.Thompson, 'The Register of the Archdeacons of Richmond, 1442-77', YAJ, XXX (1931) and XXXII (1936).
12. NYRO, Lawson of Brough Papers, ZAL 3/17.
13. VCH, North Riding, ed. W. Page, I (1914). The following two paragraphs are based on an analysis of the parochial and manorial histories, pp. 36-390. (See Map 2).
14. PRO, SC 6/1085/20.
15. H.L. Gray, 'Incomes from land in England in 1436'. EHR, XLIX (1934), p. 617. The figures given by Gray are generally accepted to be underassessed.
16. For ministers' accounts of Snape see M.Y.Ashcroft, 'Snape in the late fifteenth century', North Yorkshire County Record Office Journal, 5 (June 1977), 20-58.
17. According to a rental of 1478-9 the Harcourt moiety of Bedale was worth £49 (see NYRO, ZBA 11/8/1/23).
18. H.B.McCall, The Family of Wandesforde of Kirklington and Castlecomer (1904), p. 319.
19. A.J. Pollard, 'The Burghs of Brough Hall, c 1270-1574', North Yorkshire County Record Office Journal, 6 (April 1978) pp. 9-10.
20. A.J.Pollard, 'Richard Clervaux of Croft: a North Riding Squire in the Fifteenth Century', YAJ, L (1978), p. 154.
21. Quoted by A.R. Wagner, Heralds and Heraldry in the Middle Ages (2nd ed., 1959), p. 79.
22. CPR, 1429-36, p. 379; K.B.McFarlane, The Nobility of Later Medieval England (1973), p. 25; PRO, C. 218/17/1 Part 1/34.
23. NYRO, Clervaux Carulary, fly leaf; Lawson of Brough Papers, ZRL I/53; PRO, SC6/1085/20; DL 29/648/10485.
24. Calculated from VCH Yorks, North Riding, I.
25. J.S. Purvis, 'Monastic Rentals and Dissolution Papers', Miscellanea, III

58

(Yorkshire Archaeological Society, Record Series, LXXX, 1931), p. 42.

26. *Valor Ecclesiasticus*, V, ed. J. Caley and J. Hunter (1834), p. 235. The gross income was £188. 16s 2d. Its sister house at Egglestone held property worth £65. 5s. 6d. gross in 1535 (*Ibid*, p. 236).

27. For example, the holding of Jervaulx Abbey in the vill of Brough. See Pollard, *North Yorks. Journal*, p. 9.

28. R.B.Dobson, 'The Later Middle Ages, 1215-1500' in *A History of York Minster*, ed. G.E. Aylmer and R. Cant, (Oxford, 1977) pp. 55-6.

29. In Yorkshire about a quarter of the chantries dissolved in the middle sixteenth century were established after 1480 (C.Haigh, *Reformation and Resistance in Tudor Lancashire* (1975), p. 71). A good example of Richmondshire foundations is provided by the Burgh family who founded three chapels in 1474, 1491 and 1505 which were endowed with property to the value of £8 of rent *p.a.* (Pollard, *North Yorks. Journal*, 6, p. 9).

30. R.S. Schofield, 'The geographical distribution of wealth in England, 1334-1649'. *EcHR*, 2nd series, XVIII (1965), p. 504.

31. H.L. Gray, 'Incomes from Land', *EHR*, XLIX, pp. 635-6. One wonders whether the incomes of knights and esquires were not as underassessed for taxation as those of the baronage. See T.B. Pugh & C.D. Ross. 'The English Baronage and the Income Tax of 1436', *BIHR*, 26 (1953), p. 1ff.

32. M.J. Bennett, 'A county community: social cohesion amongst the Cheshire gentry, 1400-1425', *Northern History*, VIII (1973), pp. 24-44, reveals a very similar pattern in another northern county earlier in the century.

33. Pollard, *YAJ*, L, p. 160; *North Yorks, Journal*, 6, p. 26.

34. *Ibid*.

35. *A Visitation of the North of England, C. 1480-1500*, ed. C.H. Hunter-Blair (SS, 1930), pp. 106-7; Pollard, *YAJ*, L, p. 160-1.

36. *Visitation*, ed. Hunter-Blair, pp. 92-4; J. Raine, 'Marske in Swaledale'. *YAJ*, VI (1879-80), p. 54.

37. *Ibid;* J.W. Clay, *The Extinct and Dormant Peerage of the Northern Counties of England* (1913), p. 32.

38. McCall, *Wandesforde*, p. 198.

39. University of York, Borthwick Institute of Historical Research, Probate Register, Vol 5, f. 133v; T. Horsfall, *Notes on the Manor of Well and Snape* (Leeds, 1912), p. 31, from the Inquisition Post Mortem. Mr. Keith Dockray has pointed out to me that Inquisitions post Mortem of the North Yorkshire gentry are generally a fruitful source of information on enfeoffments.

40. NYRO, Lawson of Brough Papers, ZRL 1/33; *Testamenta Eboracensia*, II, ed. J. Raine (SS, 1855), p. 246; *Testamenta Eboracensia*, III, ed. J. Raine (SS, 1864), p. 265.

41. NYRO, Clervaux Cartulary ff. 147-7d.

42. McCall, *Wandesforde*, p. 99.

43. NYRO, Lawson of Brough Papers, ZRL 1/48.

44. NYRO, Clervaux Cartulary, f. 146d.

45. Thompson, *YAJ*, xxxii, pp. 127-8.

46. McCall, *Wandesforde*, p. 327.

47. NYRO, Clervaux Cartulary, ff. 155-6.

48. See Raine, *Testamenta Eboracensia*, III, p. 292.
49. *Plumpton Correspondence*, ed. T. Stapleton (CS, 1889) esp. pp. lxv-xciv.
50. A.Gooder, *The Parliamentary Representation of the County of York, 1258-1832*, II (Yorkshire Archaeological Society, Record Series, XCI, 1935), pp. 3-6.
51. *Plumpton Correspondence*, ed. T.Stapleton, pp. 31, 33.
52. I am grateful to Dr.R.A.Griffiths & Professor Ross for pointing this out to me.
53. Pollard, *YAJ*, L, pp. 164.
54. NYRO, Clervaux Cartulary, fly-leaf; PRO, SC6/1085/20.
55. A.J.Pollard, 'The Northern Retainers of Richard Nevill, earl of Salisbury', *Northern History*, XI (1976 for 1975), p. 54.
56. PRO, DL 29/648/10485.
57. Pollard, *North Yorks. Journal*, 6, pp. 13-15.
58. PRO, SC6/1085/20; DL29/648/10485; see also below p. 56.
59. W.C.Metcalffe, *Book of Knights Banneret, Knights of the Bath and Knights Bachelor* (1885), 6-7.
60. NYRO, Clervaux Cartulary, f. 154.
61. Ibid. ff. 167d, 155-6.
62. BL. Harley MS. 433, f. 118; *CPR, 1477-85*, p. 482.
63. BL, Harley MS. 433, ff. 93, 287 (Sir John Conyers), 50d (Richard Conyers), 85 (Markenfield), 53d, 61d (Mountford).
64. Hay, *Anglica Historia*, pp. 11, 39; *York Civic Records*, II, ed. A.Raine (Yorkshire Archaeological Society, Record Series, 1941), pp. 9-10. For the most recent discussion of the disturbances created by some of Richard III's followers see M.A. Hicks, 'Dynastic Change and Northern Society: the career of the fourth earl of Northumberland', *Northern History*, XIV (1978), esp. pp. 96-7.
65. *Plumpton Correspondence*, p. xcvi; NYRO, Clervaux Cartulary, f. 150-50d; *CPR, 1485-94*, p. 175; *CP*, III, p. 404.

The Changing Role of the Wydevilles in Yorkist Politics to 1483

M. A. Hicks
Lecturer in History
King Alfred's College, Winchester

The Wydevilles are one of the most unpopular families in English history: even their biographers have hardly concealed their dislike and have accepted improbable charges made against them.[1] Yet contemporary witnesses were not unanimous in condemnation and at least one hostile chronicler was biased, as Professor Lander has shown.[2] Lander did not re-evaluate the political role of the Wydevilles in the light of his discovery, which is the purpose of this paper. It will concentrate on the benefits which the Wydevilles received from the crown, rather than on their services. The name Wydeville will cover not only the queen, her parents, brothers and sisters, but also her elder sons Thomas and Richard Grey.

All previous historians have begun by asking: who were the Wydevilles in 1464? Their family tree has been traced in the *Complete Peerage* and glossed by Lander, who observes:

> 'Quite apart from the high birth of Jacquetta of Luxembourg, the social status of the Wydevilles . . . was not as lowly as many historians have assumed'.

They were, in short, 'a decent county family' with lands in five counties, who had filled local offices since the mid-14th century, had served with distinction in France, and had started to marry into the peerage in the 1450s. While all this is true, it does not tell the whole story.

In the first place Richard Wydeville, the future Earl Rivers, was not heir of the prominent family of Northamptonshire gentry; he was son of another Richard, younger brother of the

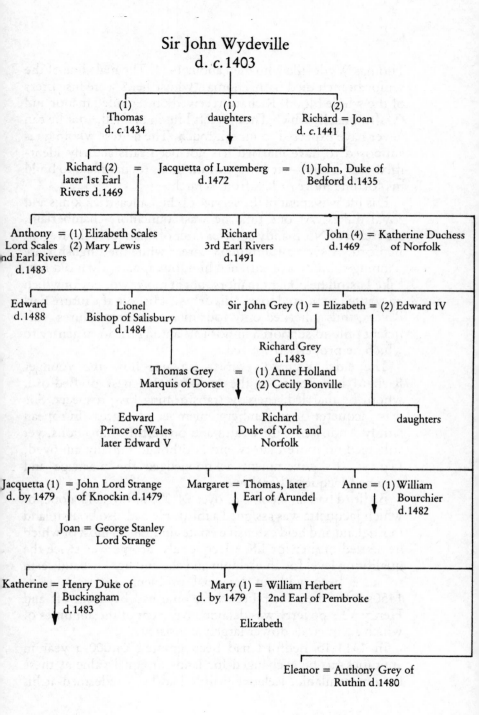

Thomas Wydeville who died about 1434. The male line of the senior branch died with Thomas, whose heirs were his sisters of the whole blood. Richard received one entailed manor and Grafton itself, which Thomas left him in his will,[3] but he can never have expected to inherit much. The heiress whom he is supposed to have married has not been satisfactorily identified, nor is it known what she inherited. Richard had to build his fortune more or less from scratch.

His life was spent in the service of the Lancastrian kings and royal dukes. At one time he was councillor, chamberlain, seneschal of Normandy and treasurer of finances to the Regent Bedford. A successful military career while the English were winning should have enriched him, but apparently it did not. Like Fastolf he bought manors, but at most two, one of which he wanted to be sold to pay his debts.[4] His son, the future Earl Rivers, thus inherited only four manors in three shires, sufficient only to support a minor role among the local gentry to which he properly belonged.

The elder Richard's career explains how the younger Richard had access to the widowed Duchess of Bedford, whom he married, thereby transforming his prospects. She was Jacquetta of Luxemberg, member of a great European family, endowed with wealth and powerful connections, yet still aged no more than twenty. Although initially annoyed, Henry VI's government acknowledged the marriage and assigned Jacquetta her dower.

Bedford had an income of over £4,000 in England alone, of which Jacquetta was assigned a third. He had also bought land in England and held extensive estates in France, most of which he settled on her for life.[5] Jacquetta's income was twice the qualifying level for an earldom and she and her husband seem to have been without financial problems until the mid-1450s.[6] By then their French income had been cut off and Henry VI's poverty was delaying payment of the annuities of which Jacquetta's dower largely consisted.

In 1414-15 Bedford had been granted £4,000 a year in annuities, to be exchanged for lands of equal value as these became available. Relatively little had been redeemed at his death, when annuities exceeded £3,000. Jacquetta's dower consisted mainly of annuities from the exchequer and duchy of Cornwall and of third shares rather than whole manors.[7] On her death her dower would revert to the crown and her husband and children would be left with only his inheritance. It was therefore sensible to make the most of her dower by using the income to buy land or by converting her life estate into something more permanent. As she held only third shares, Jacquetta had not only to improve her title to any estate but also to secure possession of the other two-thirds, which were generally granted to others. Evidently this called for expenditure or a display of royal favour which was not forthcoming. Indeed, some lands had to be exchanged for annuities, and many grants made to others from the Bedford estates included the reversion of Jacquetta's share.[8] Altogether she secured only one manor and annuities of £139 10s. 7d. a year for their children; in 1455 most of this was again restricted to Jacquetta's lifetime by act of resumption.[9] In 1461 their eight scattered manors were surely inadequate endowment for a baron.

Jacquetta and Richard needed success on the marriage market, if they were to provide for all their thirteen children. By 1461 they had concluded three marriages: Jacquetta Wydeville had married Lord Strange of Knockin by 1450; Elizabeth Wydeville married John Grey, son and heir of Lord and Lady Ferrers of Groby c.1452; and in 1460 Anthony Wydeville married Elizabeth, in her own right Lady Scales. As these baronies were older than that of Rivers, the Wydevilles were certainly marrying above themselves. They were connecting themselves with families like the Greys of Ruthin, Bourchiers, Arundels and even the House of York. But their new in-laws did not belong to the higher nobility in rank, wealth or importance. Assessed for income tax at £666 in 1436, the Ferrers of Groby barony was the richest of the three, but it was divided between the heirs male and heirs general in 1449: Elizabeth, Lady Ferrers inherited only the title and the less important estates.[10] Even allowing for her husband's Astley inheritance, she was poorer than her predecessors. Early in

1460 Rivers had provided for only two children; even after Anthony's marriage nine remained single.

Jacquetta's kinship to the king and queen could account for Richard's elevation to the Garter, to the peerage, and to the royal council. This is also suggested by his promotion in rank before becoming a councillor, but there is little other evidence that he carried weight at court. Those with undoubted influence over Henry VI secured grants from Bedford's estates which Rivers wanted himself.[11] His inability to compete for favour at a time of exceptional royal prodigality shows how modest his influence really was. He seems to have avoided committing himself politically to either Suffolk or Somerset, perhaps because his primary interests were military. He served repeatedly in France, rising to be seneschal of Gascony and (like his father) lieutenant of Calais. His useful military talents may have contributed to his pardon in 1461 and his reappearance in the council by 1463, as he certainly had little influence with Edward IV.[12]

The Wydevilles clearly had too few lands to qualify as leaders of county society, let alone maintain a peerage, for which martial talents were not enough. A lucky marriage gave Rivers wealth, connections and opportunities, enabling him to rise from the lesser gentry to become a potentially impoverished peer. Everything depended on Jacquetta's dower and her life, so he remained an upstart, in spite of attempts to construct a noble past. Such a background hardly fitted his daughter as queen and, as Professor Ross has shown,[13] Jacquetta's lineage was not enough either.

Nevertheless Elizabeth Wydeville did marry Edward IV as her second husband. Professor Lander has refuted the assertion of earlier historians that Edward was so blindly enamoured that he allowed the Wydevilles 'unbridled licence' in pursuit of their desires. Elizabeth, he pointed out, received a smaller dower than her predecessor. Lord Rivers became an earl, treasurer and constable of England, but otherwise received only minor rewards. His son Anthony received only four grants before 1469. None of Elizabeth's other brothers or sons received anything during Edward's first reign. These grants were relatively small, 'especially when compared with those made to . . . Lord Hastings and Lord Herbert' or the Nevilles, who certainly 'took more from the royal bounty in titles, lands, offices and money grants than did the Wyde-villes'. Lander's interpretation rests explicitly on the comparison of grants to the Wydevilles with those made to other royal favourites. The contrast is telling, but it begs two questions: what provision was appropriate for the Wydevilles and what had Edward to give?

In 1461 Edward enjoyed all the crown lands plus those forfeited by a third of the nobility and many gentry. Such vast resources gave great scope for patronage, permitting him to raise obscure proteges to the high nobility. Usually a king's capacity to give was severely limited, for the only lands normally in his hands were escheats. His everyday patronage consisted of favours of relatively short duration. When endowing a duke or earl, kings seldom had enough lands and made up the requisite income with annuities instead. There was thus a natural check on royal generosity. To endow his Tudor half-brothers with the minimum income appropriate for an earl, Henry VI had to recover property formerly given to others.[14] If 1,000 marks was all a king's half-brother was worth, what was suitable for a father-in-law or brother-in-law?

By 1464 most forfeitures had been given away, together with the county of Chester and much of the duchies of Lancaster and Cornwall. Edward could not endow the Wydevilles on the scale of the early 1460s; comparisons with Herbert, Hastings and the Nevilles are therefore inapplicable. They could only be so endowed by permanently disinheriting the crown or by recovering property formerly given to others. Lands could be resumed by persuading grantees to surrender them, which meant buying them out at full valuation, or by forcing grantees to give them up. Edward could either incur great expenditure or make enemies of committed supporters. The principal beneficiaries of his patronage had been those to whom he owed most, who had influence with him, and whom he was least willing to offend. He understandably declined to redistribute patronage in the Wydevilles's favour.

What did Edward regard as appropriate provision for the Wydevilles? One pointer is Lord Rivers's earldom, which morally obliged Edward to make his hereditary income up to 1,000 marks. Edward did not do this, making only two grants in tail, but he did give Rivers two great offices and an additional income of £1,586 as councillor, treasurer and earl.[14a] Rivers's income was certainly doubled to over three thousand pounds, more than that of any immediate contemporary other than Warwick and Clarence. On his death, his heir Anthony was to keep the constableship, which would suffice with his Wydeville and Scales possessions to sustain the estate of earl. Moreover, Anthony received several minor grants, together with the Isle of Wight and Carisbrooke castle. These had been given to Sir Geoffrey Gate, who exchanged them with Anthony in return for four manors elsewhere, two from Jacquetta's dower: the king merely renounced his reversionary rights and confirmed the arrangement.[15] When the Earl of Worcester went to Ireland as deputy in 1467, he sold his offices in England: Anthony secured the constableship of Portchester castle and Rivers the constableship of England, probably at Edward's expense. Another manor obtained by Rivers was surrendered by the queen for compensation elsewhere[15a] and Lord Mountjoy gave up the treasurership of England for a barony, a small annuity in tail, and 1,000 marks in cash.[16] Edward's patronage was more substantial than Lander allowed.

The other way in which the Wydevilles were advanced was by marriage. By the end of 1466 five of Elizabeth's sisters had married the Duke of Buckingham, and the heirs of the Earls of Kent, Essex, Arundel and of Lord Herbert; her elder son had married the Duke of Exeter's heiress; and a brother had married the Dowager-Duchess of Norfolk. Generally regarded as of the king's making, these matches have commonly been condemned as offensive to the magnates, especially the Nevilles. Professor Lander, however, traced this inter-

pretation back to the *Annales* of the pseudo-William
Worcestre, a Neville partisan whose hostility was due to bias.
Even this chronicler made no comment about three of the
marriages and objected to the others with varying intensity. In
only one instance, so Lander argued, had anyone outside
Warwick's immediate circle grounds for offence, and in this
one case — the Herbert match — it was not the marriage itself
which was condemned, but the bridegroom's creation as Lord
Dunster.[16a] There was little reason to suppose that the marriages gave much offence. Again Lander's remarks are per-
suasive and were followed by Professor Ross in his *Edward
IV*, in which he pointed out that 'other Yorkist noblemen had
no scruple about allowing their sons and daughters to marry
the queen's kinsfolk', even when they 'had a free choice in
their . . . marriages'.[17] Grounds exist, however, for doubting
whether Edward was as passive and the Wydevilles as innocent
as Lander would have us believe.

Let us begin by looking once more at the only marriage for
which the contract survives, that with the Herberts. As Mr.
Pugh pointed out, Herbert sought the freehold of two lordships held at farm and for a term and also Jacquetta's third
share of St. Briavels and the forest of Dean. Herbert believed
that Edward's consent could be secured by the Wydevilles,
who agreed to do their 'effectual part and devoir and cause our
Souerayn Lord the King' to comply. The resultant patent was
based on a petition by Rivers, which recited Jacquetta's surrender of St. Briavels specifically for the benefit of Herbert.
Rivers's success is hardly surprising, since the contract was
made 'at the instance of our Souerey Lord the King and his
pleasure'. Evidently Edward was willing to make concessions
and raised no difficulties about granting the reversion of lands
already held by the two parties. Since one lordship was farmed
at 100 marks,[18] Herbert's inducement beyond the marriage
portion was substantial.

The same pattern emerges in other cases. When William
Bourchier married Anne Wydeville, Edward verbally prom-
ised lands worth £100 a year and a lump sum of unknown size.
In payment he granted forfeited land in East Anglia and a

licence to ship 1,000 woollen cloths.[19] It was presumably the contract for the Arundel marriage which is behind a grant in 1467 to the earl for life, with remainder to his son Thomas and the latter's heirs male by Margaret Wydeville, who was described in the patent as daughter of Earl Rivers and the Duchess of Bedford, mother of the queen. Apparently this was what Arundel wanted: before making the grant, Edward had to obtain the surrender of Lord Say, to whom he had previously given it.[20] The marriage of the Duke of Buckingham was in the king's gift and it was again the king who 'made the marriage' between Thomas Grey and Anne Holland, the Exeter heiress.[21] One wonders what inducement was offered to Lord Grey of Ruthin to marry his heir to a Wydeville. A few suggestions may be made. First of all, Grey became Earl of Kent a few months after his son's marriage. Secondly, Edward pandered to his dislike for Herbert's advancement in North Wales, near his lordship of Ruthin, by substituting Grey for Herbert as chief justice of Merioneth and constable of Harlech castle. Finally, Anthony Grey received a substantial grant of forfeited lands.[22]

The other marriages were more complicated. That between Thomas Grey and Anne Holland was arranged at Edward's behest, on payment of 4,000 marks by the queen, and in place of an existing understanding with the Nevilles. The Duke of Exeter was an unreconciled Lancastrian, whose lands were forfeit, but his duchess was the king's elder sister. She was granted the whole inheritance for life, together with some forfeited manors. In 1466 she settled her jointure and five other manors on Elizabeth's feoffees, probably in trust for the marriage. She was allowed to convert her life estate into tail and in 1469 the ultimate remainder was reserved to the queen, her heirs and assigns.[23] Evidently, come what may, Elizabeth wanted the Holland inheritance.

Lander says that the 'diabolical marriage' of Katherine, Duchess of Norfolk and Sir John Wydeville — a sexagenarian and a teenager — was not unusual. Her career was certainly nightmarish for the Mowbrays, as she retained most of the family estate for half a century and her fourth marriage threatened their reversionary rights. The Wydevilles, however, were interested primarily in her dower and jointure from her third husband, Viscount Beaumont, as their son had been attainted and the reversion belonged to the crown. In 1467, following their marriage, the reversion of six Lincolnshire manors was granted to him, with remainder to his heirs male. He later had seisin of these and certain other manors in her right.[24] On her death, which might well have been soon, he would have a substantial estate with which to endow a second marriage and family. One wonders whether Katherine married him to protect herself against powerful reversionary interests, such as the Duke of Clarence and Lord Hastings, or because the Wydevilles themselves threatened her security of tenure. Had Sir John been satisfied with the reversion on her death, there could be no objection, but it was surely improper to secure immediate possession by marrying the old lady.

Evidently strong inducements beyond the portion were needed for magnates to marry their offspring to the Wydevilles: on the open market Herbert's heir could hardly have commanded a larger portion. Incentives were even needed for those already related to the Wydevilles. Edward was willing to commit resources to alliances from which he had nothing to gain, as the Wydevilles's partners were steadfastly loyal. Probably he provided £100-worth of land to four couples and at least one portion. He was offering patronage that would otherwise have been withheld: if the recipients could have obtained it some other way, they would have had no incentive for a Wydeville marriage. Edward enabled the Wydevilles to outbid all other competitors on the marriage market, probably aggrieving others apart from the Nevilles. Without Edward's support the marriages would not have occurred.

The Norfolk marriage illustrates how royal favour could be used to wring concessions from others. Edward might intervene directly on the Wydevilles's behalf: for example, he tried to foist Sir Richard Wydeville on the Order of St. John as prior. Likewise, when Maud, Lady Willoughby was induced in 1465 to convey sixteen manors of her Cromwell inheritance to Anthony Wydeville, probably for fear for her Lancastrian husband, Sir Gervase Clifton, royal pressure was employed.[25] More frequently, with or without Edward's knowledge, the Wydevilles exploited his power to extort concessions or to render rival claims inoperable. Realising by 1466 that his wife would bear him no children, Anthony persuaded her to re-settle her inheritance on him jointly, with remainder to his feoffees rather than her heirs. Again it was Anthony who seized Caister castle on the pretext that John Paston was a royal serf. It was he who bought lands at North Mymms (Herts.) and then denied that it was copyhold or owed any service. His mother — or was it his father? — bought an invalid claim to a manor they coveted.[26] They were apparently ready to pursue any avenue of gain, however trifling and unworthy of their attention.

The Wydevilles could reasonably expect dower for the queen and some provision for their main line, but they should surely have supported other relatives themselves. Edward, however, felt obliged to provide for them all. Each sister-in-law was to be at least a countess and his stepson was to be a duke. What else, one wonders, did he plan for Sir John and Sir Richard Wydeville? Some grants to the Herberts, Bourchiers and Arundels were effectively patronage to the Wydevilles, who might conceivably have secured them for the main line, had they not placed their daughters first.[27] Moreover, Elizabeth received not only her dower, which was several times adjusted in her favour, but her Ferrers jointure and at least £866 13s. 4d. to support the Stafford boys and her elder daughters.[28]

The family did not depend wholly on royal favour, as Elizabeth and Rivers could attract and reward dependants. As early as October 1464 Elizabeth was making appointments under her great seal.[29] Her officers were not chosen for her, though key figures must have required Edward's approval: this was assured for her chamberlain, their mutual kinsman Lord Berners. Kinship, neighbourhood and service account for her choice of Sir Humphrey Bourchier and Jacques Haute as her carvers and John Dyve and Robert Isham as her attorney- and solicitor-generals.[30] Even had she wished, she could

hardly have staffed her household exclusively from Wydeville dependants. Some were certainly king's servants and
Elizabeth wisely engaged Edward's law officers as counsel.
Unlike her household, her estates were already staffed and her
nominees took over only gradually. Besides, her exercise of
patronage had to be reconciled with her financial needs, just as
the exchequer was primarily an organ of royal finance rather
than of patronage for her father. Rivers as treasurer distributed
most offices, leases and custodies to people unconnected with
his family, but some went to his son, to dependants or to
political allies.[31]

The hub of the connection was Elizabeth's household,
where she was surrounded by her sisters and sister-in-law, her
sons and daughters, and by more distant relatives like the
Hautes, Fogges, Hastings and Donnes. Her brothers committed themselves politically to a prospective kinsman,[32] but
Rivers was more cautious. Probably it was he and Jacquetta
who resolved to advance their younger children, even at the
expense of the main line: Jacquetta was to provide for all her
offspring in her will.[33] Presumably Rivers decided family
policy, just as he directed Elizabeth's affairs without formal
authority.[34] His elder sons had access to the king but Rivers's
own influence seems more important, chary though he was of
exercising it. He used Elizabeth as intermediary: she could
secure new grants, convert feefarms from estates into outright
grants, and could pass them on by surrendering them.[35]
Presumably she adopted this technique because Edward
would not make an outright grant. He was not subservient to
the Wydevilles, but had other advisers and recipients of his
bounty.

Among those with access to his ear in 1465 were twenty
councillors, the chief officers of state and household, and
assorted nobles.[36] Some, already related to the queen, hastily
strengthened their ties, while others forged new ones, so the
Wydevilles gained that acceptance among the nobility and
politically influential which emerged in the pageantry of
Elizabeth's coronation, the tournament with the Bastard of
Burgundy, and the marriage of Margaret of York. Impressive

though their rise was, they were never the sole source of patronage and power: 'the Ryvers been [never] soo hie that I coude hardly scape thorw theym'.[37] Others retained or even increased their influence. Notable among these were the Bourchiers, several of whom served Elizabeth, but who retained their own independent influence with Edward. A closer alliance was forged with another favourite, Lord Herbert. Their marriage alliance was fortified by favours secured for him by Rivers and the queen.[38] The advance of the Wydevilles and Herberts at the expense of the Nevilles was marked by Edward's increasingly anti-French foreign policy, which the former actively promoted. The Wydeville marriage gave the Nevilles several grounds for offence and the plans of Herbert, already at odds with Warwick, threatened him and Clarence. The violence of Warwick's enmity forced the king's favourites to make common cause against a common foe. As members of the extreme anti-Neville faction, however, the Wydevilles could not command support from all their relatives against Warwick: some could work with him or even maintain friendly relations.

We are now in a position to consider the charges of Warwick's 1469 manifesto,[39] which claimed that Edward's favourites had insinuated themselves into his counsels to the exclusion of the lords of his blood and had then given him bad advice to their own profit, securing grants beyond their deserts, and denying or perverting justice. The manifesto is propaganda, but should not be wholly dismissed, as it depended for its effect on its relevance and topicality. Moreover Warwick practised what he preached, objecting neither to the influence of his own nor the king's kin, but to that of the upstarts — Rivers, his wife and sons, Herbert and others. These were indeed those with most influence on Edward, the principal channel of his patronage and the beneficiaries from it to an almost unprecedented degree, and hence beyond their deserts. They did use their power to extort and to pervert justice. Their elevation had not been designed to counterbalance the Nevilles, for Edward did not share their deep hatred for his Neville relatives. Nor was this achieved: the favourites were defeated in 1469, when the Wydevilles proved of no military use. Their influence and gains were excessive, yielded no corresponding advantage, and were therefore politically indefensible, as Edward himself came to realise.

Past experience may explain why Edward was less generous after 1471. True, he made no major grants during his second reign, but there were some spoils of victory in the great offices distributed in 1471. None fell to the Wydevilles, who even failed to secure those earmarked for them. Perhaps this reflects Edward's offence at Anthony's projected pilgrimage, possibly the slight weight that he attributed to Wydeville support, but it certainly marked a less generous attitude to his in-laws. Instead of elevating every member of the family, he did little for Anthony and his own stepsons, virtually nothing for Sir Richard and Sir Edward Wydeville. For what remained of their influence Elizabeth was even more important, yet in spite of her mediation there were painful moments when Edward preferred other claims to their own.[40] Yet, as we shall see, they established their power on a more solid base.

Elizabeth was more concerned about her sons than her brothers. Her two eldest sons Thomas and Richard Grey were frequently with her, the king and their royal stepbrothers,[41] and indeed they became Edward's intimates. Thomas did not inherit the Ferrers and Astley estates until 1483, but his marriage was effected, he was created Earl of Huntingdon, and in 1473 he and his wife were conveyed lands jointly, which he kept after her premature death.[42] In 1474 the queen concluded another marriage between him and Cecily Bonville, the Bonville and Harrington heiress and a stepdaughter of Lord Hastings. Elizabeth was to keep the inheritance until Cecily was sixteen, perhaps to cover the £2,500 paid for the marriage, but in fact these revenues were pure profit as Edward credited the cost against Hastings's debts to him.[43] Now Marquis of Dorset, Thomas steadily built up his power in the West Country, where he was a royal commissioner and administrator of the lands of his mother and the duchy of Cornwall.

After Clarence's fall he secured the wardship and marriage of the young Earl of Warwick and the custody of nine manors. Finally, in 1483, his infant heir was betrothed to the daughter of the late Duchess of Exeter by her second husband. She, of course, had no title to the Exeter estates to which Elizabeth held reversionary rights, so they were settled by act of parliament on her and her fiancé. A substantial estate was allocated to Dorset's younger brother Richard Grey,[44] hitherto unendowed.

The interests of Anthony, now 2nd Earl Rivers, were more diffuse. He had missed out on patronage in 1471, had lost his hold on Calais and the constableship, but had been compensated with a £200 annuity.[45] Without the treasury and his mother's dower, with only his own lands and those of Scales and Wydeville, he should have been a poor earl, but was apparently cushioned by a foreign pension and the profits of trade.[46] His own scanty estates were scattered, but they would ultimately have been doubled by grants made after his return to favour in 1473.[47] Strangely Anthony waited eight years from the death of his first wife until his second marriage to Mary Lewis, a teenager with modest estates in Essex. Stranger yet, after painfully accumulating estates, Anthony planned to divide them between his brothers,[48] neither of whom was married. The three brothers's apparent unconcern about the future prosperity of their family, or even its continuance, contrasts with their personal greed. One wonders what was the point.

They were just as grasping after 1471 as before. Anthony recovered the manors lost to Sir Geoffrey Gate without relinquishing the Isle of Wight and retained his wife's inheritance after her death in 1473, to the loss of her heirs.[49] In 1474 he was granted the reversion of nine manors on the death of Philippa, Lady Roos, widow of the attainted Lord Roos, of which she had been granted the use in 1461. She was still living in 1482, when Anthony was impatient and anxious to make good his estate. He speculated how two manors had passed to others. If their title was bad, he wrote, he would enter the manors: Lady Roos would forfeit them if she had suffered a fraudulent recovery. He wanted her husband's inquisition post mortem and her patent inspected, to see if her grant was made according to statute, or whether there were any other weaknesses of which he could take advantage. Had she committed any waste whereby she could forfeit her estate? What knights fees and woods were there? Were any lands in the accounts not properly part of her lordship? But no loopholes were exposed.[50] Simultaneously he was scrutinising the accounts of the Warwick feoffees, whose trust was certainly open to attack, but was already under assault from heirs more legitimate than he.[51] He inquired, in passing, about the lands of the late Sir Henry Lewis, his father-in-law. Lewis held little at his death, but in marrying his daughter Rivers may have hoped to recover lands lost by Lewis's attainder and to obtain a share of the possessions of Edmund Beaufort, Duke of Somerset, Mary Lewis's grandfather.[52] When drafting his will, Anthony had pangs of guilt: he ordered the righting of any wrongs regarding the Scales inheritance, moveables seized from Lady Willoughby, differences with Sir John Guildford, and enclosures at Roche Fen in Middleton (Norf.). Anthony's memory was adjustable: he could have mentioned other shady dealings, and his conscience nevertheless let him leave the Scales inheritance to his brother Edward, whose title was even worse than his own.[53] Like Anthony, his brothers would pursue any course of advancement: each sought manors on inadequate titles, one wholly false and the other based on non-observance of a trust a century old.[54] The brothers's limited success shows how restricted their influence was outside Wales.

By 1483 Prince Edward's council was the principal organ of government and justice throughout Wales and was dominated by the Wydevilles. These results were achieved by degrees, not all at once. In 1471 Edward created his son Prince of Wales, Duke of Cornwall and Earl of Chester, granted him the appropriate estates, and set up a council and household for him. Nevertheless Edward retained the income from the estates and delegated only estate administration and temporary appointments to the council: hence the membership of Alcock and other pure administrators.[55] The other councillors were Edward's kinsmen and ministers and the prince's councillor, chamberlain and steward. The latter were Edward's choice: Thomas Milling, the prince's chancellor, had received the queen in sanctuary during the Readeption and had earned the gratitude of her, her husband and son; Sir Thomas Vaughan, the chamberlain, was treasurer of Edward's chamber; and Lord Dacre of the South, the steward, had long been a royal favourite. All were already royal councillors, so the prince's council was little more than a committee of the royal one to which minor functions had been delegated. His household was also small and unimportant. Vaughan's and Milling's new responsibilities had to be reconciled with other duties: in 1472 Vaughan carried the prince at a ceremony at Westminster,[56] where Milling normally resided with the prince's great seal. The prince, like his sisters, may have stayed in the queen's household, but at this stage there is no evidence of undue influence by her or her blood.

There was a radical change in 1472-3. A much larger expenditure was envisaged in November 1472, when the prince was granted the issues of his estates, all alienations and appointments were revoked, and he was authorised to recruit retainers.[57] Next year he moved to Ludlow with an enlarged household and council. Councillors were appointed to the border commissions of the peace and marcher lords agreed individually with the king about peace-keeping in their Welsh lordships. Together these measures constituted a coherent plan for Welsh government. In the principality, Chester, Flint and the border shires the council would have direct authority, in the lordships of the duchy of Lancaster and earldom of March indirect authority through their chancellors as councillors, and in independent lordships it would co-operate with the lords. This change from a private and administrative status is reflected in the prince's move to Ludlow, outside his estates but centrally placed, and in the addition of lawyers and marcher lords to the council.[58]

The council was intended to remedy defects in Welsh justice, perhaps in response to petitions in parliament. One wonders, however, if this particular remedy was promoted by the Wydevilles because it was advantageous to them. The first council, as chosen by the king, included few of them, but by the end of 1472 they dominated it. The more eminent councillors — royal dukes, ministers and bishops — probably left everyday affairs to the officials, who lacked the stature to gainsay Elizabeth and Rivers, even had they wished. In practice, they do not seem to have so wished. Milling was Elizabeth's protégé, Fogge her kinsman, and Dacre, Vaughan and Alcock were all to enjoy the friendship and favour of her and Rivers. The Wydevilles had strong motives to control the prince, for their future would depend on him after Edward's death. Meanwhile control of his administration and patronage was desirable, and in the future — certainly when he was fourteen years of age — more could be expected. Actually, as we have already seen, wider powers were conferred in 1472.

Edward aimed at effective rule in Wales, not the creation of a power base for the Wydevilles, and carefully divided and limited authority. Power rested not with the prince's officers, but with his council, which operated his signet, which in turn moved his great seal and the seals of his principality, palatinates and lordships. Control in finance did not rest with the treasurer and controller of his household, but with the queen, Alcock and Rivers, who had keys to his coffers.[59] Rivers's official powers were slender. Probably he was expected to spend little time at Ludlow. It was not he nor Milling who presided over the council, but Alcock, a former master of the rolls and chancellor of England, who was continually with the prince.[60] He should have directed matters, but More testifies to Wydeville dominance,[61] which emerges clearly from the records: payments were made on warrants under Rivers's seal; his order sufficed to present a priest to a chantry and to move the chancery seal of Carmarthen; another time, when ordering repayment of a bond, he personally changed the phrase 'I will' to 'my lord wills', but the arrangement was his and his seal sufficient warrant.[62] Power rested not with the judicial council in London, but with the council in the Marches, to which bishops, magnates and lawyers seldom came, and which must often have consisted solely of Alcock and household officials.

At first Edward planned moderate reform in Wales: most appointments were confirmed and personnel changed only gradually. Co-operation was intended with marcher lords, four of whom were councillors: most important was Lord Ferrers of Chartley, uncle of the young Herbert Earl of Pembroke. Pembroke had a Wydeville wife. So too had the Duke of Buckingham. It may have been Wydeville influence that gave Buckingham livery of his estates long before he came of age.[63] He entered an indenture of the marches, employed Wydeville protégés in key administrative positions,[64] and sat on border commissions with his brothers-in-law Rivers, Maltravers and Strange and the councillors Shrewsbury and Ferrers.[65] Evidently Rivers, Alcock and the council did co-operate with those about them.

Since Prince Edward's household grew under Wydeville direction, one might expect it to consist of their clients, but apparently it did not. Some members had neither Wydeville nor royal antecedents. Relatively few estate officers were imported, particularly in Wales, where local ministers were generally natives and their superiors were absentees. All automatically became servants of the prince, to whom they could henceforth look for local patronage, access to royal bounty, and ultimately for advancement on his accession. Ambitions and loyalties focused on the prince rather than the king, forming an affinity like that around other heirs to the throne. In his entourage one can distinguish menials and administrators without previous ties, numerous but without stature as individuals, and a few royal servants, whose interests were increasingly identified with those of the prince. Examples of the latter are Vaughan, who resided with the prince rather than the king by 1475,[66] and Sir Richard Croft, a Yorkist retainer holding office in Wales, who became an active partisan of the prince. Most important were the Stanleys, whose stranglehold on Cheshire was initially threatened by the prince's council,[67] but who later entered his service. George Stanley received preferment and his uncle Sir William had become steward of the prince's household by 1483.[68] Once Stanley predominance in Cheshire was recognised, as it was by 1482,[69] they had more to gain from the prince than the king. In the late 1470s the prince was replacing absentee officials with his own men. By 1482-3, when Rivers could raise several thousand men from Wales and Stanley another 4,000 from Lancashire and Cheshire, a major connection had been constructed.[70]

In 1478 Prince Richard married the Mowbray heiress. Like his elder brother he had a chancellor, seal, household and council to manage his estates. His council, like that of Prince Edward, comprised the queen and a group of magnates and bishops, few of whom were Wydeville supporters. Some appointments were made by the council, others by it with the assent of the queen, a formula also found on Prince Edward's estates. It was Elizabeth who mattered, for Richard resided with her and Rivers treated his affairs as their own. The king retained a residual interest,[71] but the marriage gave the Wydevilles control of the important Mowbray estates, retinue and patronage, which they were understandably reluctant to relinquish.

The affairs of Dorset, Rivers, Elizabeth and the princes were five distinct spheres of Wydeville influence, but in practice they scarcely differentiated between them. Rivers used Prince Richard's treasurer and Prince Edward's cofferer as his own agents, paid Prince Edward's bills with his own money, appointed two of his councillors as deputy-butlers, employed their parliamentary patronage for his own nominees, and exploited offices granted by Prince Edward to strengthen his grip on King's Lynn.[72] There was some interchange of personnel at the top, where Lord Dacre of the South, steward of Prince Edward, became queen's chamberlain,[73] and Sir William Allington, attorney-general of Prince Edward, was deputy to Rivers and chancellor of each prince in turn.[74] There can be little doubt that the princes's households — and the princes too — identified themselves with the Wydevilles. By this I don't mean that their loyalty to the king was in question — of course it was not — or that their prime loyalty in any way lessened their allegiance to the king. Instead, under the umbrella label of loyal Yorkists and even king's men, they belonged to the faction of the prince, which was directed by the Wydevilles. In the same way Lord Hastings, whose loyalty to the king was equally committed, belonged to the faction opposed to the queen. This connection of Prince Edward was stronger than those of Rivers and Dorset, and more enduring than that of the queen. On Prince Edward's accession his connection would become a specially favoured group of the king's affinity; the queen's following would die with her. In 1483 Gloucester and Buckingham had to execute some and dismiss others in Edward V's household.[75]

In 1478, directed by the Wydevilles, all the king's relatives and servants combined to destroy their common enemy, Clarence. His destruction was the fruit of the Wydeville marriages of the 1460s, for at least four of the bridegrooms were actively involved.[76] By Edward V's accession four of the marriages had ended by death, none producing an adult heir, and family ties had slackened. Elizabeth still supported her brothers and was surrounded by her sisters, but male Wydevilles had a narrower outlook. Anthony's will ignored female relatives and remembered only his brothers and his nephew Richard Grey.[77] His next brother was to leave all he could to Dorset rather than to his sisters and their issue, his coheirs.[78] If this reveals close ties between Elizabeth's brothers and sons, it shows those with their in-laws to be weak. They no longer agreed on priority of aims, each pursuing his own interests, and in Wales Elizabeth, Rivers and Grey preferred their own advantage to that of their marcher kinsfolk.

The principal development was the break of the Wydevilles with the Herberts. The creation of prince and council of Wales had always been at the expense of the young Earl of Pembroke, whose father had dominated all Wales in the 1460s. In 1471 Haverfordwest was transferred to Prince Edward[79] and by 1473 Pembroke's entail as chief justice of South Wales was annulled. This did not mark a rupture with the Wydevilles, for he was appointed steward and constable of Haverfordwest, chamberlain and chief justice of South Wales, and steward of Carmarthen for life, and was granted 340 marks a year in annuities and regards, 80 of them entailed on his issue by Mary Wydeville, the prince's aunt; his uncle Ferrers was a councillor and constable of Aberystwyth; and his mother received Wydeville support in a struggle with Clarence over Dunster.[80] The decisive break occurred in mid-1478 and the crucial factor may have been the death of his Wydeville wife:[81] the Wydevilles felt no qualm about disinheriting her daughter. The earl lost the lordship and earldom of Pembroke to Prince Edward, receiving instead lands elsewhere and the earldom of Huntingdon, and was deprived of all his offices, regards and annuities in South Wales; his uncle Ferrers was replaced as constable of Aberystwyth and one William Herbert — perhaps an illegitimate kinsman — as receiver of Haverfordwest. The result was achieved by coercion, in which king, queen and royal council combined.[82] At a stroke Herbert influence in the principality and Pembrokeshire was supplanted by that of the Wydevilles.

This illustrates the Wydevilles's steady advance in Wales, which Edward formally recognised in 1483. He nominated Milling, Alcock and Martin to local bishoprics and gradually relinquished lordships of the duchy of Lancaster and earldom of March. Increasingly they intervened outside Wales and entertained petitions from other lordships. Such infringement of franchises had been envisaged by neither king nor marcher lords, who were now virtually unrepresented on the council. Border lords who were Wydeville kinsmen — Buckingham, Maltravers, Strange and Grey of Ruthin — might reasonably have been added, but never were; nor did they share the prince's patronage. The Wydevilles's advance at the expense of established lords may well have alienated them. This could explain the hostility of Buckingham, whose ambitions in Wales are beyond question.

Wydeville aggrandisement at this time was at the expense of others, who were given vested interests in change. The principal instances are the seizure of Pembroke and the re-settlement of the Holland and Mowbray inheritances: Prince Richard had retained the Mowbray estates after his wife's death, to the disinheritance of the heirs.[83] Nor are these the only examples, as they threatened Gloucester's tenure of the Beaufort inheritance and Hastings's hostility is well attested. The Wydevilles remained unpopular. Such factors may explain the support for Gloucester of Northumberland, Neville and Howard, but did any play a part before the decisive arrest of Rivers? Animosity for the Wydevilles should have prevented their dominance of Edward V's early councils, presumably attended by all the magnates at Edward IV's funeral, but it did not. Bereft of the king and their military power by Anthony's capture, the Wydevilles were defeated long before the usurpation.

Rivers could be seized because of divisions within his family. Doubtless he, like his sister and nephew, wanted their influence perpetuated and favoured an early coronation rather than a protectorate, but he did not regard Gloucester as an enemy. He went out of his way to meet him and unnecessarily placed himself in the duke's power; following a convivial evening, his arrest was a surprise.[84] If he saw Gloucester as a friend and had no grounds for enmity, one wonders whether More was right in charging the queen with unthinking hostility to the king's kindred?[85]

Until 1464 the Wydevilles were least among nobles, nursing tenuous ties with the great, poorly endowed and politically impotent. Afterwards they exploited Edward's sense of obligation to integrate themselves among the higher nobility. Their new patronage was still distributed among existing kinsmen and dependants; their military might, on the evidence of 1469-71, was nil. Later, appropriating the power of the princes, they established a regional hegemony and a powerful and committed retinue, thus becoming more than a court party.

Since there were so many of them, patronage was spread thinly, but they did much better than Lander thought. Throughout they exploited their influence to extort concessions, an activity for which they had an inordinate appetite; at least that other grasping family, the Nevilles, normally had some basis for their claims. Worst of them all, on the evidence, was Anthony; far from doing harm to no-one, as Mancini would have us believe,[86] there was nobody he hesitated to harm. None of them, in pursuit of advantage, worried much about repercussions or feared to make foes.

It is a severe criticism that Edward left them unchecked and sanctioned their shady dealings, especially as he was dominated by nobody and quite capable of refusing their blandishments. He helped them if it was not at his expense or to his disadvantage; hence the alienation and transfer of reversions, which enabled them to build on what they had. This attitude also coloured his regional policy, for he had no desire in the early 1470s to revive the Welsh and northern lieutenantcies of the previous decade. But once the Wydevilles and Gloucester had re-established them, Edward concurred and gradually conceded other estates and powers. The Wydevilles's growing power at the expense of others again generated factions within the political consensus that ultimately undermined the crown. As only they benefited, not Edward or his sons, their influence, as Professor Ross observed, was malign.

Notes

Except where otherwise indicated, all references to MSS. sources in these notes refer to documents in the Public Record Office, London: e.g. C139/77, n. 5, n. 7, n. 10.

1. E.g. their alleged responsibility for the death of the Earl of Desmond, D.MacGibbon, *Elizabeth Woodville 1437-92* (1938), pp. 42-3.
2. J.R.Lander, *Crown and Nobility 1450-1509* (1976), 110n. The next eleven paragraphs are based on *ibid.* pp. 104-25; *C.P.* xi. pp. 15-21.
3. G.Baker, *History and Antiquities of the County of Northampton* (2 vols. 1822-30), ii. pp.162, 252-3.
4. Certainly 'Shalford' (Beds.) (*Register of Henry Chichele, Archbishop of Canterbury, 1414-43*, ed. E.F.Jacob, ii(Cant. & York Soc. xlii), 608) and probably the Mote, Maidstone (Kent).
5. C 139/77; *C.P.R. 1461-7*, pp. 169-70; E.C.Williams, *My Lord of Bedford 1389-1435* (1963), p. 247.

6. A £60-annuity was twice left uncollected for five years before 1454; afterwards it was collected promptly, E 101/143/13/1-6.

7. *C.P.R. 1413-16*, pp. 259, 370; C 139/77.

8. *Ibid. 1436-41*, pp. 133, 260.

9. *Ibid. 1436-41*, pp. 438, 479, 523; *1441-6*, p. 453; *1446-52*, pp. 185, 205; *Rot. Parl.* v. pp. 310-11. For the next paragraph, see *C.P.* v. pp. 356-61; xi. p. 507; xii. i. p. 356.

10. C 139/119/10/2; H.L. Gray, 'Incomes from land in England in 1436', *E.H.R.* xlix (1934), p. 617.

11. E.g. Cardinal Beaufort, the Dukes of Suffolk and Warwick, Lords Cromwell, Beauchamp of Powicke and Sudeley, *C.P.R. 1436-41*, pp. 133, 260, 384, 407; *1441-6*, pp. 400-1; *1446-52*, p. 174.

12. Historical Manuscripts Commission, *78 Hastings*, i. pp. 301-2.

13. C.D.Ross, *Edward IV* (1974), pp. 89-90.

14. B.P.Wolffe, *Royal Demesne in English History* (1971), p. 137, 250sqq; *Rot. Parl.* v. pp. 251-2.

14a. *C.P.R. 1461-7*, p. 516; *1467-77*, p. 19; C.L.Scofield, *Life and Reign of Edward the Fourth* (1923), i. p. 398. Rivers received £200 a year as councillor, not 200 marks, E 404/73/1/17.

15. *C.P.R. 1461-7*, p. 535; *C.C.R. 1461-8*, p. 380; *1468-76*, no. 595; *Feet of Fines for Essex*, iv, ed. P.H.Reaney and M.Fitch (1964), p. 61; E 159/243, Rec. Mich. 6 Edw. IV m.2; Hill. 6 Edw. IV m.5.

15a. Passenham (Northants.), DL 37/37/8,/13.

16. 'Annales rerum anglicarum', *Letters and Papers illustrative of the Wars of the English in France*, ed. J.Stevenson (Rolls series, 1864), ii.ii. p. 788; Scofield, *Edward IV*, i. pp. 397-8; *C.P.R. 1461-7*, p. 444; *1467-77*, pp. 19, 41. Mountjoy was satisfied, later remembering Rivers in his will, but Warwick was displeased, Worcestre, *Annales*, p. 785; *Testamenta Vetusta*, ed. N.H.Nicolas (1826), i. p. 334.

16a. Lander, *Crown and Nobility*, pp. 110n, 114.

17. Ross, *Edward IV*, p. 94.

18. T.B.Pugh, 'The magnates, knights and gentry', *Fifteenth-century England, 1399-1509*, ed. S.B.Chrimes, C.D.Ross and R.A.Griffiths (1972), pp. 92-3; Cardiff Cent. Libr. MS. 5. 7, ff. 52-4, 57; *C.P.R. 1461-7*, p. 119; C81/809/ 1960.

19. *C.P.R. 1467-77*, p. 25; *1476-85*, p. 179; C81/806/1814.

20. *C.P.R. 1461-7*, pp. 125, 547.

21. Worcestre, *Annales*, p. 786.

22. *C.P.R. 1461-7*, pp. 271, 352, 355, 457, 467; *1467-77*, p. 485; *C.C.R. 1461-8*, p. 283; *C.P.* vii. p. 164.

23. *C.P.R. 1461-7*, pp. 7, 104-5, 533; *1467-77*, pp. 32-3, 37-8. For her jointure, see DL 41/2/8.

24. *C.P.R. 1467-77*, p. 19; C 140/31/12/2.

25. Scofield, *Edward IV*, i. p. 499n; *C.C.R. 1461-8*, p. 330.

26. E 149/226/6; CP 25(1)/294/74/37; *Essex Feet of Fines*, iv. p. 62; *Paston Letters and Papers of the Fifteenth Century*, ed. N.Davis (2 vols. 1971-6), ii. p. 374; William Worcestre, *Itineraries*, ed. J.H.Harvey (1969), pp. 188-9; Baker, *Northants.* i. pp. 353-4; Westminster Abbey MS. 4784.

27. E.g. when Jacquetta's dower was surrendered, see above p. 63.
28. *C.P.R. 1461-7*, pp. 463-4; *1467-77*, p. 110.
29. A.R. Myers, 'The Household of Queen Elizabeth Woodville, 1466-7', *Bulletin of the John Rylands Library*, 1 (1967-8), p. 455. This paragraph is based on *ibid.* l. pp. 207-35, 443-81.
30. Bourchier, Haute and Dyve were relatives; for Isham, see *C.C.R. 1447-54*, p. 257.
31. E.g. C 81/1633/22,/27,/36.
32. Davis, *Paston Letters*, i. p. 540; ii. pp. 571-2.
33. Baker, *Northants.* i. p. 354.
34. E.g. B.L. Additional MS. 48031 f. 42v.
35. E.g. to her father and Herbert, see notes 15a and 38.
36. C 49/59-65; E 28/89/21,/23,/24,/37,/40,/41. For what follows, see G.Smith, *Coronation of Elizabeth Wydeville* (1975 edn.); *Excerpta Historica*, ed. S.Bentley (1840), pp. 176-212, 227-39.
37. *Great Chronicle of London*, ed. A.H.Thomas and I.D.Thornley (1938), p. 208.
38. C 81/1633/36. Elizabeth surrendered Crendon (Bucks.), Haseley and Pyrton (Oxon.) in his favour, DL 37/37/20,/22; R. Somerville, *History of the Duchy of Lancaster* (1953), i. p. 138n.
39. This paragraph is based on *Chronicle of the first thirteen years of the reign of Edward IV*, ed. J.O.Halliwell (Camden Soc.x, 1839), pp. 46-9.
40. E.g. Rivers's hopes of the captaincy of Calais were rapidly quashed, *C.P.R. 1467-77*, p. 450. Rivers used Elizabeth as intermediary with the king against Hastings, T.More, *History of King Richard III*, ed. R.S.Sylvester (Complete Works, ii, 1963), p. 225.
41. E.g. B.L. Harleian MSS. 48 f. 80; 158 ff. 119v, 120v. For the next phrase, see D.Mancini, *Usurpation of Richard III*, ed. C.A.J.Armstrong (1969), pp. 66-7.
42. *C.P.R. 1467-77*, pp. 373-4; *1476-85*, p. 336.
43. *Ibid. 1467-77*, pp. 456-7, 514; *1476-85*, p. 36.
44. *Ibid. 1476-85*, pp. 139, 174, 212, 263, 283-4; *Rot. Parl.* vi. pp. 215-18.
45. *C.P.* vi. p. 372; *C.P.R. 1467-77*, pp. 178, 206.
46. See Scofield, *Edward IV*, ii. p. 7; E.W. Ives, 'Andrew Dymmock and the Papers of Antony, Earl Rivers, 1482-3', *B.I.H.R.* xli (1968), p. 219n.
47. *C.P.R. 1467-77*, pp. 421, 423; *1476-85*, p. 261.
48. *Excerpta Historica*, p. 246.
49. *C.P.R. 1476-85*, p. 365; C 149/226/6; see also *C.C.R. 1468-76*, nos. 1550-1, 1567.
50. *C.P.R. 1461-7*, p. 87; *1467-77*, p. 423; E 315/486/2,/4,/29.
51. E 315/486/29; tor the background, see M.A. Hicks, 'Career of George Plantagenet, Duke of Clarence, 1449-78' (unpub. Oxford D.Phil.thesis 1974), pp. 317-24.
52. For her potential title, see *Rot. Parl.* vi. p. 454.
53. *Excerpta Historica*, pp. 246-8.
54. Baker, *Northants.* i. pp. 352-4; ii. p. 152; DL 42/19 ff.22v-23.
55. *C.P.R. 1467-77*, p. 283; *Rot. Parl.* vi. pp. 9-15. The following five paragraphs are based on R.A.Griffiths, 'Wales and the Marches' in *Fifteenth-century*

England, pp. 159-62; D.E.Lowe, 'The Council of the Prince of Wales and the Decline of the Herbert Family during the Second Reign of Edward IV (1471-83)', *Bulletin of the Board of Celtic Studies* xxvii(2) (1977), p. 278-97. For what follows, see *C.P.R. 1467-77,* p. 283; Scofield, *Edward IV,* i. p. 546; A.R.Myers, *Household of Edward IV* (1959), p. 22; Davis, *Paston Letters,* i. p. 524.

56. C.L.Kingsford, *English Historical Literature in the Fifteenth Century* (1913), pp. 383, 386.
57. *Rot. Parl.* vi. p. 15; *C.P.R. 1467-77,* pp. 361, 365, 449.
58. *C.P.R. 1467-77,* p. 366.
59. J.O.Halliwell, *Letters of the Kings and Queens of England* (1848), ii. p. 143.
60. E.g. SC 6/1210/6 mm.3d, 6; /1225/3 m.9.
61. More, *Richard III,* p. 14.
62. SC 6/1210/6 m.5 (attached bill); /1225/7 m.5.
63. C.Rawcliffe, *The Staffords, Earls of Stafford and Dukes of Buckingham 1394-1521* (1978), p. 125.
64. E.g. Richard Isham, *ibid.* p. 198.
65. KB 9/334/85,/87.
66. He receives money for the prince, e.g. SC 6/781/6 m.7d.
67. *Rot. Parl.* vi. p. 46; SC 6/781/2 mm.3-5.
68. SC 6/782/5 m.5; B.L. Sloane MS. 3479 ff. 53v, 55.
69. *Hall's Chronicle,* ed. H.Ellis (1809), p. 331.
70. *Ibid.*
71. DL 29/454/7312 mm.4-5; see below.
72. *Excerpta Historica,* pp. 247-8; Ives, *B.I.H.R.* xli. pp. 222-3; E 315/486/8; *C.P.R. 1467-77,* pp. 366, 410. He was steward, constable, ranger, farmer of the demesne and warren of Castle Rising (Norf.), SC 6/933/8-d; C 1/46/25. The next three paragraphs are based on Lowe, *art. cit.;* Griffiths, *art. cit.*
73. *C.P.R. 1467-77,* p. 283; B.L. Additional MS. 6113 f. 97v.
74. *C.P.R. 1467-77,* p. 410; SC 8/344/1281; DL 29/454/7312 m.4.
75. More, *Richard III,* pp. 19-20; Mancini, *Richard III,* pp. 78-9.
76. Buckingham, Maltravers, Bourchier, Strange and Grey: Hicks, 'Clarence', pp. 169-72, 177, table VII (ii).
77. *Excerpta Historica,* p. 248.
78. PROB 11/8(P.C.C.44 Milles).
79. *Rot. Parl.* vi. p. 10.
80. *C.P.R. 1467-77,* pp. 204, 330, 364; SC 6/1225/3 mm.3, 5, 8; /1207/14 m. 4-d.
81. She was dead by 1479, Baker, *Northants.* i. p. 354.
82. SC 6/1225/7 mm.4-6; Lander, *Crown and Nobility,* pp. 183-4.
83. Pugh, *Fifteenth-century England,* p. 111.
84. Mancini, *Richard III,* pp. 74-5; More, *Richard III,* pp. 17-18.
85. More, *Richard III,* p. 7.
86. Mancini, *Richard III,* pp. 66-9.

Baronial Councils in the Later Middle Ages[1]

Carole Rawcliffe, History of Parliament Trust.

It was in 1885 that Charles Plummer first drew attention to the importance of the work and membership of baronial councils. Predictably for one who enriched our historical vocabulary with the term 'bastard feudalism', his chief purpose was to provide evidence in support of Justice Fortescue's strictures on venality in high places. 'And whi', asked the judge while discussing the evils which had brought the royal council into disrepute,

> myght not then men make be meanes off corrupcion somme off the seruantes and counsellers off somme off the lordes to moue the lordes to parciallite, and to make hem also ffauorable and parcial as were the same seruantes or the parties that so moved hem? Then couude no mater treted in the counsell be kept prive. Ffor the lordes oftentymes told ther own counsellours and seruantes that had suyd to hem ffor tho maters, how thai had sped in ham, and who was ayen ham. How mey the kyng be counsellyd to restrayne gyvinge a wey off his londe, off gyvinge off offices corrodeis or pencions off abbeyis by suche grete lordes to other menys seruantes, sithyn thay most desire such giftes ffor thaim selff, and thair seruantes?[2]

Other contemporary evidence certainly bears out the view that, even if it was not deployed in such devious practices, the influence exercised by councils and individual councillors could be immense. Edward IV's shrewd and often-quoted assessment of John Mowbray, duke of Norfolk's most prominent adviser, Sir William Brandon, is well enough known, thanks to the busy pen of John Paston. 'Thow thou can begyll the Dwk of Norffolk, and bryng hym abow the thombe as thow lyst', Edward is said to have warned, 'I let the wet thow shalt not do me so, for I vndyrstand thy fals delyng well j-now'.[3] Yet even the most strong-minded and most independent landowner was obliged to lean heavily on the William Brandons of this world. The management of his estates, the protection and pursuit of his legal rights, the supervision of his business in parliament and the implementation of administrative reforms all required expert help, although the nature, extent and significance of this help are hard to establish because so little evidence has survived that we cannot now speak definitively about the composition or activities of any one baronial council. To do so we would need complete sets of ministerial accounts and court rolls, household books, memoranda and private correspondence. Even then, our knowledge would be incomplete, since the medieval accountant, being oblivious of the interest his labours would arouse in twentieth-century historians, is often sadly negligent in drawing our attention to conciliar activities. Whereas references to the names of lawyers retained to give counsel and the payments made in the course of their duties are quite common, the more routine administrative tasks performed by estate officers and neighbouring landowners in their capacity as councillors are less easy to discover, and for this reason scholars have inevitably concentrated upon the legal aspect of seigniorial councils. The temptation to make generalisations based upon the procedure or practice found on particular estates is, moreover, one that not all historians have been able to resist. However similar they may appear in work and composition, we must remember that every council was essentially a pragmatic institution, intended to deal with specific — indeed, often unique — financial, legal and administrative problems.

Our second difficulty is to be found wherever deliberative and advisory bodies come under review. Political theorists differ today in their estimate of the relative power of contemporary institutions: how much harder is it for us to determine the extent to which a fifteenth-century nobleman was influenced by his councillors. Returning to the duke of Norfolk, who was perhaps a rather more decisive character than may at first be supposed, we can see how delicately balanced the relationship between a lord and his advisers could be. The following account of a council meeting held at Framlingham in September 1472 is of particular interest, since so little of what actually went on 'behind the scenes' has survived. Our informant is John Paston, preoccupied as ever with an attempt to regain Caister Castle from the duke, who had by this date obtained control of the property and was not prepared to relinquish it again in a hurry. 'Syr', John reported to his brother,

I haue ben twyis at Framlyngham sythe your depertyng, but now the last tym the consayll was ther I sye yowyr lettyr, whyche was bettyr then well endyghtyd . . . I took myn owne auysse and delyuerd it to the consayll, wyth a propocysion ther-wyth as well as I kowd spek it; and my wordys wer well takyn, but your letter a thowsand fold bettyr. When they had red it they shewyd it to my lady (the duchess). Aftyr that my lady had sen it I spak wyth my lady, offyryng to my lord and hyr a bettyr, so as ye myght depert, wyth-ought eny some specyfyid. She wold not dell in that mater, but remyttyd me a-yen to the consayll, for she seyd and she spake in it tyll my lord and the consayll wer agreid they wold ley the wyght of all the mater on hyr, whyche shold be reportyd to hyr shame; but thys she promyseid, to be helpyng so it wer fyrst meuyd by the consayll. Then I went to the consayll and offyrd befor them youyr seruyse to my lord, and to do hym a plesure for the haueing ayen of your place and londys in Caster. . . . So they answerid me your offyr was more then resonabyll, and if the mater wer thers they seyd they wyst what conscyence wold dryue hem to. They seyd they wold meue my lord wyth it, and so they dyd; but then the tempest aros and he gaue hem syche an answer that non of hem all wold tell it me. But when I axid an answer of hem they seyd and som lordys or gretter men meuyd my lord wyth it the mater wer your. Kepe consayle.[4]

I have quoted this passage in full because it shows how much secret diplomacy and protracted debate could go on before matters of policy were finally decided. It also provides a vivid illustration of that perennial item of conciliar business, the property dispute. Many examples of activity in this field can be cited: in 1421, for example, the advisers of Richard Beauchamp, earl of Warwick, were attempting to reach an acceptable agreement over the fate of the Berkeley estates with the councillors of the rival claimant, James Berkeley, whose reluctance to comply with their demands must have occasioned great rejoicing among the legal fraternity for another six years at least. The earl's council had, meanwhile, to deal with other problems, such as the bishop of Lincoln's claim to pasture rights at Uppingham, and a challenge by Berkeley's father-in-law, Sir Humphrey Stafford, to Warwick's title to the manor of Perton. The property had recently been purchased on the authority of the council and under their direct supervision, presumably while Warwick was abroad, and therefore unable to direct matters himself.[5] This is not the place for a discussion of the litigiousness of the late mediaeval landowner: suffice it to say that most, if not all, baronial councils included a group of lawyers, retained specifically for their professional services. On great estates they were known collectively as the council learned, and they formed a corporate and distinct group with clearly defined tasks to perform. An inner circle of lawyers, who were usually employed as estate staff as well as counsel in the legal sense, remained at hand to advise on other problems, but most of their colleagues were engaged as specialists, either on a short-term basis to work on one or two important cases, or for a more indefinite period. Many items of business which never reached the courts came under their cognizance, since prudence demanded that expert advice should be sought before litigation was even contemplated. The lawyers 'and others' retained as members of the Black Prince's council were, for instance, greatly concerned by the loss of feudal incidents brought about through enfeoffments-to-uses. In the early 1360s they spent considerable time scrutinising the conveyances made by several tenants in chief, yet despite their assiduity they were obliged to accept the situation and recommend caution in the recovery of lost revenues.[6] At a much later date, in about 1473, Henry Bourchier, earl of Essex, referred to his council learned in the law a petition from Thomas Ormond, begging for the restitution of certain estates which Edward IV had confiscated from his father, James, earl of Wiltshire. So convinced was the council of Ormond's title and the limitations of Edward's grant to earl Henry, that it advised an immediate private settlement between the two parties.[7]

Legal or quasi-legal documents of all kinds were compiled under the supervision of a semi-permanent staff of lawyers. By the terms of his brother's will of 1506, William Hastings received an annuity of 20 marks which was to be paid in whatever manner and from whichever estates his 'councell lerned' considered most acceptable.[8] The legal experts engaged by Edward, duke of Buckingham, were beset by an unending stream of memoranda, being at one moment under instructions to report on the ducal title to certain near-destitute villeins, and at another charged with the task of petitioning Cardinal Wolsey on behalf of the duke's son-in-law and ward, Ralph, earl of Westmorland, over whose inheritance Buckingham showed a rather more than paternal concern.[9]

Such were the delays and inconveniences inherent in the English legal system that even the most acrimonious disputes were frequently withdrawn from the courts after one or two terms and settled informally by the councils of the two parties involved. Recourse to the law was often considered unnecessary from the beginning, partly because landowners like the aforementioned duke of Buckingham took recognizances which bound their employees to submit to conciliar arbitration when charged with any offences arising from the performance of their duties. It was also common for seigniorial councils to act as tribunals in quarrels arising not only between tenants and retainers, but also those with less tangible connexions who hoped to gain a prompter and perhaps more favourable settlement of their affairs than was to be had at common law. The classic instance of these developments is to be found on the duchy of Lancaster estates. The duchy council discharged so many judicial functions and examined so many cases that it gave rise to the court of the duchy chamber, which was effectively exploited by Henry VII as a court of equity.[10] Other baronial councils did not possess such powers, but nevertheless helped to fill the notorious gap caused by deficiencies in the common law courts. By our period they offered a valuable and popular alternative to litigation in the King's Bench or court of Common Pleas by providing a formal and authoritative court of arbitration before which property disputes and other civil suits were quickly and more cheaply determined. That councils could, and did, exercise an accepted and well-established form of equitable jurisdiction is clear from a recently discovered roll of evidences concerning a protracted legal dispute over the manor of Ladbroke in Warwickshire during the late fourteenth century. At various times the chief protagonists appeared before the councils of the earl of Warwick, the dukes of Surrey, Exeter and Gloucester and the bishop of Durham, although in none of these instances does the arbitration given appear either to have precluded concurrent litigation at common law or in Chancery, or to have been regarded as permanently binding upon the parties concerned. On the other hand, the clearly defined procedure, the efficiency of record keeping and the speed with which appeals were heard all point to the fact that by the mid-fourteenth century, if not before, councils had assumed a recognized and accepted place in the English legal system, using procedural forms derived from the court of Chancery and referring business to subcommittees in ways similar to those of the royal council.[11] Their intervention in private disputes — notably in matters of tenure and real estate — prompted two indignant protests from the commons in 1391 and 1393: yet it would be mistaken to see in this a sign that seigniorial councils were trying to assume a more specific status as courts of the first instance with powers to impose their equitable jurisdiction upon the population as a whole. On the basis of somewhat tenuous evidence culled from the St. Alban's Abbey estates A.E. Levett expressed the belief that through their usurpation of such jurisdiction councils were deliberately attempting to undermine manorial custom. All the admittedly limited sources which have, however, survived bear out K.B. McFarlane's contrary view that despite the semi-legal complexion of their activities at a manorial level, they were primarily concerned to improve administrative efficiency through the exploitation of existing custom.[12] On certain estates, of which those belonging to the de Vere earls of Oxford furnish a particularly good example, members of the council were often present at sessions of the manorial courts, but their recorded actions certainly do not constitute that 'singular Roman practice' described by Dr. Levett. We have instances of conciliar intervention where tenants had alienated land without permission, acquired property by suspect means and tried to fell timber before obtaining the necessary licence, but no sign of equity proceedings. Indeed, it would appear that absenteeism resulting from the award of stewardships to influential retainers and councillors was chiefly to blame for any decline in the manorial system.[13]

This is not to deny that there were cases, particularly along the Welsh Marches, where the great landowner possessed unique judicial privileges and his council was free to exercise an authority which in practice, if not in theory, went unquestioned. In Wales the law in all its forms was administered by the councillors of the leading Marcher lords, either directly as agents for the enforcement of their employers' equitable powers, or indirectly while sitting as justices in eyre. The holding of sessions presented the lord with the opportunity to commission a group of men whose dual authority as councillors *and* judges made them especially useful to him.[14]

Most noblemen kept a resident staff of lawyers in London to supervise their business at the Exchequer, in Chancery and in the common law courts. Many had attornies general, who were regular employees as well as councillors, and who worked with one or two other subordinates, depending on the amount of litigation in hand. Unfortunately, there is no contemporary English source to compare with the letters written from Paris in 1509 by Charles de la Romagière, the lawyer, political agent — and even spy — employed by Alain le Grand, Sire d'Albret, to protect his interests during his years of disgrace and exile from the capital. Like his father before him, de la Romagière was responsible for the direction of d'Albret's judicial and personal affairs, usually when they concerned his dealings with the King and the law courts. His duties can, in fact, have differed little from those of any attorney general employed across the channel, for in its work and membership the French baronial council was remarkably similar to the English.[15] The attorney general and his staff are to be distinguished from the majority of lawyers associated with any council learned, because the latter group tended to receive fees from many quarters and cannot on the whole have taken their peripheral commitments any more seriously than other retainers in the pay of several lords at once. Some members of the legal profession entered indentures which, save for the type of obligation specified, hardly differed in format from those engaging knights or esquires to serve in peace and war. In 1438 the busy Staffordshire lawyer and M.P., Robert Whitgreve, was offered a life annuity of 40s. by Sir Philip Chetwynd and his wife, Eleanor, lady Ferrers, *'pro suo bono consilio nobis impenso et posterum impendendo'*. [16] Whitgreve's connexion with the Chetwynds was never particularly strong, although this did not prevent them from paying his fee, nor he from adding them to his list of patrons. Every medieval man of property wanted to obtain preferential, if not openly partial, treatment at law by giving pensions and gifts to judges and lawyers, who in turn did not hesitate to accept ill-concealed bribes from rival litigants. In short, there is a clear distinction to be drawn between councillors whose association with the lord was only slight, and certainly not of paramount import-ance in their careers, and those who were closely caught up in his affairs, often because of a long-standing family or territorial connexion. This applies not only to professional lawyers, but also to the knights, esquires and gentlemen whose advice was sought.

Although bureaucrats and lawyers had even by the thirteenth century come to dominate what was originally a consultative body composed of a nobleman's chief vassals and peers, local gentry and lesser nobility still played a prominent part on baronial councils. An ordinance of 1487 reveals that on the de Vere estates, and no doubt on others, the tenants were trying to maintain 'knights and gentlemen from my lord's council' in support of their own quarrels. Perhaps, like the advisers of Roger Mortimer, earl of March, and Henry Bourchier, earl of Essex, members of the de Vere council were empowered to distribute liveries and retain men on behalf of the lord, a privilege which easily lent itself to abuses. [17] Geographical and tenurial relationships were crucially important in determining who sat at the council board, so that leading tenants and neighbouring landowners were often consulted even if they happened to be employed by others. Thus, at a meeting of the

Grey of Ruthin council at Foxley in Norfolk in 1467, we find William Calthorp, a shire knight of some eminence who had married into the family several years before, the notorious John Heydon of Baconsthorpe, his son's tutor, Harry Spylleman, and Robert Norwich, a local estate officer. Here the composition of the council reflects its place of meeting, since all four men had strong East Anglian connexions which do much to account for their presence in the council chamber. As Norwich's current choice of M.P., Spylleman possessed another equally valuable qualification for membership of Lord Edmund's council.[18]

It would be hard to find a great landowner who did not have a direct interest in parliamentary business at some point in his life, either through his involvement in matters of state, his tenure of high office, or as a result of private disputes over property or precedence. Without implying the existence of baronial factions in the House of Commons, it is important to stress how anxious noblemen were to have among their chief advisers men who were not only well versed in parliamentary procedure, but who also stood in their own right as prominent members of the lower house. In 1425, John Mowbray, earl Marshal's claim for precedence over the earl of Warwick came before the commons, detailed evidence being presented by their respective counsel, Roger Hunt and Sir Walter Beauchamp. In this case 'counsel' is synonymous with 'councillor': we are told that Hunt had 'of long time been of counsel with his said lord earl Marshal', and he was, in fact, to be arrested in the following year for his too energetic partisanship of the earl's cause in a riot at Huntingdon. Hunt was a lawyer, and thus possessed an added usefulness to Mowbray as his feoffee, attorney general and executor. He had been a speaker of the commons in 1420, and was again to serve in this capacity thirteen years later at the end of a long and distinguished parliamentary career. Beauchamp was no less influential in the commons — he was speaker in 1416 — and, thanks to Warwick's patronage, he also rose to occupy a position of note on the royal council.[19]

Officers of the Crown, particularly those employed at the Exchequer, were also in great demand as councillors. Many senior bureaucrats who owed their appointment to financial or administrative expertise combined a governmental post with service elsewhere. One such was John Throckmorton, whose qualifications for membership of a baronial council could hardly have been improved upon. A lawyer and treasury official (he was made under-treasurer of England in 1428 and a chamberlain of the Exchequer ten years later), he represented Worcestershire in at least six parliaments and played a significant role in local government in the Midlands. The earl of Warwick first employed him as an attorney, but by 1431 he had become his general proctor in England, and he was awarded the unusually high fee of 20 marks a year for sitting on the earl's council. The surviving accounts show Throckmorton to have been active in the pursuit of his employer's interests, and although we cannot tell how useful he proved to be in securing preference for him at the Exchequer, he was certainly chief among those to whom Beauchamp entrusted his affairs.[20]

None of this will come as any surprise to students of late medieval society, and it is perhaps stating the obvious to emphasise how far the participation of the gentry in conciliar business provided a strengthening and cohesive element in the social fabric. Their activities extended far beyond the normal round of duties as feoffees, supervisors of estate business, arbitrators in manorial courts and occasional advisers in matters of policy. Over the space of a few years in the late 1480s and 1490s, Sir John Paston was required in his capacity as a de Vere councillor to accompany John, earl of Oxford, north in the service of the King, and to assist him in the performance of his various commissions as lord admiral of England and high steward of the duchy of Lancaster. He had to collect information, hear bills of complaint and arrange for the supply of provisions. On one occasion at least he was entrusted with the delicate task of furthering the earl's interest in a law suit at the Ipswich sessions (but only 'taking such discretion as should be thought reasonable'). He also performed a number of tasks for the countess of Oxford, who made use of his position on the Norfolk bench to help one of her own servants. It was not for nothing that the wife of

Thomas Howard, the imprisoned and disgraced earl of Surrey, wrote pathetically to Paston in October 1485, begging him to intercede on her behalf with his lord so that she might be sure of his continued favour. She well knew how best to oil the wheels of patronage.[21]

Paston, Hunt, Beauchamp and their kind occupied a special place on baronial councils, because it was probably with them that the lord chose to discuss matters of a more personal or political nature. Senior councillors may quite well have exercised as much influence over the marriages of sons, daughters or even their patron himself as did the council learned where the actual terms of the contract were concerned. From March to June 1391, the Stafford council played a major part in arranging the earl Thomas's marriage to the daughter of Thomas of Woodstock, duke of Gloucester, a match of great financial and political significance, which took place after a long series of negotiations between the conciliar representatives of the two parties.[22] On learning that his kinsman, William Stonor, hoped to marry Lord Mountjoy's widowed daughter, Thomas Mill immediately set out to discover the size of her dower. It proved to be considerable. 'Thes certentees I have by my bedfelow, Thomas Powtrell', he reported cheerfully, 'which ys of councell with my seid lorde, and was of councell at the mariage makyng, when my seid mastres was maried to the son of my seid lord.'[23] It is now impossible to tell how far an inner ring of councillors could sway the lord to whom they were bound by ties of mutual dependence, although they are unlikely to have been ignorant of his most cherished plans and ambitions. The greater the lord the greater these ambitions might prove to be, and the heavier the burden of responsibility borne by his councillors. There can be little doubt of Sir William Oldhall's close relationship with Richard, duke of York, whose council he dominated from 1441 onwards, if not before. Indeed, whereas it was felt in certain quarters that York's failure in France was due to the influence exercised over him by young men, others were not slow to blame Oldhall for giving his lord ill-considered advice. This view was not shared by Henry VI, who asked for Oldhall to be sent to England in 1441 so that the experience which he had gained on the ducal council in France might be put to good use in the forthcoming peace negotiations. The fervour with which leading members of society, from the King downwards, sought to gain Oldhall's 'good lordship' in the early 1450s suggests that many regarded him as the real power behind the duke. Be this as it may, on his first return to parliament, in November 1450, Oldhall was made speaker by a House of Commons which was at once hostile to the court party and favourably disposed towards York. Subsequent allegations of his complicity in the duke's projected *coup* at Dartford and other supposedly Yorkist risings cannot now be proved, although by 1453 he was considered the most suitable scapegoat for duke Richard's political indiscretions.[24]

Baronial councils must, from time to time, have become involved in international affairs, if only because of the private interests which they were supposed to protect. In January 1468, for example, the French ambassador reported to his royal master, Louis XI, that he had had communication in London with the council of Richard Neville, earl of Warwick, and in particular with John, lord Wenlock, with whom he was anxious to discuss matters of foreign policy relevant to the earl. Wenlock's connexion with the Kingmaker dated from 1459, and his rapid advancement under Edward IV obviously owed much to the support of his powerful friend, to whom he remained staunchly loyal throughout the political vicissitudes of 1470 and 1471. *A propos* of his treasonous betrayal of the town of Calais to the fugitive earl in 1471, Philippe de Commynes remarked 'qu'il servait tres bien son Capitaine, mais tres mal son roi — qu'ant au dit seigneur de Warwick, jamais homme ne tint plus grand loyaulte.'[25] Here was a man who could be trusted with the most delicate matters, and whose role as a councillor may be interpreted in the fullest sense.

Turning from high policy to the minutiae of administration, the indispensable part assumed by baronial councils in the management of great estates is immediately striking. They exercised particular authority when the landowner was either a minor or an absentee, although not even the most diligent *rentier* could hope to run a complex of scattered farms and receiverships without the help of a semi-permanent supervisory body. This type of business was usually dealt with by a specialist group composed of senior estate and household personnel, together with a few lawyers. There was an increasing tendency as the fifteenth century wore on for small itinerant commissions composed of no more than three or four councillors to make regular tours of inspection from one manor to another. Despite the extent of their commitments, no item seems to have been too trivial to bring before them, even though the inevitable backlog of administrative problems which grew up as a result often caused delays where none had previously existed. On one occasion in 1511, the most senior councillors of Edward, duke of Buckingham, compiled a detailed memorandum on a heriot worth no more than 7s 4d., and did not consider it beneath their corporate dignity to draft instructions for the use of carters passing through Madeley Park in Staffordshire.[26] This apparent obsession with small-scale economies is no less evident on other estates, particularly when repairs and allowances came up on the agenda. In about 1414, the lessee of lord Bourchier's manor of 'Stok Hall' in Langford was permitted to take expenses of 2s 2½d. for riding up to London to discuss his lease with the auditors, 'de mandato consilii domini'.[27] Likewise, some sixty years later, the councillors of Henry Percy, earl of Northumberland, decided that the forester of the lordship of Prudhoe could have an allowance of 13s. 14d. because his tenement needed attention.[28] Another important aspect of every council's administrative work was its function as a court of audit. The examination of ministerial accounts appears to have been undertaken by a few officials, among whom one or two auditors were inevitably to be found. The auditors of Elizabeth Woodville joined every year with other members of her council in touring her estates to inspect account rolls and lists of arrears, from which they compiled a valor of all the property in her possession. On a more general level they supervised the drawing up of leases and the arrangements made for the purchase or exchange of property. Although routine in nature, decisions like this do not seem to have been reached without reference to the Queen herself, since frequent meetings took place at Windsor in her presence.[29] The councillors who travelled with Lewis Robessart, lord Bourchier, from London to Stanstead in 1425 had to consider the question of a possible reduction in the rent due from the manor of Messing, and this was eventually 'allowed by my lord at Stanstead Hall before his council for default of value'.[30] While on a visit to Hicking in Norfolk, Anthony, lord Rivers, was advised by his council learned to increase the rate of fines imposed for respite of homage upon his mesne tenants. As a typical Woodville, the earl needed no second prompting to adopt these measures, although we cannot assume that either he, or any other nobleman, merely attended council meetings to provide a rubber stamp for business already settled in advance.[31] A harsh, reforming landowner like the third Duke of Buckingham sometimes found himself at odds with his council, if only because its members, being more in touch with local opinion, were realistic as to what might be accomplished. His refusal to reduce either rents or entry fines in the lordship of Newport met with resistance on the part of his council, as they were aware how much ill-feeling would be generated by such a move.[32] Yet, in common with other noblemen, the duke relied heavily upon his advisers when it came to reforms within his own domestic establishment. Like the fifth earl of Northumberland, whose household book of 1511-12 was drawn up as a provisional assignment of revenues by his council, so, not long after, Buckingham and his councillors tackled the problem of listing all the household staff, their salaries and their duties in an attempt to cut down running cost.[33]

This inner ring of experienced administrators did more than offer useful suggestions and effect necessary economies. It was from among his most trusted councillors that a lord appointed his executors and feoffees — a choice of great importance in view of the long minorities which beset many noble families during the later middle ages. A degree of continuity, so vital in the running of a large estate and household, was thus assured, for the council, above all, was a repository of knowledge and skill which could be drawn upon at all times. On becoming a life member of the 2nd earl of March's council in October 1397, Sir Hugh Cheyne, an old family retainer, promised that if his lord died first he would continue to advise his heirs and nobody else. The earl's concern for the future was born of experience, since he had only just come of age after several years as a royal ward, during which his late father's council had effectively assumed control of the running of his property. Circumstances were, moreover, to justify his desire for administrative stability: his death at the battle of Kells in 1398 again left the house of Mortimer without an adult head and saw a return to rule by the council.[34] The advisers of a lord who died without issue would often transfer their loyalties to a younger man in genuine need of assistance. Thus, on the death of John, duke of Bedford, some of his retainers, including Sir John Fastolf and Sir Andrew Ogard, joined Richard, duke of York, becoming prominent members of his council. They and the others who counselled the duke during his early years in France were at first concerned with military matters, although some, such as Sir Walter Devereux and Sir William Oldhall, were to involve themselves more closely in his personal affairs and, eventually, his attempt upon the throne.[35]

A young and still inexperienced nobleman could also rely upon the services of councillors engaged by other members of his family. The letters written by Edward, duke of Buckingham, to his 'olde good frend', Sir Reginald Bray, leave us in no doubt as to the latter's influence over the affairs of his effusive correspondent, whom he first encountered while running the estates of Lady Margaret Beaufort, the duke's aunt and guardian. 'In my most herty wyse I recommand me unto yow', wrote Buckingham shortly after he came of age,

and in the same thank yow ffor your grett ffavore schende me at all tymes in my causes, wheryne I beseche yow of contynuans. And that, as I have bene, I may alweyes be bolde to troble yow in any poore seutes and causys, besechynge yow, Master Bray, to gyve credens unto that my broder Herre [Henry, future earl of Wiltshire] schall brek fferther with yow on my behalff. And iff hyt whar in me too doo thyng unto your pleasure by eny meane ther is none woldbe more glad therto, as knowyth god, who have yow in his blessyd kepynge.[36]

As a leading minister of the Crown, Bray was no doubt the recipient of many such testimonials to his personal power, and he probably derived a substantial sum from the fees paid to him for 'good counsel' by noblemen anxious to maintain an interest at court. Influence, expertise and professional skills were sold at a premium, so that a shrewd lawyer or official could supplement his income by offering advice to several lords at once. On his own admission, the business-like Sir John Fastolf made a virtual career out of his services as a councillor, for besides extracting a fee of £20 a year from Richard, duke of York, 'pro notabile et laudabile servicio ac bone consilio', he was at various times retained to sit on the councils of Thomas, duke of Clarence, Thomas, duke of Exeter, Humphrey, duke of Gloucester, John, duke of Somerset, and John, duke of Norfolk.[37]

The monetary rewards to be gained from advising even one lord could be substantial, although they varied according to the status of the recipient and the practice current on a particular estate. Both the Staffords and the Beauchamps paid their lawyers 40s. a year, while it was understood that permanent staff such as auditors and receivers would attend council meetings without any further remuneration. The knights, esquires and local landowners who gave counsel almost always received some form of fee or annuity — perhaps from stewardships — but one cannot always tell if the money was awarded to them primarily as councillors. Indeed, since many of them combined their advisory duties with administrative work of some kind or another, distinctions of this kind are often meaningless. By 1448, Sir William Oldhall was being paid over £84 a year by the duke of York, who not only made him chamberlain of his household and steward of his lordships of Clare and Thaxted, but also supplemented his wages with an annuity of £51. Oldhall was, as we have seen, far more than a councillor, and York's generosity shows clearly enough how much value he placed upon his loyal service.[38] Few lords appear to have devised a standard scale of pay for councillors recruited outside the legal profession, preferring to offer rewards on an ad hoc basis. Members of the duchy of Lancaster council (which is comparatively well documented) were not appointed formally with a specific wage or fee, although their expenses were always met.[39] Elsewhere more distinguished individuals could usually expect a reward commensurate with their rank and potential usefulness to the grantor. Thus, in June 1490, the earl of Northumberland gave an annuity of £10 by his own letters patent to his 'heartily beloved friend', the prior of Tynemouth, who had been 'deputed and assigned' to serve on the Percy council.[40] Of even more importance than the fee was the reward for assignments successfully completed. Anthony Browne, a de Vere family councillor, used his influence as a member for Great Bedwyn in the parliament of 1547 to steer matters of great concern to the earl of Oxford through the commons, and was paid £6 13s. 4d. by way of thanks. When a young man, his colleague, Anthony Stapleton, received £10 from the earl's mother to pay for 'his learning at the common law', a bequest which was followed up with the award of an unusually generous fee of 10 marks a year. Stapleton must have spent a good deal of time and effort on his employer's affairs. His appointment as recorder of Colchester, which he obtained in 1544, almost certainly came to him through this valuable connexion, since, as in most aspects of contemporary life, the real rewards and benefits of service accrued through patronage.[41] The councillor of a great nobleman was *ipso facto* 'a man of worship' to be courted by the ambitious and preferred above others in such matters as local elections to parliament. In 1472, Sir John Paston's friend, the influential James Arblaster, sent the bailiff of Maldon a homily on the facts of political life. 'It wer necessary for my lady [the duchess of Norfolk] and you all', he wrote,

> to haue thys perlement as for on of the burgeys of the towne of Maldon syche a man of worchep and of wytt as wer towardys my seyd lady, and also syche on as is in fauor of the Kyng and of the lordys of hys consayll nyghe abought hys persone; sertyfyeing yow that my seyd lady for hyr parte, and syche as be of hyr consayll, be most agreabyll that bothe ye and all syche as be hyr fermors and tenauntys and wellwyllers shold geue your voyse to a worchepfull knyght and on of my ladys consayll, Syr John Paston, whyche standys gretly in favore wyth my lord Chamberleyn, and what my seyd lord Chamberleyn may do wyth the Kyng and wyth all the lordys of Inglond I trowe it be not vnknowyn to yow. . . .[42]

Paston was not, however, returned, presumably because my

lady's husband, the duke, was not then as enthusiastic a patron of the Pastons as his wife. It is nevertheless clear that the rank of councillor bestowed a tremendous social *cachet*, which in turn brought additional fees, patrons and opportunities for advancement. The above-mentioned Sir Walter Beauchamp was probably made a royal councillor and treasurer of Henry VI's household through the good offices of his lord, the earl of Warwick. His appointment in 1428 as one of the small and highly paid group of attendants upon the young King seems also to have been contrived by the earl, who then held office as Henry's governor.[43]

The penalties of failure are less well documented, although councillors could be dismissed under a cloud for giving bad advice. On the recommendation of two local men whom he had retained as members of his council, Ralph, lord Cromwell, decided to enclose certain common land which he believed to be part and parcel of his newly-acquired manor of Deephams in Edmonton. Alarmed at the 'great injury and wrong likely to grow by the said lord Cromwell and his council', the neighbouring landowners planned a protest meeting at Edmonton, and in August 1438 some of the most eminent men in the county gathered with their tenants and other interested parties to petition Cromwell for the restitution of their rights. That lord Cromwell had acted rashly and without examining his legal position is clear from his immediate and total surrender to their demands. His advisers were, he assured, 'never to be of his clothing nor of his counsel after that time for their untrue information', an apologia which suggests that both were being punished as much for the harm they had done his reputation as for their ignorance about his property rights.[44]

Occasionally a lord found it necessary to sue members of his council for negligence or malpractices on their part. Thus, in about 1446, John Holland, duke of Exeter, began an action in Chancery against two of his advisers for allegedly pocketing the money which they had taken as compensation from a man accused of murdering one of his employees.[45] The suit which Edward, duke of Buckingham, brought against his receiver-general, Thomas Cade, for defaulting upon the recognizances he had entered at the time of his appointment may in fact have been planned as an act of revenge for a real or imagined betrayal of confidence on Cade's part. The latter was said to have disclosed the secret deliberations of Buckingham's privy council, which had met at Thornbury to discuss how the duke might raise an armed bodyguard to protect him on his projected visit to Wales.[46] Revelations like this must often have been made by men with divided loyalties or opportunists ready to exploit any situation to their own advantage. On the other hand, any councillor whose conduct aroused undue suspicion could very easily be dropped from a body whose membership was by nature fluid and imprecisely defined.

Yet, as an institution, the seigniorial council played a major part in cementing the relationship between the lord and his retainer. How far the steady growth of these quasi-autonomous tribunals within the body politic influenced the Crown's attitude to the baronage raises another question which must largely remain unanswered. It is tempting to suggest that certain changes in central government were brought about, partially at least, in response to developments in the work and jurisdiction of the councils set up by leading subjects of the realm. As we have already seen, the duchy of Lancaster council gave rise to the court of the duchy chamber with a clearly defined field of action, and in turn provided a model for the courts of wards and liveries, general surveyors and augmentations. Henry VII's council, with its phalanx of lawyers forming the *consilium domini Regis in lege eruditum*, its inner, or privy council, made up of the King's most trusted servants, and its strong concentration on judicial business, stands as a large-scale version of the seigniorial council with augmented legal powers, although we cannot tell if Henry VII was directly influenced by the practices which he observed on the estates of the nobility.[47] We may, perhaps, detect in the setting up of the court of poor men's requests an attempt not only to bring quick and relatively cheap justice within the reach of the common man, but also to emulate the facilities which baronial councils had to offer in this respect. No doubt the early Tudors were anxious to curb the expanding jurisdiction of these bodies by tackling the inadequacies of the legal system which had initially stimulated their growth. Some cross-fertilization of ideas must have taken place, for in essence the baronial council was a microcosm of the King's and the estates it served to run a microcosm of the kingdom.

Notes

1. I would like to thank Dr. A.V. Antonovics, Dr. R.I. Jack and Dr. L.S. Woodger for providing me with a number of references which have been gratefully incorporated into this paper.
2. Sir John Fortescue, *The Governance of England*, ed. C. Plummer (Oxford, 1885), pp. 145, 308-10.
3. *Paston Letters and Papers of the Fifteenth Century*, ed. N. Davis (2 vols., Oxford, 1971-6), i. p. 544.
4. *Ibid.*, pp. 578-79.
5. C.D.Ross, 'The Estates and Finances of Richard Beauchamp, Earl of Warwick', *Dugdale Soc. Occasional Papers*, XII (1956), pp. 11-13. Over the year ending at Michaelmas 1418 alone, the earl's council sustained expenses of almost £107 while dealing with these property disputes. A further £26 was spent on incidental payments and *douceurs* to officials at Westminster (British Library, Egerton Roll 8773 mm. 2d-4d).
6. K.B. McFarlane, *The Nobility of Later Medieval England* (Oxford, 1973), pp. 217-18.
7. P.R.O. C.146/7039.
8. *Testamenta Vetusta*, ed. N.H. Nicolas (2 vols., London, 1826), ii. p. 477.
9. See C. Rawcliffe, *The Staffords, Earls of Stafford and Dukes of Buckingham, 1394-1521* (Cambridge, 1978), chapter 8, *passim*, for a general discussion of the ducal council at work. I must thank Miss M.M. Condon for showing me a recently discovered, and as yet uncatalogued, memorandum in the P.R.O., which deals with duke Edward's custodianship of Ralph Neville's estates.
10. R. Somerville, 'The Duchy of Lancaster Council and the Court of the Duchy Chamber', *T.R.H.S.*, 4th ser., xxiii (1941), pp. 173-76.
11. J.B. Post, 'Courts, Councils and Arbitrators in the Ladbroke Manor Dispute', *Medieval Legal Records*, ed. R.F. Hunnisett and J.B. Post (H.M.S.O., 1978), pp. 290-339.
12. *Rot Parl.*, iii. pp. 285-305; A.E. Levett, 'Baronial Councils and their Relation to Manorial Courts', *Studies in Manorial History* (Oxford, 1938), pp. 21-40; K.B. McFarlane, *op. cit.*, pp. 214-15.

13. These references are taken from the papers of the late Susan Flower (Essex R.O. T/Z 92/2/3, 3/4). Sadly, her work on the de Vere family during the later middle ages was incomplete at the time of her death. Her draft chapter on the de Vere council contains a great deal of valuable information about the administrative work of baronial councils, and has been of considerable help to me in writing this paper.

14. R.R. Davies, *Lordship and Society in the March of Wales, 1282-1400* (Oxford, 1978), p. 168.

15. A. Luchaire, *Alain le Grand, Sire d'Albret* (Paris, 1877), pp. 101-14. For further evidence of French baronial councils at work see *ibid.*, pp., 57, 97-98, and M. de Maulde-la-Claviere, *Histoire de Louis XII* (6 vols., Paris, 1889-93), i. pp. 347-49.

16. 'The Chetwynd Chartulary', ed. G. Wrottesley, *William Salt Arch. Soc.*, xii (1891), p. 313. This annuity hardly compares with the fee of £10 granted to him under the same terms by Humphrey, duke of Buckingham, his chief patron and employer (Walter Chetwynd's 'Collections for a History of Pirehill Hundred', *ibid.*, (1914), p. 98).

17. G.A. Holmes, *The Estates of the Nobility in Fourteenth Century England* (Cambridge, 1957), pp. 130-31; Longleat Ms. 237; Essex R.O. T/Z 92/3/4.

18. *The Grey of Ruthin Valor*, ed. R.I. Jack (Sydney, 1965), pp. 51-52, 69, 139.

19. *Rot. Parl.*, iv. pp. 267-75; J.S. Roskell, *The Commons and their Speakers in English Parliaments 1376-1523* (Manchester, 1965), pp. 207-8, 348-50.

20. Ross, *op. cit.*, pp. 11-13; *History of Parliament: Biographies 1439-1509*, ed. J.C. Wedgwood (London, 1936), pp. 851-52.

21. *Paston Letters and Papers*, ii. pp. 445, 447-49, 458-64, 466-68, 477-78, 486-87.

22. Staffs. R.O. D.641/1/2/4 m. 5.

23. *Stoner Letters and Papers*, ed. C.L. Kingsford (2 vols., Camden Soc., 3rd ser. xxix, xxx, 1919), i. pp. 123-24.

24. J.S. Roskell, 'Sir William Oldhall, Speaker in the Parliament of 1450', *Nottingham Medieval Studies*, v (1961), pp. 96-97.

25. Commynes, *Mémoirs*, ed. J. Calmette and G. Durville, (Les Classiques de l'Histoire de France Au Moyen Age, 1924), I, 196. *Anchiennes Cronicques d'Engleterre par Jehan de Waurin*, ed. L.M.E. Dupont (3 vols., Societe de l'Histoire de France, Paris, 1853-63), iii, 186 *et seq.*

26. Rawcliffe, *op. cit.*, p. 150.

27. B.L., Egerton Roll 2181 m. 8d.

28. J.C. Hodgson, 'Percy Bailiffs' Rolls of the Fifteenth Century', *Sirtees Soc.*, cxxxiv (1921), p. 94.

29. A.R. Myers, 'The Household of Queen Elizabeth Woodville, 1466-7', *Bulletin of the John Rylands Library*, 1 (1967-8), pp. 456-58, 460.

30. Longleat Ms. 352. Occasionally the lord himself travelled with his councillors to examine evidence and arbitrate in disputes. In 1496, for instance, George, earl of Kent, and his council visited Ruthin to settle a disagreement between the burgesses and one Margaret Exmewe who had allegedly infringed the borough's right of free warren (P.R.O. S.C.2/223/22 m. 3).

31. *Paston Letters and Papers*, ii. p. 438.

32. Rawcliffe, *op. cit.*, p. 153.

108

33. Longleat Ms. 457; J.M.W. Bean, *The Estates of the Percy Family 1416-1537* (Oxford, 1958), pp. 137-38.
34. Holmes, *op. cit.*, pp. 77-78.
35. J.T. Rosenthal, 'The Estates and Finances of Richard, Duke of York (1411-1460)', *Studies in Medieval and Renaissance History* (University of Nebraska), ii (1965), p. 181.
36. Westminster Abbey Muniment 16062. See also 16053 for another letter couched in similar terms.
37. McFarlane, *op. cit.*, p. 36; Rosenthal, *op. cit.*, p. 190.
38. Roskell, *Commons and Speakers*, p. 242 n. 1.
39. Somerville, *op. cit.*, pp. 164-65.
40. *Registrum Abbatiae Johannis Whethamstede*, ed. H.T. Riley (2 vols., Rolls Series, 1872-3), ii. p. 218.
41. Essex R.O. D/DPr/140, 141; Colchester Town Hall, Banham Ms. 23.
42. *Paston Letters and Papers*, i. pp. 580-81.
43. Roskell, *Commons and Speakers*, pp. 348-50.
44. D.O. Pam, 'The Fight for Common Rights', *Edmonton Hundred Hist. Soc.*, new ser. xxvii (1973), p. 12.
45. P.R.O. C.1/71/102.
46. P.R.O. C.P.40/1021B, Trinity 10 Hen. VIII, rot. 625, 1024, Easter 11 Hen. VIII, rot. 308d; S.P.1/22 f. 58.
47. *Select Cases in the Council of Henry VII*, ed. C.G. Bayne and W.H. Dunham, Selden Soc., lxxv (1956), pp. xix-xlvii.

Ruling Elites in the Reign of Henry VII

M.M. Condon,
Public Record Office,
London

This paper offers a discussion of the idea that Henry VII's reign witnessed a significant modification of the prevailing social structures of the later middle ages. Detailed further study is still required at the county and local level in order to understand properly all aspects of the interaction between governors and governed, and, thereby, the full complexities of this difficult and still largely obscure reign, but some suggestions can be advanced meanwhile.

Before the twentieth century, England was dominated by ruling elites, to a large extent divisible under the headings of court, country and church. Their personnel varied for political reasons and beyond the needs of natural renewal. Even more fundamentally, there was a response to changes within society itself and to relationships within the elites. In this respect, Henry VII's reign was not unique, but neither can it be satisfactorily explained in terms of earlier models or merely as a continuation of the Yorkist polity. After the initial two or three years of the reign, there was a remarkable stability within the ruling groups, with little of the faction characteristic of the reign of Edward IV, and, still more, of Henry VI's. The King's power was increasingly felt in the country generally, partly through the action of men dominant at the centre of power and acting under the King's direction. It became a power structure dominated, to a remarkable degree, by the King himself. This fact may have contributed to an absence of faction in the reign, except between those who belonged to the elites and those who did not, and except for the perpetual struggle for influence at local level which could still occasionally assume a national importance, especially when concerned with the north of England.

The first problem is one of definition. An elite may be described as an exclusive body to which admission is desirable. Although not neccessarily static in composition nor in the scope of its powers, it should be capable of regeneration, whether by election, imposition from without or by co-option. In a heavily structured society, elites existed at every level. In this paper they are seen through the King's eyes and are those with which the king himself was most concerned. This perspective results in two most important omissions from our study. The towns lie outside the trilogy of court, country and church and are ignored. Nor is more than passing consideration given to the power and status of the nobility at the local level, which, in turn, contributed to its standing in the body politic as a whole.

The third element in our trilogy is of least importance and easiest to define. Henry VII's bishops were not, in general, outstanding men. Baronial influence on episcopal appointments under Henry VI gave way to royal initiative under the Yorkist and first Tudor kings.[2] Lawyers became more typical than theologians upon the bench of bishops, and a seat thereon became more regularly a reward for administrative service.[3] Dr. Knecht's discussion of this change, through an analysis of the composition of the bench at the beginning and end of each reign, is misleading in suggesting a static situation. Henry VII did not merely imitate the practice of Edward IV. There is a real shift in royal policy. This becomes apparent on analysing, not the appointments as they occurred at some arbitrary point in time, but the bishops themselves. Edward IV's preferments show, at least in his later years, a change from the policy of Henry VI, but the appointments of Henry VII show a more extreme change, whether by comparison with those of Edward IV or as compared with the wider trends of the later middle ages.[4] Of the 16 bishops first appointed to English sees by Edward IV,[5] eight (50%) were doctors learned in the law, and six (38%) were theologians. Of 27 similar appointments made by Henry VII, 16 were lawyers, mostly learned in the civil law (57%), and only six (21%) were theologians. These latter were appointed only to minor and less wealthy sees, although some who became prominent in the work of the council could hope for translation at some later date. Most of Henry's theologians were, nevertheless, administrators, even if his policy was not wholly consistent. That Henry's transformation of the bench of bishops into a body predominantly curial in aspect and legal in training was a conscious act of policy is revealed by developments elsewhere.

A similar pattern is traceable in the royal household. Here again a greater degree of secularization occurs under Henry VII. The office of dean was often a route to a bishopric. Two of Edward's deans, both theologians, died in office before they could hope for episcopal preferment. In Henry VII's reign, Geoffrey Simeon died in office in 1508, but he had been prominent in the council's work as a court of equity, especially in the court of requests, where he sat as a president. William Atwater may have been a product of the occasional piety of Henry's later years, but he too continued in a conciliar role. The legal training of Henry's four other deans, in addition to their constant proximity to the King, may explain their conciliar role in attendance on the King's own person. Three of Henry's four almoners were theologians,[6] but their status outside the household depended primarily on their abilities rather than on their office. It may not be altogether a coincidence that, in place of the able but abrasive Fox, two comparative nonentities (Henry Deane and William Warham), became archbishops of Canterbury in succession to Cardinal John Morton.[7]

Dr. Knecht suggests that in the long term this secularization of the bench may have enervated its religious leadership. Throughout Henry VII's reign, service to the state even to the detriment of the church was exacted as a conscious act of policy. William Smith, for example, petitioned in vain to be allowed to leave the Marches of Wales in order to pay some attention to his neglected see,[8] and Richard Redman, bishop of Exeter, had to fine with the King for permission to reside in his diocese.[9] The appointment of Italians to the sees of

Worcester and Bath in return for services at the papal curia was a logical extension of such an attitude.[10] The church, of course, was not unused to rule by delegation. Many of her lesser dignitaries also were habitually non-resident.[11] Although the bishops, in the wider social context, remained part of the ruling elite of Henry VII's England, their office was a subordinate part of their national role. They shared influence with their junior colleagues, doctors and prebendaries of the church, active in the council of the King. Moreover, Henry VII showed towards the bishops as temporal lords that same ruthlessness as he displayed towards their secular counterparts. Even Fox paid £2,000 for a pardon.[12] Most bishops paid heavily for the restitution of their temporalities, even if a large element in the payment was a composition for the profits of the vacancy.[13] Many suffered for the laxity of their prison keeping.[14] All were subject after their deaths to Henry's revival of the practice of taking multures, following searches by the council amongst 'old presidentes' in the exchequer.[15] Several bishops, as lords of a separate judicial system no less than other lords in their franchises, experienced royal interference in their courts and suffered charges of praemunire.[16]

Of all the ruling elites, the bench of bishops was perhaps the most malleable in terms of direct royal intervention. Mortality enabled Henry rapidly to stamp the mark of his own personality and personal choice upon its members. This, however, is not true of the second great elite dominating the medieval scene. Fortescue was not alone in underscoring the traditional claim of the nobility to dominance within the body politic when he gave them pre-eminence even over the King's great officers.[17] The same point was made, for example, by the rebels led by Warbeck who complained of the lowly birth of the men who influenced the King and ruled the country to the exclusion of its traditional leadership.[18] Admission to the nobility passed primarily by inheritance, over which Henry could exert little direct control. There might be occasional exceptions: for instance, the confirmation of the title of Welles to his uncle and of Devon to Edward Courtenay. Nevertheless, two of the most notable features regarding membership of this elite under Henry VII are the absence of men of the King's own blood and the fact that Henry created so few peers. Henry was himself an only son. Thus, unlike the situation under Edward IV, there was no centre within the King's kindred for rival political tensions and no obvious focus for political discontent. For much of the reign he had no adult heir and Arthur died before he could achieve a recognizable political identity. The second son, Henry, was kept close about the household of his father.[19] Of the King's uncles, Jasper, duke of Bedford, had a long record of loyalty to the Lancastrian cause. But his rewards, though great, removed him from the centre of the political stage, with commissions in Ireland and Wales. As Bedford left no heir of his own body, his lands and offices reverted to the crown and some of his servants, including his secretary, Thomas Lucas, King's solicitor from 1497, passed into the royal service. John, lord Welles, was always a minor if loyal figure; though he sat frequently both in council and on commissions in his native Lincolnshire.

Through his mother's third marriage, and more immediately through the circumstances of his own accession, Henry VII was linked with the Stanleys. Thomas Stanley became earl of Derby; William, his brother, became chamberlain of the King's household. Both eventually were confirmed in part of their Ricardian gains and were generously compensated for the loss of the remainder,[20] though William's possessions returned to the Crown through his forfeiture for treason in 1495. Thomas sat with some regularity in council, though he was as frequently away from court, preserving a powerful local influence. He was not included amongst the King's feoffees of 1949, when provision was made for the performance of the King's will.[21] Henry's sense of obligation to the Stanleys, in so far as he felt any, did not outlast the earl's lifetime. Moreover, once the Stanleys' considerable local power was abused to the King's disparagement, Henry's reaction was swift, and the whole Stanley family was bound in recognizances for future good bearing.[22] Both James, warden of Manchester and later bishop of Ely, and Edward were indicted for illegal retaining.

The indictment against Edward Stanley is annotated in the King's own hand, an indication of his personal interest.[23] The sole debt to the Stanleys acknowledged by Henry was undoubtedly their political service. Ultimately their place in the body politic was determined by their status in council.

The Queen's kin could not even claim the obligation of political service. The dowager Queen herself was either stripped of or relinquished her lands in 1487; they were then granted to the Queen.[24] Cecily, duchess of York, the Queen's grandmother, was no longer a political force, though to some extent she bought her security by her cultivation of the King's household and council by grants of offices on her estates.[25] Thomas, marquis of Dorset, paid the penalty for his vacillation in 1483-85. Although admitted of council he never recovered his standing, even in terms of membership of commissions of the peace. In 1492 he was bound in a series of obligations and feoffments which, if put into effect, could ultimately have brought about his disinheritance.[26] The one person whose influence was paramount was the King's own mother, Margaret Beaufort. She was granted extensive estates by her son and her standing within the locality was sufficient to attract litigation to her courts.[27] From her household a constant stream of people emerged to find employment in Henry's household, council and service. In addition, she had the oversight of several important wards, including Edward, duke of Buckingham. This absence of the King's kindred from the nobility removed an element which had been a constant force, sometimes cohesive and often disruptive, in political life throughout the fifteenth century.

The small number of peerage creations is equally important. Despite an actual decline in the numbers of the peerage, including the continuance in the Crown of the titles of York and Gloucester and the failure of the male line of no less than 18 peerage families during the course of his reign,[28] Henry VII created very few peers. As a deliberate act of policy this was in part a product of the relative strength of the King's position. Even Henry VIII felt compelled to add substantially to the peerage at a time of crisis in the 1530s. It was also a product of a shift in the balance of power amongst the elites, from the use of the traditional noble councillors of the King, to councillors who held positions about the King only by the King's concurrence and whose authority was the delegated authority of the Crown and not derived from land or title. This was paralleled by a shift in the power balance at local level towards men in the second stratum of society, supported by interference from those of the King's councillors on the spot and active intervention by the central government. The weakness of this arrangement was that it ignored the many bonds which tied the nobility and gentry one to the other, through lordship, intermarriage and community of interest, although these in turn might be disrupted by royal intervention or regulation, especially at times of crisis, and certainly were curtailed as an act of conscious policy by Henry, particularly in his later years. Such curtailment was achieved by the use of enquiries, informations, prosecutions, bonds and forced enfeoffments. The same process of regulation, with a shift towards direct reliance on the gentry, is visible in Henry's policy towards retaining. If prosecutions themselves were erratic —exemplary rather than sustained, and only partially effective — Henry also attempted a system of control in the Crown's interest through licensed retaining. This was to be closely regulated by the council, to which detailed returns were to be made,[29] though the combination of penal legislation and royal licence seems to have caused some confusion in the shires at large,[30] and may be more significant in theory than in practice. Also, as Edward had done at the beginning of *his* reign, Henry could and did build up the power of men whom he trusted in areas of unrest. But the estates and franchises so granted were limited in extent. In only two cases, those of Robert Willoughby and Giles Daubeney, were they accompanied by titles of nobility.

Henry's policy is perhaps seen most clearly — though in no case carried to its logical conclusion, for circumstances and tradition proved too strong — in his treatment of the peripheral areas of his realm; in Ireland, where he was least successful,[31] Wales and the north. In all three areas Henry's handling of power groupings shows some uncertainty, punctuated by a more aggressive policy. In Wales the sole attempt at a radical interference with traditional elites was abortive. Reginald Bray, who briefly succeeded Arthur's lieutenant, Jasper, duke of Bedford, on the latter's death in 1495, was far too heavily committed at the centre of government to be spared for the governance of the principality. Moreover Bray, unlike Bedford, neither held land in the area himself nor was he given any such power base by the King.[32] The final settlement was a compromise, which has its parallels in the Yorkist and Henrician settlements, and was successful enough for Henry VII's lifetime. Even after Arthur's death a King's council under William Smith, bishop of Lincoln, continued to be active in the more vital area of the Marches, leaving Wales itself in the hands of a local leadership, albeit one loosely tied to the Crown through the household and council. The functions of the council in the marches were primarily judicial.[33] Its membership consisted largely, though not entirely, of local gentry, many of whom were councillors also of the King.[34] These were supplemented by professional lawyers and administrators, who also assisted a London-based council in the administration of the Prince's lands.[35] A quarter of a century of dislocation had already disturbed traditional loyalties and structures and perhaps assisted an extension of royal control that was given formal expression in the indentures of the Marches.[36]

Although the north had been similarly disturbed, the dislocation may have been less fundamental, permitting a return to traditional policies promulgated from a position of relative strength. From the early years of the reign, when first rebellion and then the threat of a new Scottish war, precipitated by a border quarrel, alike demanded the King's personal and immediate intervention, the north was an urgent problem.[37] Henry's first solution was the traditional one of harnessing the loyalty and influence of the most prominent local magnates. In the north-east this involved the restoration of a chastened earl of Northumberland.[38] Although the continuing need to maintain a military presence in the north may have helped to bolster traditional ruling structures, the earl's unexpected death in 1489 forced a change of policy. The fifth earl was a minor who would never enjoy the influence held by his father. This fact he would bitterly resent, the more so in that Henry, recognising his potential capacity for mischief, tried to undermine the foundations of a power already eroded by minority and political miscalculation. Under the nominal authority of his second son, Henry now gave power to the earl of Surrey. Although Surrey's standing and ability commanded influence, he had no territorial power base in the north. His only mandate was the King's authority, continually renewed but never assured, whilst his own wings were clipped by piece-meal restoration of his estates, making him dependent upon the King's continuing favour.[39] It is unlikely that Surrey was the head of a King's council. More probably he governed with the assistance of his own servants and those of the King's council normally resident in the north. Within this partial power vacuum the King's authority was yet more directly asserted from 1494 by Richard Fox, keeper of the Privy Seal, and bishop of Durham. In these years Fox was prominent in negotiations with Scotland, a diplomatic activity which itself directly affected the balance of local forces. From 1499 a new element entered the picture — William Sever received a commission as surveyor of the King's prerogative, an office potentially prejudicial to the noble interest because of the sharp eye kept by Sever for the King's feudal and fiscal advantage.[40] In addition, a more determined effort was made to exploit the King's own position as a northern magnate by means of reforms in the duchy honours, though Henry's policy proved unrealistic save in purely administrative terms.[41]

By 1500 the achievement of a lasting truce with Scotland and, if less important, the majority of the earl of Northumberland made possible, and perhaps required, a change of approach. The earl of Surrey returned south to become, in 1501, treasurer of the Exchequer. In the last decade of the reign Henry's policy definitely moved towards a rejection, or at least a modification, of the authority of the traditional elites exercising power in the north. Although this change of policy did not survive either its author or his chosen instrument, it was the forerunner of Henry VIII's council in the north. Thomas Savage, who became archbishop of York in 1501, had been dean of the chapel of the household and president of the council attendant on the King, in which his considerable authority was exercised in a mainly judicial capacity. He was now given a commission as president of the council in the north, with councillors named and appointed by the King. Significantly these did not at first include the earl of Northumberland,[42] though he had been sworn of the King's council since 1498.[43]

The establishment of an autonomous King's council in the north did not mean the total supplanting of the authority so exercised by a traditional elite. The council itself seems to have included some of the minor barons.[44] Savage, too, was a member of a prominent northern family, though its estates were in Lancashire rather than Yorkshire, and he was quite capable of advancing his own interests as well as the King's. It was a quarrel over rival jurisdictions, combined with Savage's dual exercise of authority in his own and the King's name, which brought both the earl of Northumberland and the archbishop before the King's council at Westminster under heavy obligations to keep the peace: a situation which in itself suggests both the aggression in, and the limitations of, Henry's conciliar policy.[45]

The same may also be said of his policy in the west March. Again the military significance of the March suggested a reliance on the local nobility. Henry's policy rested on the exploitation of traditional rivalries and relied upon minor baronial power rather than the major peerage. Although his power cannot be compared with that of the Percies, the earl of Westmorland was again eclipsed. The third earl was a shadowy figure and not a councillor, whilst the long minority of his heir led to an exploitation still more brutal than that of the earl of Northumberland.[46] Whereas in the East March Henry continually divided authority amongst a number of nobles and gentry, in the West March he relied principally on lord Dacre, although Dacre's tenure of office was insecure and he, too, suffered fiscal and feudal harassment.[47] In the long term, the constant renewal of the King's commission encouraged greater baronial influence and independance. This, however, seems not to have become apparent before Henry's death. The effectiveness of the King's council in London, combined with the ability and loyalty of Dacre himself, did at least promote royal authority in that area. But although unruly local gentry might be bound under heavy recognizances for their allegiance and good bearing, and might also occasionally be brought before the King himself, the very frequency with which such action was forced on the Crown, particularly on charges of retaining and riot, hints at an almost inevitable superficiality in any changes in the structure of power at a local level in the more remote areas of the realm.

In his policy towards the north, Henry attempted a redistribution in the balance of power, partly in favour of the lesser northern families, but also, and more fundamentally, by overlaying the traditional structure of power with the newer elite of the King's council. This he combined with a more direct application of the royal authority. In using local forces, Henry pursued a policy of fragmentation of interest, whether by dividing authority or by avoiding the continous, if uncertain, tenure of office by one man.[48] The same process of dislocation in the Crown's interest underlay the *quo warranto* proceedings against several northern lords concerning their franchises,[49] and also the assertion of more direct royal control over the office of warden of the March itself.[50] This is further illustrated by the occasional difficulty which the earl of Northumberland experienced in exercising his good lordship, and by the way in which he, like many other lords, was unable fully to realize his mesne lordship in matters of feudal tenure. A charge of ravishment of ward involving the daughter of Sir John Hastings brought him into the Exchequer and Common Pleas, and he was finally to compound with the council learned for a fine which effectively clipped his wings for the rest of the reign.[51]

The process of recognizance, and the consequent disturbance of the feudal order was the most effective, and certainly the most interesting of the ways in which Henry attempted to contain the independance of his nobility, although its political advantages were finite and eventually produced a dangerous reaction which was itself a measure of short-term success. Likewise, the example made of nobles who practised retaining and riot or, in exceptional cases, the feoffments made in the King's interest on noble lands, might tend to contain the use to which a noble might put his still vital authority. Ultimately this centralising royal influence would disrupt the relationship between elites, for it meant influence of the Crown in the locality in channels other than the dominant lord. In the short term there do seem to be changes in the position of the nobility under Henry VII even as against the reigns of Edward IV and Henry VIII. The absence of King's kin and Henry's parsimony in conferring titles of nobility meant that he would not be surrounded by nobles of his own choosing. This, combined with other factors (such as the strength of his position, his unconventional upbringing and his intensely personal rule) necessarily affected their position. In addition, there were long minorities in several peerage families, especially important in the crucial formative years of the reign; whilst second generation nobles rarely received the authority enjoyed by their fathers. Mention has already been made of the Stanleys and of the earl of Northumberland who, though sworn a councillor in 1498, was not even given the immediate entry to the council in the north which he considered his natural right.[52] The contrast between the active political career of John, lord Audley, Richard III's treasurer, and the relative obscurity of his son, James, may be one reason behind the latter's rebellion in 1497. Robert, lord Broke, son of Henry's steward of the household, was not a councillor, even if, following a petition to Bray and a fine with the king, he succeeded to his father's Cornish offices. Like other nobles of his generation he, too, was bound to the King for livery of his lands and his father's pardon.[53] If George, third lord Abergavenny, was employed far more extensively in the King's service than his father had been, and was sworn a councillor in 1498, he also the more nearly experienced the King's displeasure.[54] The duke of Suffolk's heir succeeded only as an earl, and with a diminished inheritance.[55] Successive earls of Kent saw their influence curtailed, earl Richard's lands were carved up amongst Henry and his councillors and he himself was placed in ignominious tutelage.[56] The duke of Buckingham had serious grievances which could not find utterance until the next reign.[57] One measure of this shifting balance of power lies in noble representation on commissions of the peace. The duke of Buckingham, for example, was not appointed to the Staffordshire commission until 1503, though he was on the Surrey commission from 1499, the year of his majority. Edward IV had been still more severe, excluding Buckingham's father from both counties. In this both Edward IV and Henry VII showed awareness of the importance of local rule. Richard III's more widespread commissions to Buckingham were no less a political act.[58] Nevertheless, there was a difference between the policies of the two Kings. Under Henry VII the peers enjoyed a less extensive mandate. Only Bedford was appointed to commissions throughout England.[59] But even this situation contains its own paradox, indicating how far the influence of the nobility was still necessary to Henry for the maintenance of peace at local level. Perhaps partly as compensation for a relative eclipse at the centre of government, peers are recorded in increasing numbers as participating in the work of the sessions in the latter half of the reign.[60]

Henry did not exclude the nobility from the council and actively cultivated their presence at court. Yet few nobles could claim any real influence with him save for Oxford, Bedford, perhaps Derby and the small household-administrative group.[61] Even these were subjected to the control exercised by Henry over the peerage in general. Thus Daubeney was heavily fined for illegal embezzlement at Calais, in which he was said to have taken pay for the ancient rather than the actual establishment of the town,[62] and was also forced to make over his interest in his French pension to the King.[63] He was bound by obligations for payment of the fine at days, and by his will he assigned certain land to feoffees, the issues to be used for these payments. Yet this punishment even Dudley thought over severe.[64] The novelty of Henry's policy lies in the extent to which he carried the use of such recognizances, rather than in the instrument itself; of this Professor Lander has made a preliminary study.[65] He suggests the increasing use of such bonds as a means of politically disabling the nobility: though any final analysis must await not only a more detailed investigation of the basis on which the bonds were given but also a study of the level of forfeiture and the Crown's success in enforcing fines and penalties. This last may well have borne most heavily on the nobility. The system itself was self-perpetuating, since the corollary to a forfeit bond was a further recognizance for the payment of a fine by instalments. At the same time, the very authority inherent in nobility might work in the Crown's interest since, given on behalf of lesser men, it might accord ill with honour to be in breach of the bond's condition.[66] Lander demonstrates, too, the penal severity of Henry's conditions for the reversal of attainder, calculating that in all at least four-fifths of noble families in England were under some form of restraint for at least part of the reign. By virtue of their wide estates the nobility also suffered, perhaps unduly, from Henry's commissions of concealments. The scale of these was such that for the year 1505-6 alone 93 returns survive showing alienations, minorities, idiocies and intrusions, including one of nearly 40 years before.[67] Seizure of land into the King's hand could mean loss of feudal incidents; whilst if a lord acted too precipitately in defence of his rights it meant process in the King's courts. The earl of Northumberland was not the only magnate to be prosecuted for ravishment of ward.[68] Henry VII himself had a very clear conception of his aims in pursuing such policies, though they may later have been obscured by the avarice for which chronicle tradition appears to be only too justified. Polydore Vergil echoes the words of a conversation between the King and the Spanish ambassador when he wrote that

> The King wished as he said to keep all Englishmen obedient through fear, and he considered that whenever they gave him offence they were actuated by their great wealth . . . All of his

subjects who were men of substance when found guilty of whatever fault he harshly fined in order by a penalty which especially deprives of their fortunes not only the men themselves but even their descendants, to make the population less well able to undertake any upheavals and to discourage at the same time all offences.[69]

In this atmosphere the earl of Kent's alleged comment that 'the Kynges grace undoyth no man' was surely a little disingenuous.[70]

It is difficult to ascertain the place of the nobility in the channels of patronage: that is, in the route to the King's ear by which a petitioner might gain his desires. Evidence so far accumulated tends to point away from the nobility and towards the council and household. This may have become increasingly true with time, as the council learned and delegated committees of councillors assumed responsibility for certain matters of grace: particularly pardons and grants of wardship, which were reduced to a common denominator of a financial composition with the Crown.[71] One symptom of this is surely the way in which councillors and household men amassed annuities and stewardships at the gift of nobles, bishops and religious houses. If Reginald Bray held annuities of, amongst others, the earls of Northumberland, Devon and Ormond, lord Dynham, lady Hastings and lord Audley, it was surely Bray who was the dominant partner.[72] In terms of personal profit it was the councillor who achieved the greater rewards. Beyond the ready employment in the shire, beyond the enhanced personal status that led Dudley, for example, to use his title of King's councillor as proudly as any peerage,[73] beyond the position of influence and the receipt of offices and casualties in the King's gift that were so accessible to him, the councillor could use his position for personal aggrandizement: most notably in the land market, where he was exceptionally well placed to exploit political and legal disadvantage and economic misfortune.[74] Councillors were cultivated and their support enlisted through their employment as feoffees-to-uses.[75] A similar picture emerges from their employment as executors and supervisors of wills. Receivers' accounts throughout England show the extent to which they were felt to command influence and thus merit annuities in cash or office. The wills of lord Lisle and his wife, who died after him, epitomise this relationship. Lisle desired Bray to be his 'good and especialle mediator' to Henry VII. To Lisle's wife Bray became 'my most single goode frende in this worlde'.[76]

The nobility and episcopate readily present themselves as elites witin society at large but are clearly no more than a part of the ruling elite within that process of governance with which this study is concerned. Within the shire, the framework of rule was provided by land and wealth, affinity and patronage, authority and office and by the compromise between self-interest and the maintenance of the King's peace in which royal patronage was but one, though the most dominant, regulating factor. There remain, then, three elites requiring consideration. One is the network of county officials, especially the sheriffs, justices of the peace and the special commissioners operating within the shire, where overall trends are more important than the ever-changing personnel of authority. The second is the King's household, a group to be reckoned with throughout the medieval period, although its use as a power base was constantly changing. The third elite, wherein the uniqueness of Henry's reign perhaps lies, is the council.

The first group is the least important in the context of this paper. Tenure of office as J.P. or sheriff was of limited duration. They were essentially executive officers rather than governors, and were subject to dominant local influences as well as being subservient to royal mandate. At the same time, though the development was over a period longer than the reign of Henry VII and not unique to it, the transfer of executive power did assist the encroachment of royal authority upon the rule of all other groups. There were, however, subtleties in this relationship; for lords joined with councillors, household men, local lawyers and their own retainers to form the upper stratum of county society.[77] Justices of the peace, sheriffs and the lesser figure of the escheator form a homogenous group and a significant proportion of sheriffs and MPs were drawn in each county from members of the bench.[78] This means that a relatively small, if expanding, section of county society dominated all the rest; the more so as in most counties the burden of the shire's work was borne by a portion only of the current members of the bench, of whom the gentry element were the most prominent.[79] Local gentry were being added to the bench in increasing numbers, accounting almost entirely for the expansion in the actual numbers of men appointed to commissions of the peace during the reign.[80] Despite this, and in contrast to the situation at the end of the century, there is little to indicate manipulation of the lists.[81] Nor was there any need to afforce a commission which always contained a number of lords, bishops and lawyers who were members of the King's council. The gentry element included also a number of household men and councillors who might exercise an influence disproportionate to their numbers. This can be seen in indictments returned for Suffolk, where James Hobart sat more than any other JP and where the returns include an unusually large number of matters affecting the King's rights. Similarly, in Hereford sessions tended to approximate to a meeting of the Prince's council, differing from it only in the manner and matter of its jurisdiction; whilst in Surrey offenders could even be bound over specifically to await the next sitting of Bray and Dynham at quarter sessions.[82] Moreover, the commission could always be over-ridden by a special commission of oyer and terminer, or strengthened by the unwonted presence of an unusually large number of peers and councillors already members of it. The growing importance of this elite is suggested by the increasing responsibilities devolved on it by statute. As the same men were frequently included in special commissions to assess subsidies and other taxes, they were exceptionally placed to affect the lives and prosperity of their fellows within the shire. A greater degree of interference is apparent in the office of sheriff. At times of crisis, responsibility passed to the King's council and household. No less than five councillors were appointed as sheriffs in 1485, besides others later to become councillors, and a high proportion of household men.[83] In

1497, in the aftermath of the Cornish Rebellion, the sheriffs originally chosen were replaced by household men in seven counties, comprising four shrievalties.[84] There was similar interference in at least five other years, despite the fact that a man was often named for sheriff for several years before finally being pricked.[85] The position of the sheriff within the shire is well enough known. Not only was he the direct representative of the King's authority. He was also open to influence within the shire, at elections, in empanelling jurors or in due process of law. As a figure crucial to a King to whom litigation by common law process was a principal instrument of authority, the sheriff was subjected to tight control. For many the burden of shrieval office carried heavy consequences in later years when their recognizances were deemed to be forfeit for transgressions real or alleged.[86] Others were the subject of specific prosecutions on penal statutes, whether for taking bribes, allowing prisoners to escape or otherwise failing in their duties.[87]

The second group, the household, is more readily recognizable as an elite. Again, Henry VII's use of his household was not startlingly new. Even Henry VI had employed his household extensively in the process of government: though in his case in particular it must remain an open question how far the household governed the King and how far men desiring positions of influence could insinuate themselves about the King's person. In examining the household one of the problems is to ascertain how far men were absorbed into it as a way of harnessing their influence within the shire and how far they were delegated office and authority within the shire because of their position within the household. Of this duality of perspective the Crown itself was not unaware.[88] In 1485 at least the choice was very much a military one, influenced by the proven loyalty of Henry's companions in exile, of those who had participated in Buckingham's rebellion and of those who had supported Henry at Bosworth: together with a strong admixture of Stafford retainers and servants, the adherents of the King's mother.

In a recent paper to the Royal Historical Society, Dr.

Morgan has elaborated on the use made by Edward IV of his household.[89] The reign of Henry VII is not dissimilar. The comments of the Croyland chronicler[90] could be applied with equal justice to Henry VII who, for example, like Edward IV, granted such offices as the constables of castles generally, though not exclusively, to his household knights and esquires. Military expeditions were conducted largely by and through the household. But there are differences between the two reigns. The most noticeable is Henry's treatment of major household offices. These were left vacant for long periods at a time: a pattern from which only the chamberlainship was exempt and in which the cofferership grew immeasurably in stature.[91] Another, more vital, difference is Henry's great extension of chamber finance, important because of the disturbing influence which it enabled the King to exert upon all ruling groups. Chamber finance meant more than an agency for the amassment of revenue. It was the hub of an administrative system. The concentration of cash and administration in the King's own hands removed a whole dimension from the political scene. It gave the King financial and, in consequence, political independence. As a tool of personal government, using books constantly perused by the King himself and including memoranda pertaining to political matters dictated by Henry and constantly brought to his attention, it provided the King with the means to supervise his policy closely and with which to execute it. Thus the offence of the earl of Northumberland was noted several months before action was begun in the courts; the possibility of raising an aid for the marriage of the King's daughter was considered two years before the parliament which compounded for it was summoned.[92] Chamber finance, in conjunction with conciliar control, radically changed the channels of patronage for certain matters of grace, as the whole transaction was reduced to a financial one. This is not to suggest that the King's grace had ever been free. But the rational and extensive application of conciliar control in the King's interest did tend to curtail the special pleading associated with such petitions. The need to pay and outbid became a pressing necessity. John Shaa, for example, promised 500 marks that Thomas Frowyk should be appointed chief justice of the Common Pleas 'as largely as he that last was gaff therefor'.[93] Equally revealing is a cancelled entry relating to the speakership of the parliament of 1497. Lord Daubeney bid the fee of the speaker that Sir Robert Sheffield should have the office. This is cancelled and above there is an interlineation of a bid by Bray for Thomas Englefield, who was indeed appointed, Thomas Lovell himself heading the delegation that preceded his 'election'.[94] Even prominent councillors felt the full impact of a system so closely controlled by the King. If Bray remained immune during his lifetime, his executors paid 5,000 marks for a pardon, suffered prosecution for alleged customs offences and even saw the provisions of Bray's will disturbed partly through the King's ruthless legalism in pursuit of his prerogative rights.[95]

Finally, the council. How can this be considered an elite at all? Was it not merely an organ of government, albeit a policy-making one? Omnipotent under the King, its relationship with Henry, its membership and functions were the keystone of Henry VII's government. Few men had any real influence with him. He was a strong King who could manipulate, though never entirely supplant, even had he wished so to do, the authority of traditional elites in society, and in this he was master of his own policy. There is a remarkable unanimity amongst contemporary observers and chroniclers, including the hostile comments of rebels against his rule, in emphasising the King's independence and naming those few men who could command influence. Morton, Fox, Bray, Lovell, Daubeney and, latterly, Dudley, were the most frequently mentioned. Others added Savage and the various King's secretaries, notably King and Ruthal, whilst one astute observer noted the influence of Margaret Beaufort on her son.[96] Not all of these are encompassed within the elites already mentioned. The one factor common to them all was their membership of the King's council, and this indeed proves to be the basis of their power, both inside and outside government. It is true that they might be recategorized into their social classes, but this would illustrate rather the wide base from which Henry drew his council than say anything positive about them. Still less does it explain their importance within the state. But what then are we to make of the comments of Ayala that by 1498 Henry had shaken off the influence of some part of the council and would have liked to reduce it still further.[97] Does this not flatly contradict the present argument or else render valueless the ambassador's testimony and political judgement on this and other occasions? In fact there is a grain of truth in such comments if they are set within a fundamentally different interpretation. Henry's relations with his council did undergo a real change. Power was a dynamic, not a static, force. Throughout the reign, Henry retained ultimate control, whether in matters as major as foreign policy, or as minor as the grant of an office. Even Empson did not escape this minute surveillance. His petition for the grant of a stewardship was amended in Henry VII's own hand from a grant for life to a grant during pleasure.[98] But power within the council did become concentrated in the hands of fewer men, mostly lawyers, underlining the peripheral status of those who sat only occasionally *in consiliarios* and diminishing also the influence of the nobility as a group, though lip-service continued to be paid to their preeminence and their presence was required on all occasions of importance. Even the less prominent councillors were, however, part of a vital chain of command and information binding the King and council to the country at large. For this statutory provision was both made and realised, if in breach as well as in observance, as in bringing riots and other misdemeanours to the attention of King and council,[99] in which the council itself maintained an active interest. Although conclusions are at present tentative, there are some pointers to support Cameron's suggested modification of accepted views of the council's jurisdiction in criminal and allied actions, though it was with the council learned rather than the council in star chamber that the initiative lay. The council did use common law process, which had the incidental advantage of making the matter of record and allowing common law process to run against those accessories in whom the Crown was less interested. But the council itself might draw up or amend indictments, issue the commission by which they were found and even on occasion attend at sessions. Process might subsequently follow both before the council and at common law, and if the final end was a composition with the council for the discharge of both processes, composition and the pardon procedure were almost the only available sanctions.[100]

The basic composition of Henry VII's council was much the same as in the Yorkist period, with which there was some continuity of personnel.[101] No less than 35 of Henry's councillors had been councillors also of Edward IV, continuity being equally apparent in all strata of the council. But there were also subtle changes in the composition of the council over the course of the reign, as the *iuris periti* became increasingly prominent. Even if total figures from the reign of Henry VII and Edward IV are compared, the numerical importance of both the peerage and the ecclesiastical groups shows a decline as against the rise of the legal element. This included not only the serjeants at law, who became increasingly important, but also such men as Thomas Lovell, Edmund Dudley, who by his own choice preferred conciliar employment to a legal career, and Richard Empson, attorney general of the Duchy and recorder of Coventry.[102]

The fall in the number of secular lords was to some extent outside Henry's control. During the 1490s a number of peers achieved both their majority and a place on the council, before death had removed some of the older generation. But this decade was also the period when Henry's rule approximated most nearly to that of his Yorkist predecessors. The traumatic events of 1497 and what can only be described as his own increasing avarice, however motivated, turned his mind more sharply to repression, affecting both the use which he made of his council and the membership of it, and also his attitude to the most 'able' group in society, the peers. At all periods their presence was necessary at moments of solemnity, as meetings of 1499 and 1504 illustrate.[103] But there was a rationalization of the conciliar body, underlining the importance of those few peers prominent in the councils of the King; primarily the household and administrative group, to the exclusion of those merely the King's 'natural' councillors. Yet even the evidence of the presence lists surviving as the *Liber Intrationum*, showing a proportional attendance of the peers which varies from 25% to 36%, rising on occasion to 57%, may be misleading. Caesar's lists, however, suggest what was surely the normal situation. On the working council rather than the plenary session the balance was weighted far more heavily towards the legal element and such assiduous councillors as Sir John Risely.[104] And until the face of the council was radically changed in the last decade it is again the group who combined household office with a place on the council who were the most prominent — a group which included Guildford, Lovell, Poynings, Daubeney and Bray himself.

The importance of the council lies in its intimate association with the King in the business of government, and the King himself was usually present at its meetings. But its business was not restricted to the range of matters which preface the late sixteenth-century extracts of its *acta*, comprehensive though this summary seems in its inclusion of much judicial and executive action touching all social classes.[105] From the mid-1490s certain councillors, of whom the chief was Reginald Bray, acted in the presence of the King as a court of audit for both lands and revenue. This committee of council was later to become a conciliar court of audit under Robert Southwell and Roger Laybourne. A second court, no less the King's council though it generally sat, from 1500 at least, without the King's great officers and met under the presidency of the dean of the chapel of the household, developed (as the court of requests) a jurisdiction in equity parallel to that of the star chamber. There were similar conciliar committees leasing lands and granting offices in Exchequer patronage, or collecting fines of distraint of knighthood or organising the collection of arrears of the benevolence and thus investigating local prosperity and influence. Most significant of all was the council learned in the law, again acting with the full authority of the King's council though meeting in the duchy chamber under the presidency of

132

the chancellor of the duchy and comprised almost entirely of lawyers. It provided a third conciliar court of equity and, more particularly, supervised matters connected with the King's prerogative, whether the grant of wardships, the compounding for intrusions or the finding of them, the punishment of abuse or negligence by the King's officers, compounding with offenders for pardons, investigating treasons and perjuries and other abuses with an energy which made its presence widely felt and its members feared and hated.[106]

Henry VII turned naturally to a conciliar solution for every administrative problem. This resulted in a conciliar omni-competence which, with the growing importance of only a small part of the council, meant that councillors formed the only elite which could dominate all the rest. This could have some unique manifestations, whether in terms of the rewards to councillors themselves, their prominence in the land market, or in the system of informers and promoters who bypassed the usual channels and exerted an influence beyond their status, bringing defaulting officers, nobles, clergy, gentry, merchants and poor men to book before the King's council or subjecting them to a combination of prosecution in the King's Bench or Common Pleas and appearance before the council for the more rapid determination of process. Even the rapid expansion of conciliar justice during the course of the reign enhanced its influence, though it was an expansion due as much to pressure from litigants as to a conscious act of policy. Star chamber cases themselves are almost entirely pleadings between party and party, in which questions of title predominate, rather than criminal actions.[107] Even so, the King might on occasion intervene, stopping the action between lord Fitzwalter and John Doget, for example, and taking the case into his own hands.[108] This expansion of litigation had several side effects. One was through the council's use of arbitration, which thus involved in its processes those same classes who provided the JPs and sheriffs, though the council often retained the ultimate decision in its own hands. A second was the further extension of the system of recognizances, which were usually taken not only for appearance but also for good abearing and often for allegiance from parties suing or brought before it.[109] These were not necessarily cancelled, and could be forfeit for breach of the condition. Even some recognizances given for appearance were later deemed to be forfeit, and suit followed in Common Pleas as on a plea of debt.[110] Such actions may, however, have had on occasion a political motive, for defendants include men of the stature of the lords Clifford and Dacre.[111] The council itself was of sufficient status and authority to try and condemn the powerful offender, whether in disputes between party and party or for matters involving breach of the King's peace. Thus, for example, the duke of Suffolk was ordered to stay process at common law and not meddle in lands in dispute;[112] the lords Dudley and Grey of Powis, having been warned concerning the misdemeanours of their servants, were subsequently committed to the Fleet for an affray;[113] lord Hastings was heavily bound for his appearance and to keep the peace.[114] But against the determined offender even the council might have little effective sanction.[115]

The final link in this chain is the council learned, which achieved a separate institutional existence by at least 1499, and perhaps by 1498. In the context of this present study it is less important for its membership, though this was small and included some of the King's most powerful councillors who, by their membership of it, commanded still greater influence in society at large, than for its activities on the King's behalf. These have already been summarized. The council's preoccupation was with the King's causes, fiscal and feudal, and the prerogative rights of his kingship, in the broadest sense of the word. The council learned interested itself also in the maintenance of law and order, and enjoyed a jurisdiction in contempt committed in other conciliar courts, besides by-passing, interfering with and anticipating action in the common law courts. Through its pre-emptive interception of returned inquisitions, too, it could assert a manipulative influence in the King's interest significant in a society in which authority was so often grounded on personal ties and landed estate. It became increasingly prominent in the administration and enforcement of that system of recognizances which are a hallmark of Henry VII's policy of control. These, the various special commissions, and, to take a crude but easily calculated measure, the great increase in the number of pardons granted 'of special grace'[116] are all yardsticks to measure a general policy which affected an increasing number of the King's subjects. Moreover, the council, or specified members of it, were given absolute discretion over the issue of certain special commissions and other matters passing under the great seal. This delegation, unusual in Henry, was possible only because of the very close association of the council learned with the King. It was a hegemony which, combined with its use of legal process and recognizance, fed by a system of information and enquiry, and governed by astute and searching legal minds and a steady tenacity of purpose, enabled it so to dominate the whole domestic scene in the last decade of the reign. It was the King himself, and his manifestation in the corporate body of conciliar justice, who was the prime dislocating factor in the relationship between elites.

All this draws together under one head, the very personal rule of Henry VII as king. This itself is the key to the relationship of elites one to another and to society at large. Bacon has a story of how, to the great rejoicing of the whole court, Henry's pet monkey tore up the notebook in which the King had recorded the characters and demeanours of those about him.[117] This trivial incident, whether or not it actually occurred, encapsulates both the essence and the fragility of Henry's rule. It perhaps suggests, too, a certain superficiality of achievement despite all the auguries of change: an impermanence, a fragility caused in part by the tensions which Henry VII himself created in binding and dividing the ruling elites themselves.

Notes

1. For encouragement generously given and criticism offered during the writing of this paper I am particularly indebted to the editor, Professor C.D. Ross; to Dr. M.A. Hicks, Dr. C. Rawcliffe, Miss E.A. Danbury, and Mr. N.E. Evans
2. R.J. Knecht, 'The episcopate and the Wars of the Roses', *Univ. of Birmingham Hist. Journal*, vi (1957-8), 108-31.
3. The curial cleric was not, of course, an unfamiliar figure on the medieval stage. But set within the bounds of an exceptional reign, that of Henry VI, and an exceptional period of change, the Reformation, and in a context in wich the balance between lay and clerical involvement in government and administration had tipped overwhelmingly in favour of the former, this marked secularization of the clergy becomes worth recording.
4. On the latter point, see T.H. Aston, 'Oxford's medieval alumni', *Past and Present*, lxxiv (1977), 3-40, esp. pp. 27-30. Henry VII's choice of bishops has in itself helped to weight Aston's figures.
5. Welsh sees have been omitted here because many Welsh bishops were too obscure to be included in Emden's register of graduates. Initial appointments only are considered, because Henry VII made unprecedented use of the device of translation — Fox, for example, held no less than four different sees in succession.
6. These figures are based on A.B Emden, *A Biographical Register of the University of Oxford to A.D. 1500* (3 vols., Oxford, 1957-9); *ib.*, *A Biographical Register of the University of Cambridge* (Cambridge, 1963).
7. Dean and Warham were both experienced curialists, but neither was of the stature of either Morton or Fox. For an excellent unpublished study of Warham, see M. Kelly, 'Canterbury jurisdiction and influence during the episcopate of William Warham, 1502-32' (Cambridge Ph. D. thesis, 1963).
8. Westminster Abbey Muniments (WAM), 16038; noticed by M. Bowker, *The Secular Clergy of the Diocese of Lincoln* (Cambridge, 1968), p. 17.
9. PRO, E 101/415/3, f. 287: a licence for three quarters of a year paying £100 yearly.
10. Knecht, *loc. cit.*, p. 130; B. Behrens, 'The origins of the English resident ambassador in Rome', *EHR*, xlix (1934), 640-56.
11. *Cf.* the correspondence and licences for absence recorded in the Act Books of the Dean and Chapter of Wells, *HMC Report on the Mss. of the Dean and Chapter of Wells* (2 vols., HMSO 1907-14), vol. ii, especially pp. 150-2.
12. PRO, E 36/214, p. 447; pardon enrolled *CPR, 1494-1509*, p. 366. Likewise Audley (1,000 marks); Dudley included this in his list of the King's more excessive demands: BL Lansd. Ms. 127, f. 60; 'The petition of Edmund Dudley', ed. C.J. Harrison, *EHR*, lxxxvii (1972), 88, 93.
13. That the fine for restitution was a composition is clear from the frequency with which prospective bishops had previously been given custody of the temporalities, or, after preferment, were granted the issues of the vacancy: *CPR, 1485-94, CPR, 1494-1509, passim*; *cf.* PRO, E 159/273, *Brevia baronibus*, Hil. rot. 7-7d., a pardon of account save for any escapes of clerks. Yet if Redman paid merely a full assessed rate of £2,000 p.a. after a vacancy lasting almost a year, James Stanley was assessed at nearly twice as much after a

vacancy of 15 months: PRO, E 101/415/3, f.291; BL Lansd. Ms 127, f.31; *CPR, 1494-1509*, pp. 265, 514.

14. This was a genuine problem in which Henry maintained a sustained, though not necessarily disinterested concern. Both lay and clerical custodians came under heavy pressure. The penalties, initiated and enforced by the council but 'made sure in the lawe' and thus found by common law process were duly exacted (*cf.* PRO Req 2/12/151, a case of embezzlement of the fine by the messenger to whom it was entrusted). The fines themselves are too numerous to list, but are noted in both the king's bench and in the chamber books. See also R.B. Pugh, *Imprisonment in Medieval England* (Cambridge, 1970), pp. 218-54, especially pp. 236-40.

15. PRO, E101/415/3 f.283; also *ibid.*, ff. 285, 288. The first recorded mention was in 1497 E101/414/16, f.259.

16. See now *Spelman's Reports*, ed. J.H. Baker (2 vols., Selden Soc., xciii-iv, 1977-8), vol. ii, pp. 64-8; M. Kelly, *loc cit.*, discusses the implications of certain actions. If prosecution was at the initiative of private parties, and if some were no more than cross suits in an accepted tradition of vexatious litigation, the penalties on the bishop and his officials were real enough, and those against the bishop of Norwich had the active encouragement of the King's attorney, a member of the commission of the peace; *cf.* PRO, KB9/438/48-54; KB9/442/ 111; KB9/445/26; DL5/4, ff.105v, 111v.

17. J. Fortescue, *The Governance of England*, ed. C. Plummer (Oxford, 1855), pp. 150-1; noticed by J.R. Lander, *Crown and Nobility 1450-1509* (London, 1976), p. 13.

18. *The Reign of Henry VII*, ed. A.F. Pollard (3 vols., London, 1913-14), vol. i, pp. 150-55.

19. *Calendar of State Papers, Spain*, i, p. 329; BL, Add. Ms 28623 ff.11-12.

20. For an assessment of the Stanleys' gains under Henry VII, see the unpublished study of B. Coward, 'The Stanley family *c.* 1385-1651' (Sheffield Ph.D., 1968), pt. iii, though he greatly overstates the extent of Henry's confirmation *cf. CPR, 1485-94*, pp. 230-1.

21. *Rot. Parl.*, vi, 444-6.

22. Coward, *loc. cit.*, pp. 163-186 discusses both the effects of the indictments for retaining and an incident involving the interruption by Stanley retainers of the reading of a royal proclamation. *Cf.* Dudley's assertion that the second earl was 'often tymes hardly intreated and to sore', *Dudley's petition*, p. 88, 93, 26n.; BL, Add. Ms. 21480 f.191.

23. PRO, KB9/434/30. BL, Add. Ms. 59899 f.211v.

24. See S.B. Chrimes, *Henry VII* (London, 1972), p. 76. Perhaps the sole point to be made is her total absence of political influence.

25. *CPR 1485-94*, p. 189; *CPR 1494-1509*, pp. 56-7; WAM 12179 — though Daubeney, for example, held such office even before 1485.

26. J.R. Lander, 'Bonds, coercion and fear' in *Crown and Nobility*, pp. 286-8. PRO, C255/8/5/3 graphically illustrates the extent to which others were potentially involved in Dorset's fate, being a record of the process of manucaption, not mentioned by Lander.

27. *Calendar of State Papers, Spain*, i, 178. One suit concerning title was even specifically delegated by the King's council to that of the lady Margaret, though she was not the immediate lord: PRO, Req 2/4/246.

137

28. Calculated from *Complete Peerage*: 19 if Lincoln is included.
29. PRO, E 34/3: service to the King was to be exclusive. The long list of men retained with Thomas Lovell may be one such list, its size explained by his prominent conciliar status and its composition by his access to the Roos tenantry through his wardship of lord Roos, *HMC, Report on the Mss. of the Duke of Rutland* (4 vols., HMSO 1888-1905), vol. iv, pp. 559-66.
30. *Cf.* the indictments against several members of the King's household, though the retainers wore the King's badge of the red rose; or the indictments brought against the King's own mother which resulted in the enrolment of her licence in King's bench PRO, KB9/436/7, 13, 16; KB27/926, Trin. 20 Hen. VII, Rex rot. 3.
31. A. Conway, *Henry VII's Relations with Scotland and Ireland, 1485-98,* (Cambridge, 1932); Select Cases in the Council of Henry VII, ed. C.G. Bayne and W.H. Dunham (Selden Soc., lxxv, 1958), pp. 46-7.
32. Bray was Chamberlain of Chester, 1495-1500 (PRO, Ches 1/2/57) and steward of Monmouth and the duchy lands in Herefordshire (R. Somerville, *The Duchy of Lancaster* (London, 1953), pp. 636-7, 648). There is little evidence of Bray's active interest. In South Wales the vacuum was filled to a limited extent by Charles Somerset (W.R.B. Robinson, 'Early Tudor policy towards Wales: the acquisition of lands and offices in Wales by Charles Somerset, earl of Worcester', *Bull. Board of Celtic Studies*, xxi (1964), pp. 422-6.
33. T.B Pugh, 'The Magnates, Knights and Gentry', p. 115, and R.A. Griffiths, 'Wales and the Marches', pp. 163-5, both in *Fifteenth-Century England, 1399-1509*, ed. S.B Chrimes, C.D. Ross and R.A. Griffiths (Manchester, 1972).
34. The initial composition of the council may be deduced from the various oyer and terminer commissions, *CPR 1485-94*, pp. 434, 441, 488; PRO, Ches 1/2, offers evidence of its changing composition.
35. *Cf.* J.A. Guy, 'A conciliar court of Audit at work in the last months of reign of Henry VII', B.I.H.R., xlix (1976), 289-95; PRO, E 315/263 where most, and perhaps all, of the entries relate to the Prince's lands; E 163/11/27.
36. T.B. Pugh, 'The indenture for the Marches between Henry VII and Edward Stafford, duke of Buckinham', EHR, lxxi (1956), 436-41. This had been preceded by an indenture with Rhys ap Thomas in 1490, and Charles Somerset was similarly bound concerning South Wales in 1496; PRO, E.175/5/18; C255/8/5/88; *CCR, 1485-1500*, 894.
37. Chrimes, *op. cit.*, p. 71; J.A. Guy, *The Cardinal's Court* (Hassocks, 1977), p. 19.
38. M.A. Hicks, 'Dynastic change and northern society: the career of the fourth earl of Northumberland', *Northern History*, xiv (1978), especially pp. 89-103.
39. J.R. Lander, 'Attainder and forfeiture, 1453-1509' (1961), reprinted in *Crown and Nobility*, pp. 146-7; PRO, E.40/14646. R. Virgoe, 'The Recovery of the Howards in East Anglia, 1485-1529', *Wealth and Power*, pp. 12-15, presents a more optimistic assessment.
40. WAM 12247, 16028, 16073. Although entries in the chamber books can rarely be dated precisely, Sever's appointment seems to have been made in the spring of 1499: PRO, E101/414/16, f. 288v.
41. Somerville, *Duchy of Lancaster*, pp. 265-74, 524, 541.
42. PRO, E163/9/27. The council's authority seems to have been restricted to Yorkshire, although Savage's position as archbishop may have blurred this limitation, and in 1504 he could term himself 'the Kings lieutenant and high

commissionar withynne these the North parties of his realme', PRO, Req 2/3/347; Req 2/10/72; *York Civic Records*, ed. A. Raine (Yorks. Arch. Soc., Record Ser., 1939-53), iii, p. 5.

43. Bayne, *Select Cases*, p. 30.
44. An inference drawn in part from the composition of the peace commissions, and also from indictment and plea roll evidence of justices participating at sessions. (Commissions, *CPR, 1494-1509*, pp. 666-9.)
45. Bayne, *Select Cases*, pp. 41-4.
46. Cf., for example, the conciliar discussion of the inquisitions made after the death of the third earl, BL Lansd. MS. 639, ff. 33-34v.
47. Instances were listed by Dacre himself, PRO SP 1/1, ff. 71v-72; *CCR, 1500-9*, 543, records a recognizance without condition which was to hang at the king's pleasure.
48. *Materials for a History of the Reign of Henry VII*, ed. W. Campbell (2 vols., Rolls Ser., 1873-7), vol. i, pp. 242-3; ii, p. 533; *Cal. Docs. Relating to Scotland, 1357-1509*, pp. 311, 314-5, 332-5, 337, 349-51; *CPR, 1485-94*, pp. 40, 213, 314; *CPR, 1494-1509*, pp. 200-2, 213, 379, 442.
49. PRO, KB27/975, Pasch. 20 Henry VII, Rex rot. 11 (Dacre); KB27/980, Trin. 21. Hen. VII, Rex rot. 6; BL Lansd. Ms 127, f. 22v (Clifford).
50. Cf. the convoluted terms of the bill for the Lord Conyers's patent for the wardenship of the East March, which terms him warden-general 'videlicet in partibus de la Est March' and on which Dudley has noted 'this bill is made for the lord Conyers for the Est marche oonly and not as deputie to my lord prince but Immediatly by the Kinges grace as the lord Darcy was', PRO, C82/325, 16 March.
51. Initially recorded in the chamber books and subsequently annotated by Henry VII with a reference to Dudley; process followed before the council, in Common Pleas and the Exchequer, members of the council being present in court when judgement was given. The process ended with an appearance before the council learned and a composition with King and council for a pardon and the fine, secured by a feoffment on the earl's lands. A later reference suggests that the fine itself may have been augmented by a composition for offences involving retaining. PRO, DL5/4, ff. 20v, 32v, 83; CP40/974, Mich. 21 Hen. VII, rot. 419; E159/284, *Brevia Baronibus*, pasch. 2d; E36/214, ff. 479, 530; BL Add. Ms. 59899, f. 213.
52. Above, pp. 109-10, 117-8; see also *Letters of Richard Fox, 1486-1527*, ed. P.S. and H.M. Allen (Oxford, 1928), pp. 43-4.
53. WAM 16047, 9222/11; PRO, E101/415/3, f. 298; BL Add. Ms. 21480, ff. 88v, 89.
54. Bayne, *Select Cases*, pp. xxix-xxx, 30; Lander, 'Bonds, coercion and fear', pp. 289-90. Lists of New Year gifts recorded in the chamber books tend to confirm his frequent presence about court. Yet he was also several times indicted of illegal retaining, accused of treasonable words, briefly imprisoned in the Tower and eventually pardoned but heavily fined; see also PRO, KB9/430/49-59; KB9/443/2-3; KB9/441/6; C237/58/6/1.
55. Lander, 'Bonds, coercion and fear', p. 275; PRO, E101/414/6, f. 210v.
56. Lander, *loc. cit.*, pp. 290-1; *CCR, 1500-9, passim;* PRO, SC12/18/53.
57. Buckingham petitioned the council: this is to be the subject of a forthcoming article by Dr. Rawcliffe. Moreover, if Buckingham's brother was allowed to make an advantageous marriage to the widowed Cicely, marchioness of Dorset, the King's extreme interest in his financial profit from the transaction is

suggested by his retention in his own hands of Stafford's obligation (BL, Add. Ms. 59899, f. 178v).

58. *CPR, 1494-1509*, pp. 658, 661; *CPR, 1476-85*, pp. 553-580.

59. *CPR, 1485-94*, pp. 481-508; *CPR, 1494-1509*, pp. 629-69.

60. PRO, KB9/368-450, *passim*.

61. Surrey, Daubeney and, less emphatically, Broke, Ormond, Shrewsbury and Herbert. Three of these were peers of Henry's own creation, and perhaps only Daubeney and Surrey were really significant.

62. PRO, E101/640; BL Lansd. Ms. 127, f. 32v; *CCR, 1500-9*, 686.

63. BL Lansd. Ms. 127, f. 34.

64. PRO, C142/25/22, 128, 138; PROB 11/16/16; '*Dudley's petition*', pp. 88, 93-4.

65. Lander, 'Bonds, coercion and fear', pp. 267-300. The defective calendaring of the early Close Rolls, and the fact that not all bonds were enrolled, has decreased the count for the first part of the reign, although it remains true that the years after 1497 show an escalation in the number of recognizances taken. The penal use of bonds by Edward IV has been discussed by P.M. Barnes, 'The Chancery corpus cum causa file, 10-11 Edward IV', *Medieval Legal Records*, ed. R.F. Hunnisett and J.B. Post (HMSO, 1978), pp. 438-40.

66. WAM 16020; *HMC, Rutland MSS.*, i, p. 19.

67. *Cal. Inq. P.M., Henry VII*, iii, pp. 10-107. Subsequent legal proceedings in Chancery, King's Bench and the Exchequer yield evidence which would increase this count; eg., PRO, C43/1/31, 34.

68. PRO, CP40/985, Trin. 23 Hen. VII, rot. 345d (Oxford); PRO, SP1/1, f. 72; DL5/4, f. 89; BL Lansd. Ms. 127, f. 44d, 48 (Mabel, lady Dacre).

69. *The Anglica Historia of Polydore Vergil, 1485-1537*, ed. D. Hay (Camden Soc., 3rd ser., lxxiv, 1954), pp. 127-9; *CSP, Spain*, i, pp. 177-8.

70. PRO, KB9/961/52.

71. Below, p.133; this remains true even if the nobleman still had an important part to play at an earlier stage in the chain of patronage.

72. Hicks, *loc. cit.*, p. 93; Exeter R.O. Court Rolls 540; PRO, C146/3273; *Cal. Inq. P.M., Henry VII*, ii, 434; WAM 16066; PRO, SC11/828: this list is clearly not exhaustive. Other lords, including Bedford and the countess of Warwick, made grants of office: PRO, KB9/377/17; SC6/Hen. VII/1373.

73. PRO, E326/8898; CP40/979, Hil. 22 Hen. VII, *Rot. Chart*. 3.

74. Eg., Bray's landed estate, almost all acquired after 1485, suggests the extent to which that advantage could be carried. It was sufficient to endow two peerages in the reign of Henry VIII, and Dugdale estimated a value of over 1,000 marks for the purchases of 1497-1503 alone: W. Dugdale, *The Baronage of England* (2 vols., London, 1675-6), vol. ii, p. 303. The familiar case of the Plumptons, involving charges of maintenance, corruption and a feigned inquisition was extreme rather than unique, and forms of pressure applied beyond mere investment might include intercession with the King for a pardon, exploitation of unquiet titles or financial difficulties arising from recognizances due to the King.

75. This may be traced both through wills and through feet of fines, although a number of such transactions conceal a use in favour of Henry VII himself: eg. the related enfeoffments on the lands of the heirs of Thomas Green, PRO, CP40/982, Mich. 23 Hen. VII, rot. 301-301d., 309-309d., 614-8, 706; BL Lansd. Ms. 127, ff. 45d., 50.

76. PRO, PROB 11/9/13; PRO, PROB 11/12/10. See also pp.131-2.

77. The comments which follow are based primarily on a study, using patent roll, pipe roll and indictment evidence, of a group of counties falling alphabetically between Salop and Sussex. Since this essay was written, several important studies have appeared, including those of Dr. Baker and Dr. Virgoe already cited, and M.L. Zell, 'Early Tudor JPs at work', *Archaeologia Cantiana*, xciii (1977), 125-43. Dr. Zell's detailed study of Kent JPs parallels much that could be said about the present sample.

78. An average of 30-40% of the JPs were, or became, MPs either within the county studied or an adjacent county; likewise at least 50% of the sheriffs were, or became, JPs and the proportion rises to 92% in the joint shrievalty of Surrey and Sussex.

79. Although there are considerable variations between counties, perhaps only 50-60% of the 'gentry' members of the commission were active at sessions, although it was on them, rather than on the bishops, lords and lawyers, that the main burden lay.

80. In four of the counties studied the commission increased between 60% and 100% in size, though in Salop and Southampton the rise is less marked.

81. On the later sixteenth century, A. Hassell-Smith, *County and Court: Government and Politics in Norfolk, 1558-1603* (Oxford, 1974). This rich evidence does not exist for Henry VII's reign, and Virgoe's study would suggest rather the multiplicity of connections which might be involved; Virgoe, 'The recovery of the Howards', pp. 10-14.

82. PRO, C255/8/5/94; C244/146/2.

83. *CFR, 1485-1509*, 95-6; 97-8; cf. *CFR, 1471-85*, 861-2; PRO, C82/14 shows that, not surprisingly, the September commission was not a pricked list in the normal sense.

84 PRO, C82/180. These were four counties most affected Devon, Somerset, Dorset, Berkshire (and thus Oxfordshire), and also Norfolk and Suffolk. A change seems to have been contemplated in Surrey and Sussex, but in the event Richard Sackville was confirmed as sheriff. The appointment of Eggecombe to Devon was ordered by the King himself before he left Exeter: PRO, C82/331, 2 November (13) Hen. VII.

85. PRO, C82/56; C82/329; C82/330; C82/332. Again, though the theory must often have failed in practice, the mere suspicion of retainder with a lord other than the King could bar appointment: PRO, C82/332, 16 November (16) Hen. VII.

86. In 1506 prosecution was made the responsibility of the under-treasurer, John Cutte, and Edmund Dudley, *vice* Bray's executors. The terms of their commission emphasize the likelihood of forfeiture, past and future, and allowed a fixed rate of composition; PRO, E404/85 16 April 21 Hen. VII.

87. Bayne, *Select Cases*, pp. cxxviii — ix lists those cases brought by Henry Toft in *qui tam* actions: these ended in the inevitable pardon and composition with the Crown for the King's interest, PRO E36/214, p. 461. For other royal actions against sheriffs, see PRO, SC1/51/179; E101/415/3, f. 291 (John Hussey); PRO C142/19/4; KB9/440/1; KB29/135, Pasch. 21 Hen. VII, rot. 28-9; DL5/4, ff. 95v, 98, 111v, 113v, (several Northumberland sheriffs); PRO CP40/479, Mich. 22 Hen. VII, rot. 102-3d; CP40/982, Mich. 23 Hen. VII, rot.

405; CP40/983, Hil. 23 Hen. VII, rot. 495; CP40/985, Trin. 23 Hen. VII, rot. 349; DL5/4, ff. 107v, 151v-152v.

88.	*Eg.* PRO, E36/130, a county-wise list of household officers, *temp.* Henry VIII.

89.	D.A.L. Morgan, 'The King's affinity in the polity of Yorkist England', *THRS*, 5th Ser., xxiii (1973), 1-25.

90.	*Rerum Anglicarum Scriptorem Veterum*, vol. i, ed. W. Fulman (Oxford, 1684), p. 652.

91.	Published lists obscure this point, though it is symptomatic of Henry's attitude to rule within society at large. There was thus, for example, no treasurer 1488-c.1502 and no controller 1505-7, nor for the years following the death of Eggecombe in 1489 and Tocotes in 1492.

92.	Much of what follows on both chamber and council is based on detailed research on which it is hoped to enlarge at a later date. Footnotes have therefore been here curtailed, pending a fuller discussion. BL Add. Ms. 59899, f. 213; PRO, E101/415/3, f. 296.

93.	PRO, E101/415/3, f. 299; annotated with receipt of 200 marks and an obligation for £200, BL Add. Ms. 21480, f. 185.

94.	PRO, E101/414/6, f. 128. The interlineation is in Henry's own hand. For the election and presentation of the speaker, *ibid.*, f. 232; *Rot. Parl.* vi, p. 510.

95.	BL Add. Ms. 59899, f. 182; BL Lands. Ms. 127, f. 11v; PRO, E159/283, *Recorda*, Trin., rot. 5-6; E36/214, pp. 441, 475, 635; E101/413/2, p. 63; C82/245, 28 June; Kent A.O., U455/T138. The record of the prosecution for customs offences suggests an offence against the letter, rather than the spirit of the law, for the duties were paid, though not in Bray's name. *Cf.* also Dudley's comment on Henry's treatment of the executors, or the more general remarks of Vergil: '*Dudley's petition*', p. 88, 94; *Anglica Historia*, p. 129.

96.	*CSP, Spain*, i, pp. 168, 178; *CSP, Milan*, i, pp. 299, 335, 351; *CSP, Venice*, i, p. 285; Pollard, *The Reign of Henry VII*, i, 150, 152-3.

97.	*CSP, Spain*, i, 178.

98.	PRO, C82/305/13 September 23 Hen. VII; likewise PRO, DL 12/1/2/6

99.	*Eg. Letters and Papers Illustrative of the Reign of Richard III and Henry VII*, ed. J. Gairdner (2 vols., Rolls Ser., 1861-3,) vol. ii, pp. 75-84: the same offences (with others) were still being presented in 1509, PRO, KB9/953/229-61; PRO, E101/415/3, f. 297v; PRO, KB9/427/80; KB9/430/49; WAM 16057, 16020; BL Add. Ms. 59899, f. 153v; likewise, the watching brief given Darcy after riots at Knaresborough, PRO, KB9/445/29; SC1/58/53. The sheriff's oath, too, enjoined that he, if he could not himself maintain the King's rights, should 'certifye the Kyng or summe of his counsell therof, such as ye hold for certayn will say it unto Kyng' *Registrum Thome Myllyng, Episcopi Herefordensis, a.d. 1474-92*, ed. A.T. Bannister (Canterbury and York Society, xxvi, 1921), p. 133.

100.	A. Cameron, 'A Nottinghamshire quarrel in the reign of Henry VII', *Bull. Inst. Hist. R.*, xlv (1972), 35-7; *cf.* '*Dudley's petition*', p. 93, n.25; above, n.87; PRO, KB9/445/1-11; KB9/435/45; KB9/427/83-4; E101/415/3, f. 297v.; E36/214, p. 475; DL5/4, f. 157v; C82/294, 28 December. Even in 1511 action before the council and imprisonment in the Tower could follow indictment in common law: PRO, KB9/456/5; Huntingdon Library, Ellesmere Ms. 2652, f. 8v. I am indebted to Dr. J.A. Guy for a copy of this latter ms.

101. For the Yorkist council, J.R. Lander, 'Council, administration and councillors' (1959), reprinted *Crown and Nobility*, pp. 309-20. For Henry VII, the author's own research has been used.

102. Although a detailed chronological breakdown makes this still more apparent, for a thoughtful development of the general thesis, E.W. Ives, 'The common lawyers in pre-Reformation England', *THRS*, 5th. Ser., xviii (1968), pp. 154-6.

103. Bayne, *Select Cases*, pp. 30-44; *cf.* Guy, *The Cardinal's Court*, p. 12.

104. Bayne, *Select Cases*, pp. 53-8.

105. *Ibid.*, pp. 6-7; *cf.* also the thematic arrangement of Ellesmere Ms. 2652.

106. The standard account, now in need of a revision which it is hoped eventually to provide, is the seminal article of R. Somerville, 'Henry VII's council learned in the law', *EHR*, liv (1939), 427-42.

107. Bayne, *Select Cases*, pp. cxxxix, clv-viii; Guy, *The Cardinal's Court*, pp. 15-18, 53-57.

108. Guy, *The Cardinal's Court*, pp. 16-17.

109. Ellesmere Ms. 2652, f. lv; confirmed not only by the evidence of the *corpus cum causa* files, but also by Henry VII himself: PRO, C244/138-157, *passim*; DL42/21, f. 21.

110 For example, PRO, CP40/983, Hil. 23 Hen. VII, rot. 348d, 353, 353d; E101/414/6, f. 232v, 226v; BL Add. Ms. 59899, f. 153v. More generally, in 1505 a large number of obligations, including many for appearance or good abearing, were delivered to Edmund Dudley to sue for the King's profit: though not all would in practice have been forfeit, whilst the mercers sued as a body for their discharge. PRO, E101/517/11.

111. PRO, CP40/983, Hil. 23 Hen. VII, rot. 406 (obligation of 1486); CP40/985, Trin. 23 Hen. VII, rot. 374 (obligation of 1488); *cf.* SP1/1, ff. 71v-72; '*Dudley's petition*', pp. 90, 98.

112. Bayne, *Select Cases*, p. 19.

113. Ellesmere Ms. 2652, f. 6v; *cf.* PRO, C244/139/93.

114. PRO, C244/146/26. Instances might be multiplied: see also above, n. 100.

115. If the most obvious instance lies in the proclamation of rebellion in a final attempt to secure appearance, neither the council of Richard III nor that of Henry VII was, for example, able permanently to enjoin good abearing on Thomas Cornwall, Richard Corbet and Richard Croft: Bayne, *Select Cases*, pp. cxxiii-iv; 9, 14, 19, 50-1, 78-87; PRO, C244/136/111; C244/139/101, 156, 174; C244/140/80; C244/143/25; C244/147/135; C255/8/5/7, 8; E404/82/ 3 Dec. 12 Hen. VII; CP40/983, Hil. 23 Hen. VII, rot. 364d.

116. The detailed particulars of the hanaper accounts, which do not, however, survive for the last two and a half years of the reign, show a rise in the number of such pardons from an average of 20-30 p.a. in the 1490s to 50-100 p.a. in the years before 1507. The artificially inflated account for 18-19 Hen. VII has been discounted. PRO, E101/217/14, 15; E101/218/3-6, 8, 10, 12; E101/219/2, 4, 6-8.

117. Francis Bacon, *The History of the Reign of Henry VII*, ed. R. Lockyer (Folio Soc., London. 1971), p. 233.

Japan and England in the Fifteenth Century: The Onin War and the Wars of the Roses*

K.R. Dockray
Senior Lecturer in History
Huddersfield Polytechnic

Both Japanese and American scholars have long been inclined to draw comparisons between the evolution of eastern and western societies, especially the origins and development of feudalism in Japan and medieval Europe. Professor Archibald Lewis, for instance, has suggested sufficiently detailed parallels between the stages of feudalism's evolution in Japan and northern France to gladden the heart of any historical determinist.[1] The dangers of such comparative studies are legion: feudalism can all too easily become a necessary stage or series of stages through which societies must pass — and, before we know where we are, it has turned into a Marxist strait-jacket which simply hinders rather than helps our understanding of the past. In fact, the term feudalism probably raises more problems than it solves: it is an artificial concept, of strictly limited value as a tool of historical analysis and comparative study. I propose to avoid its use altogether, and also dispense with the services of Karl Marx as a philosophical companion: if I must have one at all, let it be Thomas Hobbes with his powerful emphasis on the self-interested and hedonistic character of man (perhaps with a couple of Renaissance humanist historians thrown in for good measure).

---

* For the benefit of readers unfamiliar with the history of Feudal Japan, a brief Japanese chronology and a short glossary of Japanese terms may be found in an Appendix to these notes.

I would like to thank Dr A. Saul, Dr J.A.G. Roberts and Professor G. Bownas for reading a first draft of this paper, and encouraging me to believe that — despite obvious methodological flaws and some inevitable simplification of complex issues and events — it has a certain interest. However, I do *not* claim to have identified anything more than a remarkable series of coincidences.

Actually, geography provides a much better starting point than philosophy for comparisons between Japan and England. Both countries are situated on the geographical edge of their respective continents, separated from the mainland by water; and, for both, the sea has served as a physical barrier to invasion on more than one occasion. Both countries, indeed, have developed national mythologies associated with resistance to invasion: stories of England's glorious stance against the Spanish Armada have their parallel in Japanese tales of samurai resistance to Kublai Khan's Mongol hordes in the thirteenth-century; the 'Protestant winds' which saved England in 1588 are the equivalent of the 'divine winds' or kamikaze which saved Japan in 1274 and 1281.

It *is* possible, in my view, to make some interesting comparisons between medieval England and medieval Japan. Both countries had been subjected to a species of centralised, proto-bureaucatic government by the mid-thirteenth century. In both, too, the personality and capacity of the ruler was of great importance. In England this meant the king; in Japan it usually meant the shogun (generalissimo) or his regents.[2] So, if we are going to look for Japanese equivalents to strong English kings like Henry II or Edward I, we shall have to examine the careers of shoguns like Yoritomo or Yoshimitsu; the same goes for weaklings too — Henry VI's counterpart in fifteenth-century Japan, for instance, is the shogun Yoshimasa.

The Kamakura shogunate, so called because it was centred on Kamakura in the eastern province of Sagami, was established by Yoritomo towards the end of the twelfth century. It was essentially the product of overwhelming military supremacy — and this is reflected in the use of the term bakufu (literally, tent government) to describe what was clearly a species of military rule. Yoritomo evolved a system of control based on the appointment of men from his own household to key positions in the provinces viz. as shugo (constables or governors) and jito (land stewards). During the thirteenth century this system — under the supervision of a succession of regents for the shogun — gave pre-modern Japan some of the best government it ever had. Of crucial importance were relations between the ruler at Kamakura and his powerful agents in the provinces: as long as the bakufu was able to maintain control over the shugo in particular, all went well. However, increasingly weak leadership at the centre in the late thirteenth and early fourteenth centuries encouraged growing independence on the part of provincial constables and stewards, and this eventually resulted in the collapse of the Kamakura shogunate in 1333.[3]

Limited comparisons are possible, perhaps, with England in the thirteenth century — at any rate insofar as strong and effective government depended on the capacity of the ruler and the need to get the crown/baronial relationship right. Certainly, Sir Maurice Powicke and his followers have emphasised the crucial importance of achieving a satisfactory balance in thirteenth-century England between the king on the one hand and his greater subjects on the other: thus if a king like John seemed to curtail baronial power and influence, he could find himself landed with Magna Carta; if, on the other hand, the baronage sought to usurp powers that were right-fully the king's — as they did during the crisis of 1258-1265 — this too would produce distortion. On this kind of interpret-ation, Edward I's greatness lay in his ability (at any rate until the last years of his reign) to maintain the balance between the king and the 'community of the realm'.[4]

In Japan, with the end of the Kamakura shogunate, an anachronistic attempt to restore effective imperial rule soon collapsed under pressure from Ashikaga Takauji: making the Japanese capital of Kyoto his centre of operations, he vigor-ously drove out his opponents and duly secured the title of shogun for himself in 1338.[5] However, since his enemies were sufficiently undaunted by such treatment to establish a rival court and capital in southern Japan, the stage was set for a species of civil war which lasted almost six decades (until 1392). During the course of the struggle the Japanese provin-cial nobility greatly added to their power and independence: in fact, the shugo of Kamakura times gave way to an altogether more powerful governing elite, usually dubbed shugo-daimyo (constable-barons).[6]

No very close parallels can be drawn with fourteenth-century England here, but it is certainly worth remembering what happened after Edward I's death in 1307: his son's chronic inability to handle the leading aristocratic figures of the day produced a fine crop of political crises in the ensuing decades, with complex and bitter baronial rivalries very much to the fore — and men like Thomas of Lancaster seem little less truculent, self-seeking and opportunistic than many Japanese shugo-daimyo.[7] Even the deposition and murder of Edward II in 1327 did not put an end to English baronial conflicts. Only Edward III's renewal of traditional aggressive monarchical claims in Scotland and France could do that, by transforming aristocratic feuding at home into aristocratic campaigning abroad.

In Japan, clearly, it was vitally necessary for the shogun Yoshimitsu (at the end of the fourteenth century) to achieve an effective working relationship with his shugo-daimyo. For, during the civil war, a relatively small group of truly great barons had emerged in central and western Japan. Coming, for the most part, from families who had enjoyed little or no prominence in Kamakura times, they had steadily arrogated to themselves all manner of rights and powers, as well as becoming great landowners in many cases. In theory, they exercised powers to raise taxes or settle local disputes, to serve as receivers of confiscated estates or in various judicial capacities, as representatives of the Ashikaga bakufu. And, in the last analysis, they *did* remain critically dependent on shogunal sanction. But, in practice, by the early 1390s, they had come to enjoy a very considerable degree of independence from central control.[8] There is some comparison, perhaps, between this group of powerful men in early Ashikaga Japan and that coterie of super-magnates in late fourteenth-century England with whom Richard II so signally failed to hit it off.

Yoshimitsu succeeded in establishing an effective balance of power between bakufu and shugo-daimyo which lasted well into the fifteenth century. Historians, indeed, regard him as the greatest of the Ashikaga shoguns, occupying a position similar to that of Henry V in the gallery of late medieval

English rulers. However, just as Henry V's shortcomings are now becoming more apparent than they used to be, so it is increasingly recognised that 'for all his victories, Yoshimitsu was not able to strengthen to any great extent the economic and military bases of the Muromachi Bakufu'.[9] Moving on chronologically, if Henry VI's minority can be seen to have had its firmly constructive side, so recent research on early fifteenth-century Japan shows there was no rapid decline under Yoshimitsu's sons Yoshimochi and Yoshinori. Yoshinori was murdered in 1441, however, and his death does seem to mark a useful dividing line in Japanese history — as, perhaps, does the ending of Henry VI's minority in England in 1437.[10]

Yoshinori was assassinated in Kyoto while attending a banquet and theatrical performance at the residence of Akamatsu Mitsusuke, and Akamatsu himself was responsible for the deed being done. He was the head of a prominent shugo-daimyo family, and one which has been unusually well studied. From about 1364 the Akamatsu house, in theory at least, dominated the small Japanese province of Bizen. In practice, however, Akamatsu power there (and in the other two provinces which the family came to control) was always precarious: in Bizen, in fact, it depended not on the extent of family lands in the province (they were relatively slight), but on the somewhat uncertain submission of the Matsuda house in the west and the Urakami house in the east. The heads of these two houses, indeed, served as deputies to the Akamatsu in Bizen. Since the latter were also significantly dependent on central sources of power, authority deriving from the Ashikaga bakufu, they needed to have an eye both to what was going on in Kyoto and to the state of play in the provinces which were their responsibility — but, when it came down to it, they tended to leave provincial administration very much in the hands of their deputies, while concentrating their own attention on the capital. This helps to explain why there was such a serious gap between theory and practice when it came to enforcing shogunal authority in Bizen (as shown, for instance, by the immense difficulties experienced in collecting taxation);

it also helps to explain why, ultimately, the Akamatsu lost out to their deputies in Bizen altogether.[11]

Akamatsu Mitsusuke had several reasons for planning and master-minding the murder of Yoshinori. For one thing there were significant personal animosities: Yoshinori, it seems, was notably contemptuous of Akamatsu's small stature and physical appearance generally, even to the extent of pointedly releasing monkeys in his presence on several occasions; also, the shogun executed Mitsusuke's sister, one of his own concubines, in a fit of pique, as well as confiscating lands belonging to his younger brother (which he then proceeded to bestow on his own homosexual lover!). However, Akamatsu had good political and economic reasons, too, for wishing to see the back of Yoshinori: in particular, he had excellent grounds for believing his own three provinces were about to be transferred to the same shogunal favourite.

If the Ashikaga shoguns and their agents were hard-pressed to enforce their authority in central provinces like Bizen, this was even more the case when it came to the eight Kantō provinces in eastern Japan. And if a reasonably competent English king like Henry IV had extreme difficulty in controlling a great northern family such as the Percy earls of Northumberland, how much more hopeless a task did a Japanese Ashikaga shogun face on his eastern frontier. In fact, the aggressive and self-seeking eastern magnates could, and did, disobey the bakufu with impunity — and from the mid-fifteenth century there was a major private war in the Kantō, no less significant than the Percy-Neville feud in England.

In this context, too, attention should be drawn to the very considerable evidence we have of social upheaval in early Ashikaga Japan — in particular, agrarian risings led in the main by small landowners and directed especially against the activities of government agents in the provinces. Such risings became endemic during the fifteenth century — and just as popular unrest is of some significance in understanding the Wars of the Roses (especially, perhaps, Jack Cade's rebellion in 1450), so Japanese social protest needs to be considered in the context of the Onin War. Moreover, if there were English soldiers of fortune at a loose end in the 1450s, men who were willing either to riot or to join the ranks of private baronial armies, so in mid-fifteenth century Japan there was no shortage of impoverished samurai ready either to participate in popular uprisings or to swell the forces of Japanese warlords. [12]

Until recently, historians were inclined to portray fifteenth century Japanese history in terms no less gloomy than those employed by J.R. Green when writing of the Wars of the Roses. [13] James Murdoch, for instance, could hardly contain his moral disapproval of the Ashikaga age:

In seasons of famine the misery of the farmers was unspeakable. Such of them as had the strength left to do so would crawl into the gay capital in the vain hope of finding something to keep body and soul together there . . .

(In) 1454 the famine-stricken peasants were simply left to perish in the streets, and a daily average of 700 or 800 corpses had to be taken up and disposed of. The females of the family were then consigned to the brothels, while the boys were often sold to the priests, who shaved their eyebrows, powdered their faces, dressed them in female garb and put them to the vilest of uses . . .

And in the midst of all this misery the Shōguns usually deigned to envince no tokens of compassion for the stricken multitude . . . [14]

For J.R. Green Henry VI was 'a weak and imbecile king' and his reign 'a long battle of contending factions'; for Murdoch, the shogun Yoshimasa was 'an aesthete and a dilettante', a man given both to extravagance and indolence — and, worse still in Murdoch's highly moralistic eyes, inclined not only to heavy drinking but also habitual indulgence in foul debauchery. [15]

To some extent at least the explanation for such judgements lies in the nature of the source material, especially narratives put together some time after the events. Compare, for instance, the Tudor chronicler Edward Hall's well-known strictures on the misery, murder and execrable plagues suffered by England during the Wars of the Roses with the Japanese war tales known collectively as the *Chronicle of*

Onin: these take the form of contemporary narratives (despite being put together considerably later), and emphasise that as a result of the Onin War the people 'suffered from starvation and cold' while 'the capital, its temples and its shrines' were all 'reduced to ashes'. War tales like these are almost always anonymous, and it is usually difficult to establish precisely *when* they were written. Clearly, too, there was a decline in the quality of such tales from their heyday in the thirteenth century — just as most fifteenth-century English chronicles are inferior to those of the twelfth and thirteenth. It is very difficult moreover to assess their reliability. Professor H.P. Varley, in his recent study of *The Onin War,* expresses the opinion that the *Chronicle of Onin* is a romanticised work: for instance, it may well credit the shogun Yoshimasa with decisions actually formulated in quite different quarters (as, perhaps, do some English chronicles when treating of Henry VI). Yet, Varley concludes, 'the later war tales must, apart from those passages that are obviously hyperbolic, be accepted as fairly accurate records of the times'. [16]

Personal and semi-official journals — put together by members of the aristocracy, officers of the bakufu and imperial court, and Buddhist prelates — have long been regarded as another major source of information. Many of these have the advantage of being eye-witness accounts: but it could well be that they dwell unduly on the destructive character of the war in Kyoto, and on the extent of pillaging, looting and arson perpetrated by unruly soldiers in the city. [17]

In recent years new source materials have become increasingly available, enabling historians to get behind chronicle and journal accounts of shogunal weakness, political failure at the centre, and the impact of the war on Kyoto. Indeed, many post-war scholars — using such evidence and concerned with what they regard as fundamental processes of economic and social change — have been inclined to play down the significance both of the shogunal house and the Onin War itself. Instead, they would have us concentrate on elements of vigour and growth in fifteenth-century Japanese society. [18] What follows, however, is clearly and unashamedly along more traditional lines.

In detail, the origins of both the Wars of the Roses and the Onin War prove to be notably complex, confusing and controversial. Yet it is tempting to see the basic underlying cause as the same: namely, the relationship between an increasingly weak, partisan and ineffective central government on the one hand and powerful, disruptive provincial forces (with a strong stake in what happened at the centre) on the other. For Henry VI of England, we might read the Ashikaga shogun Yoshimasa; for the feud-ridden English baronage of the mid-fifteenth century, we might perhaps substitute the personal struggles for land and power which split several Japanese shugo-daimyo families at this time. And insofar as the Wars of the Roses in England were a quarrel between the great houses of Lancaster and York, so the Onin War might be portrayed as no less a dispute between those of Hosokawa and Yamana in Japan.

Moreover, recent controversy among English historians about where the stress should be placed when examining the crown/baronial relationship has some parallel in the problem of the bakufu/shugo-daimyo relationship in Japan. Should we, in discussing the origins of the Wars of the Roses, put the bulk of our emphasis on Henry VI's personal inadequacies and the serious failings of his government and its policies? Or should we, rather, stress the importance of private feuds among the English baronage? In Japan, should we mainly concentrate on the personal shortcomings of Yoshimasa and the ineptness of his government? Or should we, instead, scrutinise most closely disputes within and between shugo-daimyo families (the 'overmighty subjects' of mid-fifteenth century Japan)? Or should we, perhaps, adopt a more Marxist line, and see if we can detect fundamental changes taking place in the 'economic bases' and 'social relations' of the two societies?[19]

For England, we have had R.L. Storey's grass-roots analysis of the Wars of the Roses as the outcome of an escalation of private aristocratic feuds; and there is certainly ample evidence of great feuds and rivalries splitting Japanese shugo-daimyo families in the 1450s and 1460s. In both countries, moreover, such feuds were accompanied by increasing lawlessness which the central government was hard-pressed to control: indeed, in much of Japan at least, Yoshimasa's government did not even try. We are particularly well-informed about the great rivalry which developed between the houses of Akamatsu and Yamana. Following the assassination of Yoshinori by Akamatsu Mitsusuke in 1441, the Yamana saw and took the opportunity to increase their power at the expense of their rivals. However, this ultimately brought the Yamana face to face with the Hosokawa, when the latter began to promote the restoration of the Akamatsu family to its former possessions and power. And, in the late 1450s and early 1460s, we find both Hosokawa Katsumoto (leader of the Hosokawa family) and his father-in-law Yamana Sōzen (nicknamed the Red Monk, and a notably irascible and turbulent magnate) building up their power for all they were worth — and, especially, building up their military factions by attracting lesser men into their service. There is something of a parallel here, perhaps, with the behaviour of great English noble families such as the Percies and the Nevilles. The Percies became stalwart defenders of the Lancastrian cause in the 1450s, while the Neville family associated itself with the house of York; in Japan, when a great succession dispute disrupted the shogunal house in the 1460s, the Hosokawa and Yamana families assumed sponsorship of the rival claimants. And, in 1467, the tremendous build-up of military force which had occurred in the capital escalated into full-scale warfare.[20]

If some English historians — for instance, Charles Ross — still put most stress on Henry VI's personal inadequacies in explaining the Wars of the Roses, so — among recent historians of Japan — H.P. Varley for one is reluctant to go along with the socio-economic school in virtually discounting the shogun Yoshimasa altogether. 'Can we fully understand the times of which Yoshimasa was a product', Varley asks, 'if we ignore the activities of the shogun and his clique of personal advisers?' To do so, he concludes, 'would be to misinterpret seriously the true nature of the Onin War.'[21]

Yoshimasa, like Henry VI, clearly lacked the qualities — especially the martial qualities — necessary for effective rule in a turbulent society. Yet, for years, Henry was treated with remarkable respect (all things considered) by supporters and critics alike, and hardly any of the baronage showed much enthusiasm for Richard of York's claim to the throne when he put it forward in 1460; in Japan the Ashikaga bakufu remained an important force in the later fifteenth century, despite its greatly reduced military strength — and, though both Yoshimasa and his government left much to be desired, the Onin War was not fought with a view to displacing either. In the Wars of the Roses control of Henry VI's person, of the main organs of government, and of London, was recognised as crucial (especially by the Yorkists); in Japan, as Varley demonstrates, the plans and ambitions of the great shugo-daimyo continued to revolve around the Ashikaga bakufu and Kyoto — hence the nature of the Onin War, and the reasons why 'it was fought for so many years in such limited space'.[22]

Yoshimasa, a younger son of Yoshinori, found himself shogun (at the age of eight) in 1443. Professor Varley considers him an enigmatic and intriguing figure, who succeeded to a shogunate already in a state of rapid decline; moreover, what effective power it still had in 1443, it had largely lost by the time he retired in 1473. Throughout his life, in fact, he seems to have been dominated by an unsavoury collection of mistresses and favourites, who encouraged him to live the kind of life of extravagance and luxury to which he was only too naturally inclined! And, if we are to believe the *Chronicle of Onin,* predominant among them was Ise Sadachika. Lecherous, greedy, always willing to accept bribes and manipulate state affairs in his own interests and those of his friends, Ise Sadachika clearly exercised a disastrous influence over his young master: he 'craved the pleasures of the flesh', declares the chronicler, and both 'engaged in lustful affairs and accepted bribery'.[23]

Yoshimasa most emphatically did not share Henry VI's modesty and chastity when it came to ladies; Henry VI, for his

part, did not possess Yoshimasa's taste for personal extravagance — though there were plenty of men in his court, as in the
shogun's, only too willing to take advantage of his misplaced
generosity towards them. Neither Yoshimasa nor Henry VI
appears to have had much enthusiasm for the day-to-day
business of government or the martial arts. Henry VI's prime
concern seems to have been with his own spirtual well-being,
while Yoshimasa was overwhelmingly pre-occupied with
entertaining on a lavish scale and the liberal patronage of the
arts. Clearly, the political ineffectiveness of both was a major
factor in explaining the onset of civil war — and if Henry VI's
most positive achievements were the foundation of Eton and
King's College Cambridge, Yoshimasa's was to encourage the
cultural flowering of Zen Buddhism at his court.[24]

In order to cover his lavish expenditure, Yoshimasa was
forced to impose heavy taxes and all manner of special levies —
and his profligacy semed especially irresponsible to contemporaries in the context of widespread economic and social
distress in the provinces. For, in the decade immediately
preceding the Onin War, the Japanese countryside suffered
appallingly from a combination of flood, famine and epidemic
disease. In an account put together in 1460, the author tells of a
woman — describing herself as 'a homeless wanderer' —
whose home province has suffered from drought for three
years; nevertheless, she has informed him, officials 'perpetrate
excesses and taxes are collected'. As a result she has been
forced 'to go to another province to seek food from others and
to beg'. In stark contrast to this, the author describes how he:

> . . . came across a group of lords out viewing flowers. They
> numbered more than a thousand on horse and a myriad others in
> carriages . . . They looked down haughtily on pedestrians and
> railed at the soldiers in front of their horses. They were in a
> frolicsome mood, stealing flowers, and some had drawn swords
> and were singing drinking songs. Others, who had vomited and
> were unable to walk further, were lying on the road. There were
> many such incidents occurring. Those who were witness to these
> happenings shuddered, while others coming upon the scene
> withdrew in surprise. They feared the powerful.

Not surprisingly, rioting was frequent, both in the country-side and the capital. In 1447, we are told, rioters set fire to buildings in Kyoto; further riots followed in 1451, 1457 and — worst of all — in 1461. In 1461, in fact, law and order collapsed altogether in Kyoto for several weeks: there was much burning and pillaging, with the houses of moneylenders being selected for special attention. Yet, in 1465, regardless of the fact that the bakufu treasury was virtually empty, Yoshimasa and his wife Lady Tomiko organised a particularly magnificent flower-viewing expedition followed by a sumptuous feast.[25] Henry VI's corrupt and partisan government in England, in the 1450s, paid similarly scant attention to its financial stability; while evidence of distress in the countryside and rioting in London is likewise not lacking.[26]

Civil war would not have been possible either in Japan or England but for the existence of powerful aristocratic families capable of raising substantial armies of retainers. Men like Edmund Beaufort, duke of Somerset, and Richard Plantagenet, duke of York, in England in the 1450s can, perhaps, be compared with warlords such as Hosokawa Katsumoto and Yamana Sōzen in Japan in the 1460s. Long before 1460, in fact, conflict had become commonplace within and between the great shugo-daimyo families: in particular, there had developed bitter succession disputes within the shogunal deputy families of Hatakeyama and Shiba. Then, between 1460 and 1465, 'the powers of the land' (as Varley puts it) 'began to gather into two great camps behind the Hosokawa and the Yamana'. And, he argues, to some extent at least:

... the confrontation of Hosokawa and Yamana may be regarded as a struggle between the party out of power and the party in, since Yamana Sōzen undoubtedly envied the pre-eminent position of Katsumoto in Bakufu councils.

Just as in England the Wars of the Roses were in part at least a conflict of 'ins' and 'outs', so the Onin War was fought to secure the benefits of shogunal patronage and political power.[27] Hosokawa Katsumoto and Yamana Sōzen, like successive dukes of Somerset and Richard of York, were concerned with matters of political advantage and (ultimately) military victory in the armed struggle which ensued: none of them, with the possible — though, to my mind, doubtful — exception of Richard of York had any really disinterested objectives in mind.[28]

The shogun Yoshimasa, with his thirtieth birthday just around the corner, decided (in 1464) that he had had enough of political life. Considering 'how difficult it was to be shogun', and in view of the fact that 'he no longer had any interest in the affairs of government', he resolved (so the *Chronicle of Onin* tells us):

> . . . to have his younger brother, the abbot of Jōdo-ji, return to secular life and succeed to the shogunacy. Then he, Yoshimasa, could retire and enjoy the pleasurers of later life to his heart's content.

The shogun's brother, Yoshimi, was forthwith ordered to return to Kyoto. However, he only agreed to do so reluctantly — and then on the strict understanding that he would not be deprived of the succession again, even if a son were born to Yoshimasa. When this had been agreed, he took up residence in the city — and, significantly, appointed Hosokawa Katsumoto steward of the household which he established there. Initially, Yoshimi was to assist his brother in performing the shogunal duties; then, in due course, to succeed him altogether.

Perhaps there is some similarity between Yoshimi's political advancement in Japan and Richard of York's securing power in England following Henry VI's nervous breakdown in 1453. However, just as Henry's breakdown was rapidly followed by his wife (Margaret of Anjou) giving birth to a son, so Yoshimasa's wife (Lady Tomiko) produced a male infant (Yoshihisa) in 1465. Yoshimasa, apparently, postponed his retirement when he heard of his wife's pregnancy; nevertheless, it seems, he was willing to abide by the agreement with his brother. Lady Tomiko was not. Like Margaret of Anjou in England, she had no intention of allowing her son's claim to be set on one side. The *Chronicle of Onin* tells how she:

. . . brooded over how she might establish her own son as the successor. She thought bitterly of Yoshimi, whom she despised, and wished for some miracle to change things. It was this desire of Lady Tomiko to place her son in line for the succession that eventually led to conflict in the land.

Lady Tomiko, in fact, seems to have been no less formidable and determined than her English counterpart — and, given that Hosokawa Katsumoto had committed himself to Yoshimi, it need come as no surprise to find Lady Tomiko approaching his great rival Yamana Sōzen. And, obligingly, the Yamana leader did commit himself to Tomiko and her son.[29]

Now that the two most powerful aristocratic figures in Japan had taken opposite sides in the shogunal succession dispute, it was perhaps inevitable that most other shugo-daimyo houses should line up behind them. The accompanying military build-up in Kyoto and its neighbourhood was considerable: troops summoned from the provinces were billeted in the city in ever increasing numbers, while the warlords organised the construction of defence works around their headquarters there. Yoshimasa, like Henry VI in England with his so-called 'Love-day' of 1458, did his rather puny best to prevent the situation getting out of hand: in particular, he warned both Yamana and Hosokawa that he would brand as a rebel whichever of them was first to fight openly in the city. In April 1467 a report anticipating 'desperate happenings tonight' proved a false alarm, but a full-scale conflagration could not long be delayed. Finally, at the end of May 1467, fighting began in earnest in the streets of Kyoto between the forces of Hosokawa and Yamana — and the Onin War can truly be said to have begun.[30]

The war lasted some eleven years in all, much of it fought in the streets of the capital itself — and the early stages of the struggle at least were marked by great ferocity and brutality. The *Chronicle of Onin* suggests that, at the war's commencement, there were 277, 500 troops mustered in Kyoto: 161,500

158

for Hosokawa and 116,000 for Yamana. Such figures, though, may well be as unreliable as their equivalents in English narrative sources. Moreover, Yamana, despite his lesser numbers, did enjoy the advantage of controlling six of the seven entrances to the city at the beginning of the war — and, certainly, he emerged triumphant from two major battles fought there in the autumn of 1467. As a result of the second battle, we are told, the city streets were littered with corpses; while Kyoto at the end of 1467 was described as 'an empty moor, from which the evening skylark rises while your tears fall'.[31]

In 1468 Yamana continued to have the best of it on the whole, and during the course of the year he was joined by the shogun's brother Yoshimi. However, there were no more full-scale battles: instead, apart from a few skirmishes early in the year, the two sides simply confronted each other from behind strong barricades, while between them lay a great trench which (according to the records) was ten feet deep and twenty feet wide.

As the years went by, the Hosokawa position increasingly came to be the stronger — but not strong enough to make possible a decisive victory. In fact the military situation was so much of a stalemate that even minor skirmishes became infrequent. Both Hosokawa Katsumoto and Yamana Sōzen professed a deep-seated desire for peace, but no solution could be found since neither came up with the sort of terms on which such a settlement could be based. The situation became so desperate, indeed, that at one point Hosokawa shaved his head and tried to take holy orders, while Yamana made the gesture of attempting ritual suicide. As for the shogun Yoshimasa, he seems to have had little time for either the war or the warlords. In 1473 he finally retired, while both Hosokawa and Yamana died in the same year.

Yet still the war continued — though, as Professor Varley emphasises, what particularly characterised the years after 1473 was its spread to the provinces. And the 'most meaningful struggles' there were:

. . . those in which assistant or subordinate chieftains seized the holdings of their absentee masters, who were still engrossed with the fighting in the Capital.

More and more troops, in fact, had to be withdrawn in order to deal with disorder in the provinces — until, eventually, the war in the capital subsided into a 'stalemate of exhaustion' when the last generals left the city in 1477.[32]

The war had been marked, at any rate in its early stages, by great disregard for human life and enormous material destruction: indeed, most of the great monuments in the city of Kyoto were destroyed and the city itself reduced to a virtual ruin long before the end. London did not suffer to anything like the same extent during the Wars of the Roses. The city's trade was seriously disrupted. Its citizens experienced much anxiety and fear, and its fabric did sustain a certain amount of damage. In 1450, for instance, the city gates were opened to Jack Cade's followers and the citizens experienced the excesses of a rebel army for the first time since 1381; there was military action in London in July 1460, and again in the early months of 1461 (when the city came within an ace of being occupied by Margaret of Anjou's ill-disciplined northern army); serious violence and lawlessness hit London again in the autumn of 1470, while in May 1471 it had to withstand the full-scale assault of the Bastard of Fauconberg and his followers.[33]

What especially horrified chroniclers and diarists in Ashikaga Japan, it seems, was the appearance on a large-scale of footsoldiers: such men, hardly disciplined at all, were able to indulge in pillaging, looting and burning on a grand scale. And, though the study of the Wars of the Roses in England does produce evidence of excesses perpetrated by the soldiery, they were on nothing like the same scale as in the Onin War.[34]

Abbot Jinson, writing in his journal shortly after the war in Kyoto ended, paints a dismal picture of its impact and consequences:

> There is nothing in the whole Empire to be glad about . . . The provinces . . . have paid no taxes since the outbreak of Onin, and (those) provinces which should obey all the orders of the Bakufu

160

pay no attention whatever to the commands of the Shōgun. The Constables say they will obey, but their deputies say that they can do nothing . . . The whole country is in a state of disobedience.

In similar vein the shogun Yoshimasa, when warned by his son Yoshihisa against the danger of further withdrawal from the world of affairs (in 1482), is reputed to have replied:

The daimyo do as they please and do not follow orders. That means there can be no government.

For England, we have John Warkworth's comment that, though the people looked to Edward IV for prosperity and peace, the first decade of his reign in fact produced one battle after another, much trouble and great loss of goods among the common people; then there are Sir John Fortesue's famous remarks on the 'perils that may come to the king by over-mighty subjects', and the desirability that the ruler should 'exceed in lordships all the lords of his realm'.[35]

Many Victorian writers were singularly unimpressed by fifteenth-century England. However, since C.L. Kingsford first seriously called into question the strictures of Stubbs and Denton on the Wars of the Roses, medievalists have been inclined to play down the impact of civil war on English society and to stress the many areas of national life scarcely affected by it.[36] There are significant signs of change, too, in the attitude of historians towards fifteenth-century Japan and the importance of the Onin War. Traditionally, the war has been seen as a significant dividing line in Japanese history, with the later Ashikaga shoguns no better than puppets and their bakufu practically bereft of power. Recently, however, scholars have been questioning not only accepted views of bakufu power post-1477 but also stock generalisations about Kyoto and its society during and after the war, the significance of provincial developments in Japan in the late fifteenth/early sixteenth centuries, and the nature of late Ashikaga cultural life. The Onin War, we are now assured, did *not* mark the absolute end of Ashikaga power: in fact, in the capital area at least, the bakufu continued to play an important role in politics and economic life. Also, instead of dwelling on the extent of material destruction in Kyoto, we are urged to direct our attention to the energy shown by the citizens in rebuilding their shattered city once the holocaust was over.[37]

In England we have all long since tired of regarding the Wars of the Roses as 'the graveyard of the feudal nobility'; the 'rise of the new men', too, has been subjected to much searching criticism, especially insofar as it is supposed to have resulted from deliberately anti-baronial policies pursued by Henry VII. In Japan, however, the Onin War *does* present us with the spectacle of an old aristocracy (the shugo-daimyo) on the one hand and 'new men' (the sengoku-daimyo) on the other. And there is little room for doubt here that, as a result of the war, most of the former lost out to the latter.

Even before the war the heavy involvement of many shugo-daimyo in the life of Kyoto had meant that they were tending to lose power in the provinces to their deputies. During the war itself this trend became very pronounced indeed: while the great shugo-daimyo became 'locked in struggle' in the capital, comments Professor Varley, 'many of these deputies took over real control in the provinces, and thereby emerged as the principal agents in the final overthrow of the constable-daimyo domains'. Very few shugo-daimyo were able to retain in later Ashikaga times the power and status they had enjoyed before 1467. The Yamana family did manage to retain authority in Bingo province until 1538 — but, from the later fifteenth century, their power was being undermined more and more by men supposedly their subordinates. In Bizen, too, the Akamatsu family not only survived the Onin War but actually managed to reassert its position somewhat during the 1470s — but its effective power base was deteriorating all the time, and by 1483 Akamatsu authority in the province had been reduced to a shadow of what it had once been. That power collapsed entirely between 1483 and 1522 (when the head of the Akamatsu house was assassinated), and the main beneficiaries were the Matsuda and Urakami families. They had served as deputies to the Akamatsu in Bizen before the war; now they emerged as fully-fledged sengoku-daimyo in the province, the Matsuda in the west and the Urakami in the east, their power firmly based on military force.[38]

During the Onin War and the years that followed, in fact, several hundred sengoku-daimyo seem to have emerged in Japan, controlling territories which varied considerably in size and were notably unstable in their boundaries. This new military aristocracy, a vigorous and assertive class, can and must be distinguished from the shugo-daimyo of pre-Onin times. They were very much men of the provinces, and were not themselves subject to much (if any) external control in practice — whether from Kyoto or anywhere else. They were, however, engaged in almost continuous warfare amongst themselves and with their former shugo-daimyo masters: as a result, the weaker among them went to the wall, and by the early sixteenth century the victorious survivors had become very powerful indeed.

The later Ashikaga age, then, was an era of political decentralisation and endemic provincial warfare, when men needed powerful lords to protect them and such lords were only too anxious to attract retainers into their service. (So close were lord/man ties in late Ashikaga times, in fact, that homosexuality — long rife in the monasteries — became second nature to many samurai as well!) By about 1560 there had come into existence a series of self-contained and effectively controlled daimyo domains throughout most of Japan, veritable kingdoms in miniature, their ruling daimyo powerful military figures exercising a practically absolute authority within their territories. Then, in the last decades of the sixteenth century, three remarkable (though very different) Japanese leaders — Oda Nobunaga, Toyotomi Hideyoshi and Tokugawa Ieyasu — succeeded in reuniting the Japanese state.[39] The climax of this process of reunification was reached in 1600, with the battle of Sekigahara. And C.P. Fitzgerald is not entirely wide of the mark when he draws a parallel between Tokugawa Ieyasu's victory at Sekigahara and Henry VII's at Bosworth in 1485:

> Both battles ended an age of civil war and brought about a lasting peace under a new, firm and enduring government. Both battles were decided by the opportunist treachery of great feudal lords

who watched and waited till they saw which side seemed to have the best chance of victory. But if these treacherous lords expected to profit from the result, in both cases they were disappointed. The new conqueror was strong enough to reduce them to a role of far less importance than that which they had hitherto played, and to deny them all chance of future triumph.[40]

Notes

1. A. Lewis, *Knights and Samurai: Feudalism in Northern France and Japan* (1974). Other useful studies of Japanese feudalism (in English) are: K. Asakawa, 'Some Aspects of Japanese Feudal Institutions', *Transactions of the Asiatic Society of Japan*, XLVI (1918), pp. 77-102; E. Reischauer, 'Japanese Feudalism', *Feudalism in History*, ed. R. Coulborn (1956), pp. 26-48; J.W. Hall, 'Feudalism in Japan — a reassessment', *Comparative Studies in Society and History*, V (1962), pp. 15-51; Peter Duus, *Feudalism in Japan* (1969)
2. Japan had, and still has, an imperial house. For most of its history, however, the Japanese royal family has been virtually bereft of power. In the thirteenth century the emperor claimed divine descent and exercised certain religious and ceremonial functions, but that was all.
3. G. Sansom, *A History of Japan to 1334* (1958), chs. XV-XXI relates the history of the Kamakura shogunate at some length; see also H.P. Varley, *The Onin War: History of its Origins and Background, with a selective translation of the Chronicle of Onin* (1967), 6-15, for a valuable analysis of the role of the Kamakura constable.
4. Sir Maurice Powicke's most important work — *King Henry III and the Lord Edward* (2 vols, 1947) — is significantly sub-titled 'the community of the realm in the thirteenth century'. A recent short study treating of this theme is R. Wickson, *The Community of the Realm in Thirteenth Century England* (1970).
5. The Ashikaga shogunate thus established lasted (in name at least) until 1573. Some authors dub this the Muromachi age (from the Kyoto suburb of Muromachi, where the Ashikaga shoguns established themselves).

164

6. Sansom, *History of Japan 1334-1615* (1961), chs. I-VII, for a detailed account of events 1334-92.

7. J.R. Maddicott, *Thomas of Lancaster* (1970) certainly presents duke Thomas in no very favourable light. C.P. Fitzgerald, *A Concise History of East Asia* (1966), p. 171, suggests a rough, if slight, parallel between the Japanese civil war of the fourteenth century and the English Wars of the Roses: a major aim of this paper is to suggest a rather more convincing parallel between the Onin War and the Wars of the Roses.

8. Varley, *Onin War*, pp. 33-48, for an analysis of the rise of the constable-daimyo in the fourteenth century.

9. *ibid.*, p. 62.

10. B.P. Wolffe, 'The Personal Rule of Henry VI', *Fifteenth-century England*, ed. S.B. Chrimes, C.D. Ross and R.A. Griffiths (1972), p. 29, for comment on the 'impressive political and social stability' prevailing during Henry VI's minority; Varley, *Onin War*, p. 61, and *Japan in the Muromachi Age*, ed. J.W. Hall and Toyoda Takeshi (1977), pp. 12-13. The latter volume consists of papers delivered at a Japanese/American conference on the Muromachi age held in Kyoto in 1973, in one of which ('Shogun and Shugo: the Provincial Aspects of Muromachi Politics', pp. 65-8) Kawai Masaharu argues that the Ashikaga house reached its zenith *c.*1394-1440, with the bakufu's success very much dependent on an effective shogun-shugo relationship.

11. J.W. Hall, *Government and Local Power in Japan 500-1700: a study based on Bizen province* (1966), ch. VIII

12. Varley, *Onin War*, pp. 65-75, for the assassination of Yoshinori and its significance, pp. 191-205, for discussion of recent work on Japanese social history (mainly along Marxist lines) and analysis of the relationship between the Onin War and provincial unrest.

13. J.R. Green, *Short History of the English People* (1878), p. 282, for the 'weariness and disgust' engendered by studying the English wars.

14. J.H. Murdoch, *A History of Japan*, I (1910), pp. 603, 604.

15. Green, *op. cit.*, p. 278; Murdoch, *op. cit.*, pp. 621-2.

16. C. Ross, *The Wars of the Roses* (1976), p. 7, for Hall's remarks, and *Edward IV* (1974), pp. 429-30, 431, for critical comments on the quality of narrative sources for later fifteenth-century England; Varley, *Onin War*, pp. 139-90, for substantial extracts from the *Chronicle of Onin*, pp. 207-11, for note on Primary Sources.

17. *ibid.*, pp. 207-8; Sansom, *Japan 1334-1615*, pp. 203-4, 238-9, for comments on the journal of Chief Abbot Jinson and the diary of Sanjonishi Sanetaka.

18. The papers in *Japan in the Muromachi Age* illustrate the range of sources now being investigated by scholars of fifteenth and sixteenth-century Japan, and the kinds of questions being asked and answered.

19. Ross, *Wars of the Roses*, pp. 37-42, for a summary of current arguments regarding the causes of the English conflict; Varley, *Onin War*, especially pp. 101-3, for recent work on the origins of the Japanese civil war.

20. R.L. Storey, *The End of the House of Lancaster* (1966), especially pp. 1-28, for the origins of the Wars of the Roses, pp. 124-32, 142-9, for the Percy/Neville feud; Varley, *Onin War*, especially pp. 76-101, for Japanese succession disputes and the failure of the government to control them.

21. Ross, *Wars of the Roses*, p. 42; Varley, *Onin War*, p. 102.

22. *ibid.*, pp. 83-4, 103-5, 109-10; Ross, *Wars of the Roses*, pp. 47-54, for the importance of controlling king and capital in 1460/1.

23. Varley, *Onin War*, pp. 70, 83, 110-5, 140; Hayashiya Tatsusaburō, 'Kyoto in the Muromachi Age', *Japan in the Muromachi Age*, p. 18, emphasises that 'the decline of the shogunate's political fortunes, which were already well advanced by the middle of the fifteenth century, attracted disasters upon the capital'.

24. Varley, *Japanese Culture* (1973), pp. 83-5, 88, for Yoshimasa's cultural interests and patronage; J.R. Lander, *The Wars of the Roses* (1965), pp. 39-41, for John Blacman's recollections of Henry VI's chastity and purity, his anger when confronted by 'young ladies with bared bosoms' about to dance in his presence, and his embarrassment even at the sight of nude men bathing in Bath. By contrast, Edward IV's liking both for women and a comfortable life compares only too well with Yoshimasa's inclinations: Ross, *Edward IV*, especially pp. 86-7, 315-6.

25. Varley, *Onin War*, p. 117, for the contemporary account of privileged lords and suffering peasants in 1460, pp. 139-41, for comments in the *Chronicle of Onin* on the extravagance of Yoshimasa and his court, pp. 51-3, 104, 111-13, 115-6 for Varley's own view of the financial condition of the Ashikaga bakufu and the behaviour of Yoshimasa's wives and favourites; see also Hayashiya Tatsusaburo (above, note 23) and J.W. Hall, 'The Muromachi Power Structure', *loc. cit.*, pp. 28-9 (for rioting in Kyoto), pp. 39-43 (for the financial weakness of the bakufu).

26. B. Wilkinson, *Constitutional History of England in the Fifteenth Century* (1964), p. 50, and *English Historical Documents*, ed. A.R. Myers, IV 1327-1485 (1969), pp. 261, 281-2, for contemporary and near-contemporary comments on the self-seeking clique surrounding Henry VI and his chronic financial position in the 1450s; Robert Fabian, *New Chronicles of England and of France*, ed. H. Ellis (1811), pp. 630-1, for a vivid description of anti-Lombard rioting in London in 1456.

27. Varley, *Onin War*, pp. 124-5; K.B. McFarlane, 'The Wars of the Roses' *Proceedings of the British Academy*, L (1964), p. 94, for a strong commitment to the view that the English civil war was 'a conflict between ins and outs'.

28. Lander, *Wars of the Roses*, p. 30, for the view that York was a political opportunist cf. Ross, *Wars of the Roses*, p. 28; Varley *Onin War*, pp. 125-6, for the 'pragmatic and entirely opportunistic' ambitions of Hosokawa and Yamana.

29. *ibid.*, pp. 143-5, for the events of 1464-5 as given by the *Chronicle of Onin*, pp. 126-7, for Varley's reconstruction.

30. *ibid.*, pp. 127-32, for Varley's reduction to order of the detailed and bewildering account of events 1466/7 in the *Chronicle of Onin*, pp. 145-77; Sansom, *Japan 1334-1615*, p. 222, for the report of April 1467; *The Great Chronicle of London*, ed. A.H. Thomas and I.D. Thornley (1938), pp. 189-90, for the build-up of troops in London early in 1458, and the reaction of the city authorities.

31. Varley, *Onin War*, pp. 131-2, where he rather rashly suggests that, given the lack of corroborative records, 'we must accept these figures (i.e. the estimates of troop numbers in Kyoto given by the *Chronicle of Onin*), even though the *Chronicle of Onin* is not noted for its numerical accuracy'; Hayashiya

166

Tatsusaburō, *loc. cit.*, p. 27, suggests that, at their maximum, the two armies were perhapa 160,000 and 90,000 respectively; Sansom, *Japan 1334-1615*, pp. 222-6, for events in Kyoto May-December 1467.

32. *ibid.*, pp. 226-8; Varley, *Onin War*, pp. 132-5, 189-90.

33. Varley (with I. and N. Morris), *The Samurai* (1970), pp. 75, 76; Hayashiya Tatsusaburō, *loc. cit.*, pp. 27-8; *Great Chronicle*, pp. 181-96, 209-20, for the impact of rebellion, riot and civil war on London 1450-71.

34. Varley, *Samurai*, p. 75, including the comment that to their 'shocked contemporaries these vicious marauders (i.e. footsoldiers) appeared as a threat to the very future of civilized life in Japan'; some English observers were little less horrified at the excesses perpetrated by Margaret of Anjou's northern army on its march south following the battle of Wakefield, notably the anonymous author of a continuation of the Croyland Chronicle, *Ingulph's Chronicle of the Abbey of Croyland*, trans. H.T. Riley (1854), pp. 421-2.

35. Sansom, *Japan 1334-1615*, p. 216, for the entry in Jinson's journal; Hayashiya Tatsusaburō, *loc. cit.*, p. 22, for Yoshimasa's remark; *Warkworth's Chronicle*, ed. J.O. Halliwell (1839), p. 12; *England under the Yorkists*, ed. I.D. Thornley (1920), p. 153, for Fortescue's comments.

36. W. Stubbs, *Constitutional History of England*, III (1878), p. 632, W. Denton, *England in the Fifteenth Century* (1888), pp. 115, 118-9, for highly critical Victorian comments; C.L. Kingsford, 'Social Life in the Wars of the Roses', *Prejudice and Promise in Fifteenth Century England* (1925), pp. 48, 64, 66, and Lander, *Wars of the Roses*, p. 20, for optimistic assessments.

37. Sansom, *Japan 1334-1615*, ch. XIV, provides a largely traditional view of Japan after the Onin War; the papers in *Japan in the Muromachi Age* illustrate changing attitudes towards (and recent research into) post-Onin history.

38. Varley, *Onin War*, p. 46; Hall, 'Foundations of the Modern Japanese Daimyo', *Journal of Asian Studies*, XX (1961), p. 321, and *Government and Local Power in Japan 500-1700*, pp. 234-5; Kawai Masaharu, *loc. cit.*, pp. 66, 77-8.

39. E.O. Reischauer and J.K. Fairbank, *East Asia: The Great Tradition* (1958), pp. 570-91, for a convenient summary of developments in Japan *c.*1477-1600.

40. Fitzgerald, *East Asia*, p. 191-2.

HOKKAIDŌ

SEA OF JAPAN

HONSHŪ

Kamakura • Edō (Tokyo)

Kyōto (Heian) •
• Ōsaka
• Ise shrine
Yoshino

INLAND SEA

SHIKOKU

PACIFIC OCEAN

Nagasaki

KYŪSHŪ

Feudal Japan

▨ – Kanto Region   ■ – Yamato Region

Appendix

1. JAPANESE CHRONOLOGY

Late 3rd/early 4th c.AD: foundation of the Japanese state in the Yamato region

7th and 8th c.: import into Japan of Chinese political, religious and cultural ideas/institutions

710: permanent capital established at Nara

794: capital moved to Heian (Kyoto)

10th, 11th and early 12th c.: political emergence of warrior chieftains in provincial Japan and decline of political power of Imperial Court and Court nobility

1180-1185: Gempei War, resulting in establishment of Kamakura bakufu by Yoritomo

1192: Yoritomo appointed shogun

1274, 1281: unsuccessful Mongol invasions of Japan

1333: fall of Kamakura bakufu

1334-6: failure of attempt at Imperial restoration

1336: beginning of civil war between Northern and Southern courts

1338: Ashikaga Takauji appointed shogun

1368: Yoshimitsu became shogun

1392: agreement ending civil war

1394: Yoshimitsu resigned, tho' he continued very influential until his death 1408

1428: Yoshinori became shogun

1441: assassination of Yoshinori at Akamatsu Mitsusuke's residence in Kyoto (nb. Akamatsu family shugo-daimyo in Bizen province, with Matsuda and Urakami as deputies)

1443: Yoshimasa became shogun (at age of 8)

1450s and 1460s: notable succession rivalries within, and feuds between, shugo-daimyo families eg. rivalry between Akamatsu and Yamana houses, succession disputes within Hatakeyama and Shiba families. Most important — rivalry between *Hosokawa* (led by Hosokawa Katsumuto) and *Yamana* (led by Yamana Sōzen), especially in context of shogunal weakness (influence of Ise Sadachika, Lady Tomiko et. al.)

1447, 1451, 1457, 1461 etc.: riots in Kyoto, in context of
provincial distress
1464: Yoshimasa decided to resign; brother Yoshimi agreed to
assist and accept succession
1465: Lady Tomiko gave birth to Yoshihisa
1466/7: military build-up in Kyoto, Hosokawa v. Yamana
May 1467: Onin War began
1468: Yoshimi joined Yamana
1469: Yoshimasa named Yoshihisa as his heir
1473: Yoshimasa finally retired; Yamana Sozen and Hosokawa
Katsumato died
1477: end of Onin War
1467-77, and after (to c.mid-16th c.): rise of sengoku-
daimyo
1542: arrival of Portuguese
c.1560-c.1600: military reunification of Japan
1568: Kyoto occupied by Oda Nobunaga
1573: fall of Ashikaga bakufu
1582: assassination of Nobunaga, followed by spectacular
career of Toyotomi Hideyoshi
1600: victory of Tokugawa Ieyasu at Sekigahara, followed by
political reunification and establishment of Tokugawa bakufu
at Edo (Tokyo)
1603: Tokugawa Ieyasu appointed shogun
c.1636-c.1641: establishment of Tokugawa 'isolationism'
1868: fall of Tokugawa bakufu and Meiji (Imperial) restoration

2. GLOSSARY OF JAPANESE TERMS

Ashikaga: dynasty in office as shoguns 1338-1573
Bakufu: 'Tent government', headed by shoguns
Jito: Land stewards
Kamikaze: 'divine winds'
Kokujin: small peasant landowners
Muromachi: suburb of Kyoto where Ashikaga shoguns
resided (hence sometimes known as Muromachi shoguns)
Samurai: warriors/knights, strictly mounted warriors with
retainers
Sengoku-daimyo: Japanese aristocracy rising during and

after the Onin War

Shiki: rights to income from land on private estates

Shoen: private estates, exempt from taxation and administrative interference from centre

Shogun: generalissimo or 'warrior monarch', who headed the bakufu

Shugo: provincial constables or governors in Kamakura times

Shugo-daimyo: constable-barons, rising during the 14th century

Yorkist propaganda: Pedigree, prophecy and the 'British history' in the Reign of Edward IV.

Alison Allan, University College of Swansea.

The deposition of the Lancastrian king, Henry VI, by Edward, earl of March in 1461 is generally considered to have been forced by political and military circumstances. Edward's father, Richard, duke of York, along with the staunch Yorkist nobleman, Richard Neville, earl of Salisbury, had been killed at the battle of Wakefield in December 1460. In February 1461, at the second battle of St. Albans, Salisbury's son, the earl of Warwick, lost custody of Henry VI (in whose name the Yorkist lords had been governing) to Margaret of Anjou, Henry's queen and the unrelenting enemy of the house of York. For Edward and Warwick to remain at liberty and in full enjoyment of their power and possessions was thus no longer possible and, early in March 1461, Edward himself assumed the dignity of the crown of England.[1]

However it was brought about, the removal of a reigning monarch demanded justifications more substantial than those of mere political necessity and personal safety. The change of dynasty from Lancaster to York was achieved against the background of over a decade of protest at the inadequacies and corruption of Henry VI's government. Popular acceptance of Edward's rule would be, to a considerable extent, dependent on his continued profession of Yorkist promises to restore order and good governance in the realm. Yet in the last resort, the legitimacy of Edward's monarchy, as distinct from its *de facto* existence, could rest only on the unimpeachable claims of hereditary right. When Richard of York had first mooted his title to the throne in October 1460, he had caused confusion and dismay, apparently confounding both Salisbury and Warwick.[2] Nonetheless, York's pedigree, which caused such

172

embarrassment in the autumn of 1460, became by the spring of 1461 the cornerstone of Yorkist propaganda and was to remain so throughout Edward IV's reign.

Duke Richard had laid claim to the crown by virtue of his descent from Lionel, duke of Clarence, second son of Edward III. (Henry VI was descended from John of Gaunt, duke of Lancaster, who was Edward's third son.) Lionel's daughter, Philippa, had married Edmund Mortimer, third earl of March; their granddaughter, Anne Mortimer, became the wife of Richard, earl of Cambridge, son of Edmund of Langley, duke of York and the fourth son of Edward III. Richard of York was the offspring of Anne and Richard. In view of these facts, Bible stories, ancient history and the legends of early Britain might not appear to have much relevance to the prosecution of Edward IV's title to the throne. Yet such material was to form the core of a significant body of propaganda in the years after 1461. For the immediate vindication of Edward's dynastic claims, only the generations of the fourteenth and fifteenth centuries were of importance; but to these were harnessed tales of earlier kings and realms to give the Yorkist king an impressive pedigree which emphasised the antiquity of the royal line he represented.

Manuscript genealogies which traced the ancestry of the ruling king through the centuries to the creation of the world were not a Yorkist innovation; many examples survive from previous reigns, particularly from that of Edward's erstwhile sovereign lord, 'he that calleth hymself, Kyng Henry the vjte'.[3] There are several clearly recognisable types among these 'biblical' pedigrees, but the essential form and content of each are the same. Beginning usually with Adam, they draw a line of descent, in some instances unbroken, through Noah's son Japhet. As they proceed, their scope narrows from the portrayal of several biblical and ancient kingdoms to the representation of British, Saxon and English royalty alone. An accompanying narrative is included and the manuscripts are, in effect, short chronicles illustrated by a genealogy.

Although some earlier Lancastrian manuscripts were updated or re-copied after 1461, four types of genealogy, appearing for the first time, predominate during Edward IV's reign.[4] There is (1) a Latin pedigree, beginning with Adam, whose text is fairly detailed and much of which is drawn in its early stages from the twelfth century *Compendium Historiae in Genealogia Christi* of Peter of Poitiers; and (2) the same text in an English translation (the two to be described hereafter as the 'Long Latin' and the 'Long English' pedigrees, respectively).[5] These are complemented by (3) another Latin genealogy of a much simpler and abbreviated form, which again (4) has a vernacular counterpart (the 'Short Latin' and 'Short English' genealogies).[6]

These genealogies, or the sources and examples on which they were based, may well have been produced originally by a cleric for educational purposes. (One genealogy of Henry VI has been ascribed to Roger of St. Albans, a Carmelite friar in London in the 1450s.[7]) The 'Long Latin' pedigree uses the preface from Peter of Poitier's *Compendium*, which offers the ensuing work as an easily assimilated biblical and historical digest for those who seek knowledge but lack the application, ability or means to study in depth. The three companion Yorkist texts, the Roger of St. Albans descent, and other comparable fifteenth-century genealogies contain similar introductory passages.[8] Biblical history figures prominently in such manuscripts. The 'Long Latin' pedigree also includes lines demonstrating the succession of popes and Holy Roman Emperors. Purely biblical genealogies continuing only to the birth of Christ were produced contemporaneously with their more lengthy royal counterparts.[9] The four Yorkist texts were not, however, necessarily created in a religious setting, since by Edward's reign there were sufficient precedents for them to be composed quite easily by an educated layman.

Whatever their provenance, as their prefaces indicate, these genealogical chronicles were destined for a secular audience. Their compilers would have been aware of the way in which their manuscripts flattered the king and, if their work was not deliberately commissioned, they probably would have sought favour by offering it to a noble or royal patron. Roger of St Albans reputedly presented his genealogy to Henry VI; its subsequent popularity was presumably a result of the acknowledgement it received from the king and his court.[10]

There is no clear proof that the initial appearance of biblical pedigrees was prompted by the monarchy itself, but it is likely that, once written, their reproduction at least would have been encouraged by the king or an ardent royalist. Simply because of the venerable heritage which they depicted, such documents were inherently propagandist. It is quite feasible that Edward IV or an adherent, sensible of the example of earlier texts, should order the production of similar manuscripts to demonstrate the new king's title to the throne. Certainly, in some of the pieces for his reign, the narrative in its latter stages was written with a bias which, even if not royally inspired, was distinctly Yorkist in tone.[11] Again, the more blatant use which was made of Edward's lineage in other Yorkist propaganda makes it improbable that the biblical genealogies were written in isolation or in ignorance of their likely influence on their audience.[12]

The extant copies of these four types of Yorkist pedigree indicate that their production in considerable numbers was consciously planned. They seem to be the output of a small group of craftsmen, probably from the secular workshops which were becoming an increasingly important source of manuscript production in the fourteenth and fifteenth centuries.[13] The 'Long Latin' and 'Long English' texts show the closest similarities. They are uniform in their layout and are written in a standard hand; they are all illuminated in a like manner with much use of gold leaf and vivid colours. There are two 'Long English' pedigrees of the same date which are the work of one scribe and which have been decorated by the same artist or artists, thereby suggesting the simultaneous preparation of a batch of identical manuscripts.[14] The earliest example of the 'long' Yorkist genealogies belongs to the opening years of Edward IV's reign and the dates of the remaining manuscripts imply that a fresh genealogy was compiled, probably at the behest of the king himself, after the birth of each of his children.[15] It has been suggested that all the biblical pedigrees of the latter half of the fifteenth century which show a marked affinity in script and ornamentation (the Roger of St. Albans text and the four Yorkist pieces) were made in a single workshop.[16] This would indicate that a particular publisher or bookseller made a point of specialising in such manuscripts, acquiring a sufficient reputation for future orders to be submitted to him.

The methods of dissemination for this type of propaganda were clearly different from those of short texts — such as poems and manifestoes — which were often broadcast indiscriminately by scattering or posting up in the streets. The biblical genealogies were executed in the sophisticated manner of works designed to please the eye. They were made in both roll and book form, presumably to cater for customers' preferences.[17] They were intended to be bought or presented, to be appreciated at leisure rather than forced upon the public's attention. As most manuscripts were produced to order during this period, they were not necessarily even kept in stock but produced only when a request was made.[18]

These genealogical chronicles include the most striking episodes of history for a medieval audience, namely, the fortunes of the British Isles in the pre-Saxon era. Hence their potential as propaganda. The traditions and myths which surrounded these early centuries largely owed their existence to the vivid picture created by Geoffrey of Monmouth in his *Historia Regum Britanniae*. His narrative, which has little foundation in verifiable fact, was completed about 1136 and achieved quick and lasting popularity. Despite the disparaging remarks of occasional sceptics, Geoffrey's vision of his country's past before its domination by the Saxons became firmly established as historical truth, and he gave the account of this period a coherence and fullness which it had hitherto lacked.

Geoffrey described the conquest and settlement of Britain by the Trojan exile, Brutus, whom he claimed was the great-grandson of Aeneas. To this legendary hero, he attributed the derivation of the name of the island (Britain) and the race which he fathered (the Britons). The tale continues through the descendants of Brutus, portraying the lives of various monarchs and dwelling much on civil wars and battles. The central chapters of the story hinge on the characters of Merlin and Arthur, whose deeds were to prove such fruitful ground for the writers of chivalric romance throughout Europe.

Geoffrey closed his work with the reign of Cadwaladr, the last British prince to have had true hegemony over Britain and who ended his days in pious exile in Rome.[19]

Chronicles which perpetuated Geoffrey of Monmouth's rendering of early British history were plentiful in the following centuries. They began with a reiteration of the accepted myths of Britain's past, moving gradually to a more accurate and historical presentation of events as the author came closer to his own age.[20] By the fifteenth century, vernacular manuscripts of this type were the most widely-read histories of the time.[21]

This fondness for the 'British history' gave Edward IV a valuable advantage over the Lancastrian monarchy because of his links with the Mortimers. In 1230 Ralph Mortimer (whose family was to be invested with the earldom of March a century later) married Gwladys Ddu, daughter of Llywelyn the Great, prince of Gwynedd. With the end of the political power of the house of Gwynedd towards the close of the thirteenth century and the eventual extinction of its male line in 1378, its royal Welsh title passed to the Mortimers and thus to Edward IV.[22] Edward was consequently able to lay claim to a British lineage which stretched back to Cadwaladr and, with a little imagination, yet further to Brutus, the supposed founder of the British race. The Lancastrian kings boasted a proud heritage from Woden, the putative father of the Saxon tribes.[23] Both Brutus and Woden could be taken back, by fabulous means, to Japhet, but although the mythical antiquity of the houses of Lancaster and York was comparable, the Britons held a special place in popular affection.

Surprisingly, despite the prominence of the 'British history' in biblical genealogies, most of the Yorkist examples do not take full advantage of the potential inherent in the Welsh ancestry which Edward possessed. The British line which, from the Saxon age onwards, becomes that of the Welsh princes, is allowed to wane at the end of the thirteenth century, following the Edwardian conquest of Wales. Only the 'Long English' manuscripts make a point of showing the union of Ralph Mortimer and Gwladys Ddu. This apparent lack of awareness may stem from the fact that perhaps in these manuscripts, the later details of Edward IV's descent from Edward

III were of the greater importance, and the earlier history of the realm merely served as an acceptable traditional setting.

Elsewhere, however, Edward's Welsh lineage was made the focal point of literature which sought to persuade its readers of the Yorkist right to the throne and that Edward was the 'true and undoubted heir of Brutus'. But this aspect of Edward's heredity was not just seen as a satisfying quirk of fate, whereby his accession, as well as restoring the correct order of succession from Edward III, gave the realm a king of British ancestry. To those in the right way of thinking, Edward's assumption of the crown marked the fulfillment of various prophecies which had foretold the ultimate re-establishment of the British monarchy and the end of years of alien domination. For although Geoffrey's history had concluded with the eclipse of the British people by the Saxons, he did not leave it as a tale without hope, but rather as one with the promise of a divinely ordained recovery.[24] These assurances quickly developed in the succeeding centuries, especially amongst the Welsh, into a confident expectation of a return to British hegemony.[25]

It is pertinent here to consider whether an appeal to Welsh sentiment played any part in Yorkist propaganda. Geoffrey of Monmouth did not write his work with any particular sympathy for the Britons; indeed on occasion he was contemptuously critical of them. But his inclusion of an angel's prophecy to Cadwaladr of the eventual reassertion of British dominion did much to inspire Welsh resistance to English rule. Thus, in 1282, in his struggle against Edward I, Llywelyn the Last was encouraged to believe that he was destined to become the first British king for six centuries, and similar hopes surrounded Owain Glyndŵr in the early-fifteenth century.[26] Yet, there is nothing noticeably Welsh about the 'British history' propaganda of Edward IV. Descended from the princes of Wales he might have been, but there was no celebration of the glories of the Welsh principalities after Cadwaladr's reign. Edward IV was, after all, in practical terms, king of England and not of a mythical British kingdom, and the conquest of Wales by Edward I had been one of the triumphs of the English monarchy. If the idea of British

178

sovereignty — which in the fifteenth century meant Celtic sovereignty — had been taken out of the realms of propaganda into practical politics, the implications for Edward's English kingship and subjects would have been horrifying.[27] The Welsh princes were only of significance in transmitting Edward IV's descent from Cadwaladr and Brutus. It was the traditions of the 'British history' that were important to the Yorkists because of their popularity with the medieval public and because they gave prestige to the monarchy. In 1461, a British king may well have acceded to the throne but certainly not a Welsh one, and as one chronicler reveals, the Welsh people scarcely felt that Edward IV had returned them to pre-eminence in Britain.[28]

Geoffrey of Monmouth did more than create an attractive history of Britain. One section of his chronicle (Book vii) was entirely devoted to what purported to be the prophecies of Merlin, proclaimed before the British king, Vortigern in the mid-fifth century, when the Saxon threat was beginning to gain momentum.[29] These pages, originally written with the first century of Norman history in mind, became widely popular independently of the rest of the work, and they were mainly responsible for inaugurating a whole tradition of prophetic writing in a similar vein.[30] In prophecies which imitated Geoffrey's in style and method, the interpretation was obscured by the use of symbols — usually animal symbols — to represent the characters involved and by the production of an often deliberately vague or ambiguous narrative.[31] In these features lies the reason for the perennial popularity of these writings in the middle ages. They could be applied and re-applied with impunity to fit new and contemporary political situations *ad infinitem* and with ever greater respect for their growing antiquity. Whatever the actual date of these pieces, they were invariably ascribed to venerable and ancient authorities; Merlin, Bede and Gildas were among the favourites, though martyrs and foreign seers were also prominent. In this way their credibility was enhanced through an appeal to figures who were popularly revered and who came from a wide historical period and geographical area. In no respect were these texts prophecies in the true sense of visions of the future;

they were written retrospectively with particular events in mind or out of wishful thinking. They were made to follow the desired course in language sufficiently contorted to convey mystery and authenticity but which, nonetheless, was clear enough to allow the intended meaning to be appreciated. By the fifteenth century a wealth of prophetic literature existed which could be drawn upon by the politically aware. Apart from the efforts of Geoffrey himself, there were many texts which perpetuated the themes of Celtic victory. A whole crop of prophecies promising glorious successes in war appeared in response to Edward III's continental ambitions. The deposition of Richard II in 1399 and the precarious position of Henry IV in the early years of his reign again prompted a spate of prophetic writing.

The use to which traditional prophecies were put in Edward IV's reign is illustrated by three particular manuscripts, two books and a long parchment roll, all the work of the same scribe.[32] In these, along with some other propagandist texts, numerous prophecies were collected together and presented in such a way as to point their relevance to the fortunes of the house of York. The full contents of each individual manuscript are not identical, but there are interpretative sections and a large number of prophecies common to all three. The most telling comparisons may be made between the two books, Vespasian E.VII and Bodley 623. Vespasian E.VII is the larger work but the majority of its texts are found in Bodley 623 as well. Ashmolean Roll 26 includes several prophecies, but it also contains two Yorkist pedigrees and it has numerous lengthy passages which elaborate Edward IV's hereditary rights.

There is one feature of the three collections which is crucial in determining the way in which their author believed the prophecies should be interpreted. Each manuscript gives a list of cognomens by which a rightful and usurping king might be identified. These symbols are drawn from the prophecies themselves and take the form of historical and legendary figures and heraldic badges. The names Edward and Henry are included in the appropriate list to make their intended application clear.[33] By using these lists the reader would have been able to explain each of the prophecies, whatever their original purpose, to the advantage of the Yorkists and the denigration of the Lancastrians. It would also have been possible to eliminate the discrepancies which would have arisen in trying to put a chronological or exact fifteenth-century interpretation on texts written for an earlier period. Ambiguities and inconsistencies could be ignored in the appreciation of the general theme of York against Lancaster. Bodley 623 and Ashmolean Roll 26 arrange each set of names in a circle headed by the name of the relevant king. Inside each circle there is a short text. The piece on Edward IV states that the names are those of the monarchs who, according to different but authentic prophecies, will win the Holy Cross. Edward *verus heres erit electus a deo*; he will be victorious against his enemies and win three crowns before he dies.[34] It is then stated that all these promises had been made by the most High God.[35] The prophetic symbols referring to the Lancastrian line are described as being the names of kings who have occupied the throne unjustly and who, according to *prophecias autenticas*, will be punished by God and whose reigns will end in sorrow because of their usurpation and deceit.

The two books open their anthology of prophecies with some explanatory paragraphs on the efficacy of prognostication and each includes a comment on recent Lancastrian and Yorkist history.[36] In these passages extensive use is made of the commentary on John of Bridlington's prophecy. This verse prophecy, and its companion prose interpretation, was originally designed to celebrate the deeds of Edward III and the Black Prince, making hopeful forecasts of a victorious future.[37] The Yorkist compiler selected some of the most appropriate sentences and rearranged and expanded them to suit his own propagandist purpose. Although he was using Bridlington to describe what had already happened, the language of the prophecy naturally put his account into the future tense. This act of making what had occurred seem as if it had long been promised was the main purpose of most of the prophecies used by the Yorkists. In Vespasian E.VII the author began with the penultimate line of the second section of Bridlington's prophecy, *Iam canis intravit. . . .* The original commentator interpreted this and the following lines as announcing that the prophet wished to suspend his prophesying because the astrological conditions were unsuitable and were making him ill.[38] The prophecy then starts afresh in the next section of the poem; there is no connection in content with the final lines of the second section.[39] Vespasian E.VII, however, takes the line quoted above and the beginning of its astrological interpretation, *Iam canis intravit .i. stella que canis primus dicitur*, adding that *canis* and *stella* symbolise *henricus maledictus*. (The 'dog' and the 'star' were included in the list of prophetic names for usurping kings, thus removing any uncertainty about the Yorkist interpretation of Bridlington.) The remaining commentary on this line and the one which follows is omitted and the text moves straight on to the exposition of section three, which details the evils which will befall the kingdom because of bad government:

> ego timeo describere . . . ista quae sequuntur, quae sunt valde nociva per pestilencias et destructiones hominum, per ignem et aquam, multis modis, et propter mala statuta sive propter regimen regni illo tempore.

The blame for these disasters is thereby assigned to the 'accursed Henry'.

Another reason given for the troubles of the realm is the suffering which will be inflicted by the bull, which Vespasian E.VII interprets as Richard. *Henricus* and *Ricardus* were probably intended to indicate Henry IV and Richard II. In identifying the bull as Richard II, the author may have been referring to the discontent and rebellion which was fomented in Richard's name even after his death.[40] Alternatively, the two names may have signified Henry VI and Richard of York, since *taurus* could equally have been used for the duke. In this case the lines on the distress of the kingdom would have been seen as a criticism of Henry VI's government.

The next lines discuss the nature of prophetic inspiration. Foolish and false prophets who claim to know the future, but who are in fact ignorant of such matters, are castigated. The author of Vespasian E.VII is, however, only writing about what is just and has been revealed by God to be just, namely the rights of the 'bull' or the kings of England, in this instance

Edward IV. The holy inspiration of his prophecy is protested:

> Sed quia ego sum instructus et doctus per Spiritum Sanctum, et oportet quod faciam secundum voluntatem sui, non accipias istam prophetiam tanquam ex voluntate et ordinatione mea procedentem sed ex voluntate et doctrina Dei, qui non fallitur, quia ipse solus Deus, et non homo nec angelus, novit futura secura.

Finally, Vespasian E. VII transcribes some lines from the ninth chapter of the third section of Bridlington, applying to Edward IV the glorious career promised to the Black Prince.[41]

Bodley 623 includes the same lines on the divine source of true prophecy, prefacing them with a sentence of similar import from the first preamble of the Bridlington commentary.[42] Then follows a piece from another chapter which declares that it is impossible for people's sins to remain permanently hidden and unpunished.[43] This would seem to have been intended as a Yorkist attack on the wrongful usurpation of the crown by the house of Lancaster. This crime had been made manifest by the virtuous house of York and retribution exacted by Edward IV in his victory over the Lancastrians. After this Bodley 623 leaves the prophecy of Bridlington and has a paragraph asserting the veracity of the works of various venerable prophets: the Sibyl in the time of King Salomon, the Eagle in the reign of King Rudhudibras, Merlin and the angel who spoke to Cadwaladr.

The application of the prophecies in the three collections can be illustrated by examining a few examples in detail. Three passages were quoted and adapted from Geoffrey's history itself. The first comes from the beginning of Book vii, which contains the prophecies of Merlin. In a pool underneath the ground on which King Vortigern had been trying unsuccessfully to build a fortress, two sleeping dragons were discovered. On awakening, the two dragons, one red and the other white, began to fight. Merlin declared that the red dragon signified the people of Britain and the white, the Saxons whom Vortigern had invited into the country.[44] For the Yorkists, the red dragon represented Edward IV, who had defeated the white dragon, the Lancastrians who were descendants of the Saxons.

The next piece from the *Historia Regum Britanniae* comes from a little further on in Book vii. It begins *Sextus hiberniae menia subvertet.*[45] Firstly, the reign of a king called *Sextus* is described. He will subdue Ireland, reunite his kingdom and, although his position will be unsure at the beginning, he will become increasingly powerful and will restore the church to its former dignity. Applied to Edward IV, these lines would have emphasised his piety and promised him a successful reign after an insecure start. The appearance of a king called *Sextus*, or one who would fulfil the prophecy, was frequently anticipated throughout the medieval period, presumably because of the attractive reign which was foretold for him.[46] The author of these three manuscripts certainly considered that the prophecy had been realised in Edward IV, since he included *Sextus* in the list of prophetic names for Edward. Many other vaticinations in his collections are headed as being about 'the sixth' or 'the sixth or Ireland', even though the texts themselves make little or no mention of *Sextus*. For example, one long prophecy attributed to Gildas, is, in fact, made up of three distinct texts and only the first, beginning *Ter tria lustra*, actually refers to *Sextus*.[47]

After *Sextus* the reign of a lynx is foretold. This animal will involve itself in numerous affairs and be responsible for the downfall of his race. Vespasian E.VII treats this part of the prophecy separately from the preceding lines on *Sextus* (Edward IV) and interprets the lynx as Henry V, presumably in an attempt to denigrate this popularly revered king. Finally, the return of the Britons to power in their native land is predicted. Dissension will erupt amongst the foreigners (the English). Cadwaladr, in alliance with the Scots, will destroy the foreigners, the Celtic peoples will flourish and the name of Britain will be used instead of the Saxon name of England. Vespasian E.VII states that the final destruction of the English and the resurgence of Cadwaladr (yet another of the names given to Edward as a rightful king) will occur in 1460.[48]

The last passage selected from Geoffrey's work relates the promise made by a heavenly angel to Cadwaladr that, because of their faithfulness, his people would eventually regain supremacy in Britain.[49] The Yorkist version adds a further

condition for the revival of British sovereignty.[50] The Britons
had been expelled because of their sins and would only be able
to return when such sins were as great in the Saxons as they had
been in the British people. These faults are listed: the negligence
and evil life of the clergy, the rapine of the magnates, the
cupidity of the judges and abominable luxury. According to
the Yorkist writer, these conditions were fulfilled with the
accession of Edward IV, in other words, the Saxons (now the
Lancastrians) had become as wicked and degenerate as the
Britons whom they had dispossessed. This catalogue of vices
can therefore be considered as an indictment of Henry VI's
government.

Several prophecies develop the theme of the alliance between
the Britons and the Scots against the English, which was foretold in Geoffrey's *History*. Some of these are reported in
various chronicles as having been popular during the Scottish
war of independence against Edward I and they were often
part of longer collections or compilations of prophecies on
Scottish history.[51] These texts would have been admitted to
the Yorkist collections not because of their Scottish content,
but because they forecast the revival of British sovereignty.
The massacre of the English nation, which was an inherent
feature of this type of prophecy, could only have been intended
by Yorkist apologists to be symbolic of the defeat of their
enemies. Edward IV was as concerned as any English monarch
to keep the Scots behind their own border: he would hardly
have wished that they should come rampaging into England to
murder his subjects. Thus, in one of the Scottish prophecies
which he appropriated, the author of these Yorkist collections
omitted several lines which described the destruction of the
English. It would hardly have been tactful of Edward IV to
allow his new English subjects to believe that he hoped that

Bruti posteritas cum Scotis associata
Anglica regna premet, marte, labore, nece.
Flumina manabunt hostili tincta cruore,
Perfida gens omni lite subacta ruet.
Quem Britonum fundet Albanis juncta juventus
Sanguine Saxonico tincta rubebit humus.[52]

One text which was especially popular in the fifteenth

century is a lengthy prophecy usually entitled 'The Six Kings to follow John' which details the reigns of King John's successors from Henry III to Henry IV. Owain Glyndwr and the Percies used this prophecy in their revolt against Henry IV; the latter was castigated as a wicked and accursed king, and a disastrous reign was foretold in which his kingdom would be divided into three and he would lose the throne.[53] The author of the Yorkist anthologies made use of this text, not in order to re-apply any part of it directly to Edward IV, but as an historical account written in prophetic terms which demonstrated the evil character of the first Lancastrian monarch, described as *talpa ore dei maledicta,* and predicted his fall *pro peccatis ante factis.* The material is rearranged and altered to prove that the monarchy should rest in the hands of Richard II's true heirs, namely, the house of York. The paragraph on Henry IV deletes the prophesied — and unfulfilled — partition of the realm and only mentions the curse which rested on the king and the destruction that would befall him. At this point, the words *terra revertetur ad asinum et ipse gubernabit totam terram in pacem* are interpolated.[54] *Asinus* was the cognomen for Richard II. In earlier versions of this work, this line was part of the history of Richard II's reign, telling how, after temporarily handing over the government to an eagle, Richard resumed personal responsibility after the eagle's death. The corruption present in the Yorkist text was probably made by those who sought Richard II's restoration. In Edward IV's reign the sentence would have implied that the crown had now returned to its rightful inheritor.

Other pieces, apart from the 'Six Kings' prophecy, relate to the deposition of Richard II by Henry Bolingbroke. For example, there is a text which begins *In illo tempore superveniet filius Aquile.*[55] This prophecy declares that *Filius Aquile* (Henry IV) will imprison the ass (Richard II) and will be raised to the Crown by the false citizens of Troy (or London), who will be held in everlasting shame by the rest of the realm.[56] Afterwards, these flatterers, who had been deceived by the *predator* (Henry IV) will mourn and regret their actions. Blood will be shed in many places. Witnessing this, and worse, the spirit of courage and wisdom will rise up in a *Brutum animal* (presumably Edward IV), who will gather his forces, devastate the predator and reign in his stead.

Prophecies belonging to the period of Edward III's conquests in France which were revived in Edward IV's reign, reflect another aspect of Yorkist ambitions. Until Edward was secure on his throne, expeditions to France would have been inconceivable. Nonetheless, optimistic forecasts of success could easily appeal to popular sentiment. Provided that Edward did not ask his subjects to dip into their own pockets, promises of military achievement could only enhance the king's image in the eyes of his people. One of the most popular of these 'foreign conquest' pieces is entitled 'The Lily, the Lion and the Son of Man'. In this, it is prophesied that the Son of Man (the king of England), in alliance with the Emperor, will overcome the Lily (a usurping French king) and assume his crown. The text piously concludes with the Son of Man's crusade to the Holy Land.[57]

Two prophecies included in the Yorkist manuscripts are not concerned to emphasise one particular political issue, but to forecast more generally a prosperous and victorious reign for Edward IV.[58] They do not dwell on the personal successes of the monarch alone, but rather on the peace and contentment which the king will bring to his faithful subjects. The two texts are essentially similar in content, differing only in their length. There are references to foreign conquest and the pieces may therefore originally have belonged to the reign of Edward III, but their sentiments seem peculiarly appropriate to the circumstances of the young Yorkist king. The devout character of the king, symbolised by a dragon, is stressed, and the suppression of lawlessness and corruption (a major complaint against the Lancastrian regime) is promised. Pride will be trampled underfoot and the king will destroy robbers and oppressors as well as his own enemies; and he will display a passion for justice.

So far, genealogies and prophecies have been discussed as two separate forms of propaganda, the one demonstrating Edward IV's royal title *via* the historical facts of his ancestry, the other portraying him as the fulfiller of various ancient prophecies. But there were those of his advocates who recognised the potential value in combining the two media in genealogies which both showed a king who was British by birth and whose monarchy was vindicated by the prophecies which it satisfied.

One such genealogy was produced by the author of the three collections of prophecies.[59] He showed four lines of descent: the heirs of Britain, the conquerors (i.e., the kings of England from the Norman conquest), the heirs of France and the heirs of Spain. These four lines finally unite in Edward IV, who is styled *dei gracia verus et indubitatus Rex istius Britanniae, Franciae et hispaniae.* At various points in the genealogy, the author copied some of the prophecies most pertinent to the house of York. The first text is the angel's message to Cadwaladr, including the conditions on which the Britons might return to power in their kingdom. Below this is a short verse, frequently encountered in fifteenth century manuscripts, which may be entirely a Yorkist creation, since it foretells quite specifically the end of Norman (i.e., Lancastrian) domination in 1460.[60] Among the remaining prophecies there is yet another which predicts British sovereignty, a very abbreviated version of the 'Six Kings' prophecy, and an account of the fate of Richard II and the eventual victory of his true heirs. The author also transcribed large portions from John of Bridlington, either to illustrate Edward III's right to the French crown or to transfer the glories promised to him and his son, the Black Prince, to their later namesake, Edward IV. The implications of these prophecies and Edward's pedigree are heightened by the coupling of the names of relevant figures in the genealogy with some of the names of rightful and usurping kings listed by this author in his three anthologies.

Another genealogy takes to much greater lengths the use of symbols to point its meaning.[61] There are three lines of descent; British, English and French. (The Spanish line is introduced later.) Under the heading of the British line, it is announced that according to Merlin, the Red Dragon signified the British people who would overcome the Saxons. We are told that the French kings are always called *Gallus* and there is a whole string of names by which the kings of England may be recognised. From the beginning, the appropriate names are attached to their owners. *Rubeus Draco*, the Red Dragon, parallels each descendant in the column of British princes, and *Gallus* likewise appears beside the French kings; whilst the English line is sometimes characterised by *Albus Draco* (the White Dragon) and sometimes by *Taurus* (the Bull). The outcome of the struggle between the two dragons is described, followed by the angel's prophecy to Cadwaladr. As the genealogy progresses, more cognomens are added, especially to the figures in the British line. By the time the names of Richard of York and Edward IV are reached, they have acquired an entire array of symbols connected with the British history and their rightful title to the English and French crowns. The point at which the true succession to the English crown becomes corrupted, namely, at the usurpation of Henry IV, is indicated by the transference of the symbols for lawful kings into the British line and the attachment to the Lancastrian line of all the appellations associated in prophecies with usurpers and oppressors. The French monarchy is similarly treated, *Gallus* passing first to Edward III and Richard II, and then to the Mortimers; subsequent French kings receive the names used for false rulers of their realm.

Propaganda of this nature — lengthy and detailed genealogies, collections of prophecies — could only have reached a restricted audience. Royal proclamations declaimed aloud, vernacular poetry, often publicly posted up and almost certainly repeated orally, might engage the attention of the majority of the king's subjects. The former dealt in simple and immediate terms with contemporary political concerns; the latter eulogised Yorkist heroes in memorable phrases and attractive imagery. The literature of pedigree and prophecy was something that had to be studied and pondered rather than taken in at a glance or a cursory reading. Vernacular literacy was becoming more widespread in the fifteenth century and straightforward biblical genealogies — especially the English texts — could be widely comprehended, but an appreciation of Latin prophecies was more likely to be the province of the well and formally educated. The message which these genealogies and prophecies declared was not vital to the security of the Yorkist dynasty, but it provided a background of historical and semi-learned argument through which the more thoughtful might realise and acknowledge the undeniable superiority of Edward IV's title to the throne. Their limited audience does not diminish the value of such texts as propaganda; the idea that propaganda must necessarily have a mass hearing is a modern conception. These Yorkist documents would have appealed to those whose support was of greatest practical importance to Edward IV, the nobility and gentry, and the increasingly educated commercial classes.

Notes

1. Charles Ross, *Edward IV* (London, 1974), pp. 30-33.
2. *Ibid.*, p. 28.
3. Two popular biblical genealogies of Henry VI are (1) a pedigree which begins with Noah (for example, B.M., Additional MS. 2732A and Lansdowne Roll 2; Bodleian Library, Bodleian Rolls 10 and MS. Marshall 135); and (2) a work ascribed to Roger of St. Albans, for whom see below pp. 173-4 (for example, B.M., Harley Roll T. 12 and Royal MS. 14BVIII; Lambeth Palace MS. 1171; John Rylands Library, Chronicle Roll 2; Queen's College, Oxford, MS. 168).
4. Lancastrian manuscripts of both the 'Noah' and 'Roger of St. Albans' genealogies were augmented in Edward IV's reign, often demonstrating a marked Yorkist bias. For example, Bodleian Library, MS. Marshall 135, Emmanuel College, Cambridge, MS. 231, and A. Wall (ẽd.), *Handbook to the Maude Roll, being a XVth century ms. genealogy of the British and English kings from Noah to Edward IV, with a marginal history* (Auckland, 1919).
5. *Catalogue of the collection of medieval manuscripts bequeathed to the Bodleain Library, Oxford, by James P. R. Lyell*, compiled by A. De La Mare (Oxford, 1971), pp. 80-83. Some manuscripts of the 'Long Latin' pedigree are B.M., Landsdowne MS. 456 and Harley Roll C9; St. John's College, Oxford, MS. 23; and of the 'Long English' pedigree, Bodleian Library, MS. Lyell 33, MS. E. Mus. 42, and Corpus Christi College MS. 207.
6. *Catalogue of Lyell manuscripts*, pp. 83, 84. For the 'Short Latin' pedigree, see B.M., Stowe MS. 72, and Bodleian Library, Brasenose College MS. 17; and for the 'Short English' pedigree, see B.M., Stowe MS. 73.
7. J. Bale, *Scriptorum illustrium maioris Brytannie, quam nunc Angliam et Scotiam vocant catalogus; a Iaphete per 3618 annos, usque ad annum hunc Domini 1557 . . . Basilea, Apud Ioannem Oporinum*, 1557-59 (2 volumes in 1), I, 94.

8. Two other genealogies with introductory passages are (1) a work which begins *Cuilibet principi congruum utile et honestum est* (Bodleian Library, Jesus College MS. 114); and (2) a very complex biblical genealogy, beginning *Veterum cronicorum narraciones ac sacre historie solacia* (Lambeth Palace MS. 1170, and Queen's College, Cambridge, MS. 22).

9. Roger of St. Albans produced his genealogy in both a biblical and a historical version: Bale, *op. cit.* One manuscript of the 'Long Latin' pedigree suggests that its scribe was working in part from a biblical version, since he forgot to extend the wording at the end of the introduction, which outlines the course of the genealogy, from Christ to Edward IV (St. John's College, Oxford, MS. 23).

10. *Dictionary of National Biography*, XLIX, 113.

11. For example, B.M., Lansdowne MS. 456 states that Henry Bolingbroke *incarceravit ricardum verum regem et heredem anglie et francie, eumque violenter deposuit . . . ipse et heredes sui coronas predictas usurparunt et occupaverunt iniuste;* and Bodleian Library, MS. Lyell 33 makes similar comments in English.

12. See below pp. 177-88.

13. H.J. Chaytor, *From Script to Print: an introduction to medieval vernacular literature* (London, 1976), pp. 17, 37; B. Boyd, *Chaucer and the medieval book* (San Marino, California, 1973), pp. 90, 93; K.L. Scott, 'A mid-fifteenth century English illuminator's shop and its customers', *Journal of the Courtauld and Warburg Institutes*, xxxi (1968), 170-96.

14. Bodleian Library, MS. E. Mus 42 and Corpus Christi College MS. 207.

15. The manuscripts can be dated by the number of Edward IV's children shown: B.M., Lansdowne MS. 456 (before the birth of Edward's first child Elizabeth in 1466 and perhaps even before Edward's coronation in June 1461, since the textual note only extends to his public acclamation on 4 March 1461); Copenhagen, Konelige Bibl. MS. Ny. Kgl. 1858 fol., noted in *Catalogue of Lyell manuscripts*, p. 83 (February 1466 — August 1467, after Elizabeth's birth on 11 February 1466); Yale University, MS. Marstone 242 noted in *Catalogue of Lyell manuscripts*, p. 82 (February 1466 — August 1467); Bodleian Library, MS. E Mus. 42 (August 1467 — March 1469, after Mary's birth in August 1467); Corpus Christi College MS. 207 (August 1467 — March 1469); MS. Lyell 33 (March 1469 — November 1470, after Cecily's birth on 20 March 1469); B.M., Harley Roll C9 (April 1472 — August 1473, after Edward's birth on 2 November 1470 and Margaret's in April 1472; this manuscript may have been written before Margaret's death in December 1472); St. John's College, Oxford, MS 23 (August 1473 — November 1475, after Richard's birth on 17 August 1473). C.L. Scofield, *The Life and reign of Edward IV* (2 volumes, Lonon, 1923; reprinted 1967), I, 393, 428, 482, 546; II, 27, 60.

16. *Catalogue of Lyell Manuscripts*, p. 82.

17. Of the extant manuscripts of these four types of Yorkist pedigree, six are rolls.

18. H.S. Bennett, 'The production and dissemination of vernacular manuscripts in the fifteenth century', *The Library*, fifth series, I (1946-47), 167-78.

19. The edition of the *Historia Regum Britanniae* used in this paper is that of A. Griscom (London, 1929).

20. L. Keeler, *Geoffrey of Monmouth and the Late Latin Chronicles, 1300-1500*

(Berkeley and Los Angeles, 1946) discusses many of the chronicles which used Geoffrey's *History* as a source.

21. C.L. Kingsford, *English historical literature in the fifteenth century* (Oxford, 1913, p. 113).

22. F.M. Powicke and E.B. Fryde (eds.) *Handbook of British Chronology* (second edition, London, 1961), pp. 48-49.

23. Both the 'Noah' and the 'Roger of St. Albans' genealogies show the descent of the Lancastrians from Woden.

24. Griscom, *op. cit.*, pp. 533-34.

25. G. Williams, 'Prophecy, Poetry and Politics in Medieval and Tudor Wales', in *British Government and Administration: Studies presented to S.B. Chrimes*, edited by Hearder and H.R. Loyn (Cardiff, 1974), p. 105.

26. Keeler, *op. cit.*, pp. 51, 60; Williams, *loc. cit.*

27. See below p. 184.

28. *Ingulph's chronicle of the Abbey of Croyland with continuations by Peter of Blois and anonymous writers*, translated by H.T. Riley (London, 1854), p. 446.

29. Griscom, *op. cit.*, pp. 348-97.

30. R Taylor, *The political prophecy in England* (New York, 1911; reprinted 1967), p. 24.

31. *Ibid.*, p. 4.

32. B.M., Cotton MS., Vespasian E.VII; Bodleian Library, Bodley MS. 623 and Ashmolean Roll 26 (to be cited hereafter as Vespasian E.VII, Bodley 623 and Ashmolean Roll 26).

33. Vespasian E.VII, f. 71; Bodley 623, ff. 71 and 71b.

34. This is a reference to the crowns of Britain, France and Spain. The French crown had been claimed by English kings since the reign of Edward III. The house of York had a title to the throne of Castile and Leon through the Spanish marriage of Edmund of Langley, duke of York.

35. In Ashmolean Roll 26, the two circles appear at the end of a genealogy of Edward IV from Louis IX of France which is on the back of the roll. The text inside the circle for rightful kings also includes some of the sentences discussed below on the divine nature of prophecy and on the eventual discovery and punishment of sins; see below pp. 181-2.

36. Vespasian E.VII, ff. 70b-71; Bodley 623, f. 18.

37. T. Wright, *Political poems and songs relating to English history* (2 volumes, Rolls Series, 1859), I, 123-215.

38. *Ibid.*, pp. 176, 179.

39. *Ibid.*, p. 179.

40. L.D. Duls, *Richard II in the Early Chronicles* (The Hague and Paris, 1975). pp 191-97.

41. Wright, *op. cit.*, I, 203-205.

42. *Ibid.*, p. 125.

43. *Ibid.*, p. 186.

44. Griscom, *op. cit.*, pp. 383-85; Vespasian E.VII, f, 80; Bodley 623, f. 83.

45. Griscom, *op. cit.*, p. 388; Vespasian E.VII, f. 117; Bodley 623, f. 84b.

46. Taylor, *op. cit.*, p. 89.

47. Vespasian E.VII, f. 85. For the earlier origins of the prophecies in this compilation, see Taylor, *op. cit.*, pp. 56-57; H.L.D. Ward, *Catalogue of*

Romances in the British Museum (3 volumes, London, 1883-1910; reprinted 1962), I, 307, 308, 317, 319; F.S. Haydon (ed.), *Eulogium Historiarum* (3 volumes, Rolls Series, 1858-63), I, 418-21.

48. Yorkist prophecies give the date of the return to British sovereignty as 1460. This may refer to the claim made to the throne by Richard of York in October of that year. It is more likely, however, to be the result of the method of dating used. It was fairly common practice in England at this time to date the beginning of the year from the Annunciation on 25 March; this would place Edward IV's accession in 1460. See C.R. Cheyney (ed.), *Handbook of Dates for Students of English history* (London, 1945), p. 5. In a chronology in Bodley 623 (ff. 37-70) the author calculated the years from the Creation to 5 Edward IV, which he took as 1464. He was thus counting the years of Edward IV's reign from 1460.

49. Griscom, *op. cit.*, pp. 533, 534.

50. Vespasian E.VII, ff. 80-81. In Bodley 623, this narrative of Cadwaladr's vision, or some part of it, appears five times: ff. 18b, 31b, 83b-84, 95b. See also Ashmolean Roll 26.

51. P. Zumthor, *Merlin le prophete* (Geneva, 1973), pp. 62-64, 71; T. Wright (ed.), *Chronicle of Pierre de Langtoft* (2 volumes, Rolls Series, 1866, 1868), I, 448-51; W. Stubbs (ed.), *Memoriale Walter de Coventria* (2 volumes, Rolls Series, 1872, 1873), I, 25, 26; W.F. Skene (ed.), 'Johannis de Fordum, Chronicis Gentis Scotorum' in *The Historians of Scotland* (10 volumes, Edinburgh, 1871-1880), I, 25, 26.

52. For example, *Memoriale Walter de Coventria*, I, 25, 26.

53. Taylor, *op. cit.*, pp. 48-50.

54. Vespasian E.VII, f. 89; Bodley 623, f. 86b.

55. Vespasian E.VII, f. 90b; Bodley 623, f. 88b.

56. When London was founded by Brutus, he gave it the name of New Troy, Griscom, *op. cit.*, p. 252.

57. Vespasian E.VII, f. 86b; Bodley 623, f. 76-76b. See also, M.E. Griffith, *Early Vaticination in Welsh* (Cardiff, 1937), pp. 15, 16.

58. Vespasian E.VII, f. 88; Bodley 623, f. 84, 84b.

59. College of Arms MS., Box 9, number 9.

60. See above n. 47.

61. B.M., Additional MS. 18268A.

The First English Standing Army? — Military Organisation in Lancastrian Normandy, 1420-1450[1]

Anne E. Curry
Lecturer in History
University of Reading

English military organisation in the later middle ages is still very much an unknown quantity. Sir Charles Oman scarcely mentions the English army in his chapter in the relevant volume of the *Cambridge Medieval History,* and both he and Ferdinand Lot are particularly weak on English military activities in the later part of the Hundred Years War.[2] It must be admitted that there is nothing in English to compare with Philippe Contamine's *Guerre, Etat et Société à la Fin du Moyen Age,* although some would argue, perhaps, that there are no equivalent phenomena to write about.[3] Where there has been some attempt to include an assessment of English military organisation, writers have been content to assume, for the most part, that the army which occupied Normandy and parts of France from 1417 to 1450 was organised along the same lines as those expeditionary forces with which Edward III had launched his attack on France in the fourteenth century.[4] The earlier period (superficially more significant, perhaps, because it marks the transition from the feudally to the contractually based army) has received the full historical treatment and has given rise to important and diverse studies.[5] There is no lack of research on the English in Normandy, but, except in the work of R.A. Newhall, the army has not been the subject of an independent and specialised study.[6]

It is clear that there were several fundamental differences between the campaigns of the fourteenth and those of the fifteenth centuries. Unlike the former, which were conducted by short lived expeditionary forces with little sustained conquest, the latter led to a lengthy occupation of Northern France, and were further complicated by the offensive commitment embodied in the Treaty of Troyes. This treaty also obliged the English to work through the existing French administrative structure, (although this requirement did not apply to military organisation and there is little evidence that French influences had any effect on the latter), because the English hold over France was intended to be one of just and acceptable possession and not of harsh, long term military occupation.[7] The problems of recruitment and organisation of the army, given such criteria and commitments, would be particularly grave. Whereas in the fourteenth century, for instance, it was rare for captains to be engaged in the war for more than one year continuously, the occupation demanded captains and troops to form what was effectively a standing army, albeit permanently stationed abroad.[8] The administration, pay, food and discipline of such an army over an extended period would produce problems of a scale not hitherto experienced by the English government.

In addition to assuming that this fifteenth-century army differed little from the expeditionary forces of the fourteenth century, many earlier works considered that there was very little change in the nature and organisation of the army of occupation over the period as a whole.[9] It is well known, however, that Bedford initiated certain reforms which placed the army more firmly under civil control, a move to be expected, perhaps, in the circumstances of an occupation whose military nature every attempt was made to disguise.[10] Given the extended duration of the occupation it could be expected that the army would change its nature, moving towards, perhaps, a more professional and bureaucratically organised force. In a successful occupation, the natural trend is likely to be towards formalisation, professionalisation and bureaucratisation of the occupying army: such developments are necessary, firstly, for the sake of the morale and efficiency of the troops themselves, and, secondly, for the sake of the civil population.[11] A study of the army in Lancastrian Normandy illustrates the care taken over both of these considerations.

Organisational models can be used to differentiate between the kinds of army in question. For instance, Weber distinguished three main types of organisation according to the ways in which authority within them was legitimised — charismatic, traditional and legal/rational.[12] The personalised army of the fourteenth century and, I would argue, of the early years of the occupation of Normandy would illustrate Weber's second category, being based upon the traditional authority of king and regent. A professional, bureaucratic army, such as we might expect to find developing during a long-term occupation, would demonstrate Weber's third category of legal/-rational authority. It would be increasingly skilful, being composed of men who were full time soldiers. Furthermore, it would possess a distinctive and formalised hierarchy, with a unified chain of command which controlled strategy and troop development. This army would be bound by impersonal ties and by a system of rules and procedures. It is my intention to examine whether the English army in Normandy did undergo such developments, and if so, whether this was the result of the deliberate policy of its commanders.

It must be pointed out, of course, that fourteenth-century armies were not devoid of certain of the above characteristics. Indeed the contractual army in itself was a move towards increasingly bureaucratic organisation, and by 1400, there was central control of booty division, prisoners and shipping, and, to a lesser extent, of weapons, pay and discipline.[13] From its origins, the war contract was never considered a purely private or commercial matter, for the recruitment of retinues of war to form an army was licensed and stimulated by royal orders, with the resulting forces coming under royal review.[14] But the prerequisite conditions for the development of military organisation as outlined above were more conspicuously present in Lancastrian Normandy and so it is necessary to look more closely at this army of occupation.

There is little to suggest that the armies of Henry V and of the early regency did not consist, like their fourteenth-century counterparts, of a collection of personal retinues with a high degree of cohesiveness within themselves but with very little interdependence with other retinues. In the conquest of Normandy, the captain was appointed, admittedly at royal command, to the control of the garrison, but the number of his retinue to serve there and the conditions of such service were dictated by the captain himself in consequence of the already established size and nature of his personally recruited force.[15] The indentures entered into between the captains and the king or regent demonstrate the relative absence of central control: only with regard to prisoners, gains of war and mustering was there any surveillance of the captain and his garrison.[16] However, control over these activities was increased by the powers of the newly instituted seneschal of Normandy.[17]

The overridingly personal nature of the army of occupation in the early stages of the war can be seen at two levels, firstly in the relationship between the captains and their men, and secondly in the relationship between the captains (and consequently their retinues) and Henry V and Bedford. This first relationship provided the basic social and administrative structure of the army in the early years of occupation. Once the military structure had been conceived in such a way, all efforts were directed towards maintaining and strengthening the pre-existing personal relationship between the captain and his men. Although the ordinances of Henry V stressed the powers of the king and his officers, the captain was always to be the first stage of complaint and punishment, and in any case, the king relied on the captains for the publication of such ordinances.[18] Once the occupation was more firmly established, soldiers were forbidden to leave their original captain.[19] For armies on the move, the captain's power was supreme.[20]

The second level of relationship was nothing new. The importance of the royal household in the Agincourt campaign was but a reflection of a similar situation in the fourteenth century, and was echoed again in the campaign of 1475.[21] The situation after 1422 was, however, to some extent quite novel. The Duke of Bedford was given quasi-regal powers in France which were not challenged until the King's visit of 1430-1432.[22] These powers were wide and varied and had especially great repercussions on military organisation and personnel.[23] To a great extent, the army in Normandy and the Pays de Conquête during his regency was regarded as his personal retinue, and most certainly his household figured prominently in the occupation, along with those whose connections with him were no less real if less formal.[24] Indeed all captains indented directly with him and were paid at his orders. He controlled the distribution of grants from the conquered lands, and, with the French council, had begun already to exercise some control over the agglomeration of retinues which formed the army.[25]

Bedford's intention — and in this he was presumably following the example of his royal brother whilst expanding trends initiated by the latter — was to establish a personally based army over which he held supreme control. In years of conquest he was ready to assign certain areas to other commanders with both military and administrative responsibilities but this did not destroy the personalised system. Early field armies tended to be made up of men of a particular and distinctive group.[26] When men in such groups brought about specific English successes, they reaped the principal rewards of the same in the form of grants of land.[27] In addition, captains and their retinues frequently received lands in the locality of their service: such men were intended to form the core of the occupation, being intended not only to continue to form the backbone of the English army in France but also the basis of English settlement.[28] As well as their less predictable yet valuable function as an incentive towards recruitment and continuing service, grants were made with the important rider that the recipient should be obliged firstly to defend his own property, and secondly, to provide a stated number of troops when necessary to defend the lands in English hands in particular or in general, without pay.[29] Royal garrisons could thus be few in number and contain the minimum number of paid troops. Once a core of settlers had been established, each with an interest in maintaining English supremacy, then the defensive force at least could be provided by them. This force would be locally based, informally organised, and for the most part non-mobile, and would, it was hoped, prove adequate if combined with the obligation placed upon the local French as well as English population to provide 'guet et garde'.[30] The English tried to avoid the need for a large, formal, paid army of occupation, not just for financial reasons but also to achieve the desire of just and acceptable possession, in appearance at least.

To recapture the areas still under Dauphinist control, however, required a larger, formal field army which could be recruited most easily along the lines of the expeditionary forces of the fourteenth century, based upon contract and personal connection. These field armies were recruited in England in the early years of the occupation and were intended to provide service for a limited period and then to return home. Such troops would not receive an interest in the occupation but their use would prove strategically preferable to the use of garrison detachments and more professional than forces serving by virtue of feudal obligation.[31] A definite and important distinction was drawn, therefore, between garrison and field forces. Further emergency or temporary field forces would be provided by the local population as a whole, English and French, by the publication of the 'ban' and 'arrière-ban'.[32]

Bedford's original plan seems to have been to create a system of defence in France (and especially in the Duchy of Normandy which was always the lynch pin of the English position) which did not require a large and expensive standing English army of occupation. Although his own power was paramount, his system left considerable initiative and responsiblity in the hands of both the captains and the local population. From hindsight, it is clear that his intention could not be realised, although the circumstances of the early occupation may have made it possible temporarily. But future military and administrative demands proved such that there needed to be a reworking and adaptation of his system which would establish a professional army within his lifetime. Certainly military circumstances were much changed after the failure to take Orleans, and thereafter, due to increasing pressure from Charles VII and to growing antagonism from the local population, the English were forced to maintain a much more rigorous and formal defensive control over Normandy and the Pays de Conquête. After the rising in the Pays de Caux in 1435 and the defection of the Duke of Burgundy with the subsequent loss of Paris and the Ile de France, the English were forced completely onto the defensive (with the exception of piecemeal offensives in an attempt to recover what they had lost), and could not hope to extend the area under their control beyond Normandy and parts of Maine.

Field armies which were larger, more mobile and which could offer service of longer duration were required at every stage, even when stress was placed upon defence. This made it necessary to send reinforcements from England almost every year, because military resources in Normandy were inadequate One reason for this was the above mentioned change in strategic demands. A second reason was that the system of feudal obligation envisaged by Henry V and Bedford had failed. Although fiefs remained in the hands of the English right to the end of the occupation, it proved impossible to enforce the requirement of residence and of providing troops.[33] The English council lamented in April 1429 that the non-fulfilment of such obligations had led to the need to send larger, more frequent and hence more expensive armies from England, an indication, perhaps, that Bedford's ideal was widely supported.[34]

Settlement policy may have worked to the disadvantage of recruitment and military service. Property allocation had given soldiers an interest in a specific locality outside which they may have been reluctant to serve. This could explain why it proved so difficult to realise the numbers of garrison detachments ordered from time to time to serve in the field.[35] Furthermore, as the war continued, estates granted to the English devalued, which may have rendered their possessors unable to afford the burden of meeting their feudal obligation.[36] The attempt to impose neo-feudalism proved unpopular when demands for service showed no signs of abating. There was growing reluctance, too, on the part of the local population to provide the service of 'guet et garde', so that responsibility for the watch had to be placed upon the paid garrisons.[37] Certainly there were few attempts after 1435 to call the Norman population to arms, and even before then, some feudal summons specifically excluded French and Norman fief holders.[38] After 1435, there was a fundamental change in settlement policy, when English captains were rewarded with pensions rather than land, thus further undermining the possiblity of a feudal army of occupation.[39] This change in policy was probably due to the necessity to buy Norman support by the restoration of lands to the dispossessed. Certainly even Bedford cooled down his policy of granting properties to the English in the later years of his regency. He may have realised, too, the military inadequacy of feudal obligation, and so turned towards a more formal, paid army of occupation. So the two elements, settlement and military service, originally conceived as complementary, if not interchangeable, were discovered to be incompatible.

The constant but necessary influx of new men in armies from England challenged the permanency of the core as established by Bedford. It can be seen that personal connections in such reinforcements would become increasingly loose.[40] Return to England was increasingly difficult or less attractive, thus leaving many surplus and unattached troops in Normandy. At the end of their contract, they were left, leaderless and wageless, and constituted a blight on military organisation and upon the English presence as a whole.[41] In addition, the loss of garrisons in the Pays de Caux, the Ile de France, and later Maine created a further surplus of disorganised manpower which may have provided a keener problem than ever shortage or manpower was to create. There must have been a considerable number of ex-soldiers who were now 'of no garrisons or retinues' and who were 'vivans sur le pays': the presence of these unattached troops was at its worst by 1437.[42] Another factor which weakened the all important personal connection was the increasing use of garrison detachments as field forces, especially during and after the siege of Orleans: indeed, indentures after Orleans gave the Regent and council a formal right to call out such troops.[43] When such detachments had been used in field forces in the early years of the occupation, precautions had been taken to ensure that an adequate garrison remained behind for defence, but such care was not a characteristic of later years when garrisons were severely depleted by withdrawal of troops for field service.[44] Additional troops, 'creus', installed in garrisons after Orleans, were made up of men not attached to the captain and constituted a further threat to the cohesive force of the personal relationship between the captain and his troops. Newhall suggests that these 'creus' were made up initially of soldiers who had fled from the battle of Patay and that they were a conscious attempt to reabsorb such men in the retinue structure, whilst also meeting a strategic need.[45] If he is correct, then this demonstrates how slow the English were to abandon the traditional form of military organisation even when it was proved to be militarily inadequate.

It may have been that there was an increasing reluctance to be tied to retinues at all when there appeared to be more lucrative and easily obtainable opportunities for self-aggrandisement outside the formal organisation of retinues. The system of the division of spoils can only have worked and have been seen to be working to the detriment of the lower ranks, especially when Bedford's ordinances gave increased control to the local population. Overall, the rank and file military population became too volatile a body: it is significant that, whereas under Bedford captains had indented on a yearly basis, in later years they indented to serve for longer and longer periods, even life; their troops, however, continued to serve on a quarterly basis, and although there are instances of relatively continuous service, many retinues show a three-monthly turnover.[46] In this way, too, a greater gulf developed between the captains and their troops. Desertion was a problem as early as 1421, but by 1429, guards had to be posted at ports to prevent soldiers crossing to England before the end of their contract. Similar precautions were taken in 1439 to ensure that none slipped away illegally under the guise of escorting the body of the Earl of Warwick back to England.[47]

Even within Bedford's lifetime, it became impossible to rely on the basic control exercised by captains over their troops in the vital area of military discipline. The protection offered to the civil population took the form of the establishment of civil supremacy over the military.[48] This was easily extended to complete governmental control over the army, which began in the crisis following Orleans and continued to the late 1430's, although with what appears to have been decreasing success.[49] This did not, of course, mean the complete overturning of the personal system: the disciplinary ordinances still called for the maintenance of strong personal control by the captains, and a weakness remained in that only those soldiers who were attached to a captain could be controlled by the disciplinary system. The development of the terms in indentures demonstrates the desire to control as many aspects of the military establishment as possible.[50] The control of personnel reflects increasing professionalisation as a result of central control, and marks a considerable change in the concept of what the army should be. This change was brought about by ordinances published after Orleans which precluded certain categories of men from service in the army. For instance, the recruitment of those who held lands, or were involved in a craft, or were merchants was forbidden.[51] The first restriction at least was in direct contradiction of the earlier policies of Henry V and Bedford. There is some indication that the motive behind such a volte-face was financial, for musters indicate that those in forbidden categories did continue to serve as soldiers although the authorities tried to ensure that they received no pay.[52] However, as the financial crisis had not reached very serious proportions in the early 1430's, it is tempting to see this regulation as part of an attempt to create a more professional army of occupation. It is interesting that these restrictions on personnel were confirmed in contemporary military theory.[53]

A further restriction placed upon military personnel after Orleans was that limiting the proportion of French who could serve in a retinue. Under the indentures of September 1430, captains agreed not to have more than half their lances French, and to have all their archers English, Irish, Welsh or Gascon, not to recruit their retinues in the neighbourhood and to maintain the standard ratio of three archers to one lance.[54] These restrictions were imposed by the English council now in France with the King, and were launched in great secrecy, an indication, perhaps, of their anticipated unpopularity with English captains and Norman soldiers.[55] In 1434, the provisos were modified to permit one-eighth of the entire retinue to be French, although there is much to suggest that this was ignored in later years by indiscrimate recruitment of the native population, and by failure to ascertain or record nationality in the muster rolls.[56]

All restrictions on personnel indicate the increasingly military nature of the occupation, a development brought about by a fundamental change in English policy after the failure to take Orleans. This change is revealed in other areas of military activity, for example in the appointments of Scales as seneschal and Talbot as marshal in c. August 1435 and May 1436 respectively. Although the nature and purpose of these appointments are still in some doubt, it is clear at least that these officers were intended henceforward as purely military commanders and not as quasi-civil administrators.[57] As a result of the activities of such men and of other field commanders (whose importance increased after the death of Bedford and who were especially strong during the period of 1435 to 1441), the deployment of forces was controlled from the centre. This was necessary especially in the years after 1435 when military needs led to an increase in the number of field armies and to more being in service at the same time. From 1438 onwards, too, there was a conscious and centrally directed effort to use in field armies those unattached soldiers who were found living off the land and who constituted a public nuisance as well as a classic case of military wastage.[58] Further professionalism on the military side is seen in the growth and significance of the group of lieutenants (which included such men as Thomas Gower, Maykin Longworth and John Burgh) who were specialists in war and who acted for many captains who were absentee or not themselves sufficiently professional. Overall, then, there was a perceptible and intentional move away from the traditional system of the early occupation towards an army under central control, with an established hierarchy of command, increasing professionalism, and an attempt at the best use of the military resources available.

The chronology of this change is difficult to establish. Indeed, the frequent inability to put a date to specific incidents as well as to general trends has been apparent in this study. It could be argued that the major turning point was the death of Bedford, and, as we shall see, this was indeed an important time. But certainly, several significant changes in orientation had occurred within his lifetime. Developments before 1430, including the formalisation of the system of muster and review itself, were at his behest, but it may be that the more significant changes from 1430 onwards were not instituted by him. Certainly his previously unassailable powers were being threatened at this time. The failure to take Orleans was more than just a strategic turning point, and even though Bedford had advised against the campaign — it is significant, perhaps, that his military leadership had been challenged and defeated by Salisbury and presumably by both the French and English councils — he suffered the acrimony of the defeat.[59] His position was weakened further by the royal visit of 1430 to 1432, when he surrendered the regency.[60] There is evidence that the men of his connection suffered a similar eclipse in these years, to the advantage of Cardinal Beaufort and his nominees.[61] The English council had discussed the preparations for this visit most thoroughly, including the military aspect of it, although it was little more than a show campaign.[62] When in France, they again involved themselves very closely in the question of the army, bringing about the regulations mentioned above. In addition, they began an investigation into the alleged oppression of the civilian population in Normandy by soldiers.[63] They also experimented briefly with the method of payment of the troops, paying them directly instead of through their captains.[64] This was surely an attempt at central, bureaucratic control which threatened the power of the captain and hence the nature of the army as a collection of separate retinues. It appears, then, that much of the change in attitude towards the army, with the resultant changes in use, was the result of decisions taken by the English council. The post-1435 period would seem to add extra weight to this hypothesis.

Bedford's powers were restored after the royal visit, but his death removed the foundation of what was left of the traditional system.[65] It also raised two fundamental questions, both of which remained areas of contention to the end of the occupation, and were closely tied up, as is well known, with English domestic politics of the 1430's and 40's. These questions concerned firstly, who should replace Bedford and, secondly, the future conduct of the war. In 1435 there was no question but that both these matters should be settled by the council in England. It was to this body that Sir John Fastolf addressed his suggestions.[66] In answer to the first question, he advocated that there should be two lieutenants for the field who would serve on a yearly basis and be answerable to the English council, and that an exclusively English council should replace Bedford's predominantly French council in Normandy. In answer to the second, he urged that the garrison system should be preserved, and that a separate and permanent field force be kept on the borders of Brittany, Anjou and Maine which could be used to reinforce the garrisons as required. This was a strategic plan along the lines already established by Bedford, although Fastolf broke with his previous master when he urged an end to wasteful siege warfare. The council followed his advice on Bedford's successor, if not on the future conduct of the war. The first tentative replacement for Bedford, the Duke of York, was appointed for one year only. Having established its prominence in 1435, the council determined the conditions under which York and later Warwick, also their appointee, should serve: in both cases they were substantially less than those held by Bedford, thus leaving many important powers in the hands of the council.[67] Certainly the years from 1435 to 1441 see the continual involvement of and interference by the latter in matters concerning the government of Normandy and the army of occupation, conducted largely through the sending of special representatives.[68]

It would have been impossible, however, to conduct a war from England, whatever the ambitions of the council and its individual members. Spheres of authority in Normandy during these years were very confusing and could have contributed to the military indecision and failure of the time. This was especially true in the years of interregnum between the appointments of lieutenants general. The Chancellor, Louis of Luxembourg, maintained some prominence, given the inexperience of York and the illness of Warwick, but his dealings with the English council again point to the prominence of the latter and his own desire to comply with their wishes.[69] On other occasions we can see decisions being taken in Normandy by the field commanders themselves.[70]

The years from 1435 to 1441 probably offered the best opportunity for the establishment of a professional standing army independent of one man's personal control, given the involvement of the English council and the prospect of cooperative command in Normandy. Indeed, in many respects the army came closest to meriting this description at this time, but never met the criteria completely. Confusion in the spheres of command may have handicapped the process, as did the general feeling of defeat, the impending peace negotiations, and the increasing financial problems. It is difficult to assess the nature of the army in 1440-1. Conclusions depend to a large extent upon the historian's interpretation of the parliamentary statute of November 1439 which made the leaving of one's retinue during the term of indenture a felony which could be punished by the civil authorities.[71] Newhall sees it symptomatic of a change towards 'a modern conception of an army', and indeed the degree of civil control imposed fits in with the general trend towards a professional army as an organ of government.[72] The statute recognised the performance of a private contract as a public duty, says Newhall, but it is difficult to see to what extent the indenture was still a private contract in 1439. On the other hand, the statute can be seen as an attempt to move back to a personalised system, by stressing the bond which ought to exist between captain and soldier and sanctioning its maintenance with the aid of state-controlled methods of enforcement. In the light of this and of events after 1441 it may be that the English found it impossible to move completely away from the traditional form of military organisation.

It is clear that York was prepared to take up his second term of office only with enhanced conditions and wider powers which approximated more closely to those of Bedford.[73] From the researches of Anne Marshall, we know that York, during this term, made a positive attempt to build up a strong circle of personal connections in Normandy, by distributing offices and military commands amongst his supporters and amongst certain veterans of the war whom he now took formally into his service.[74] This was certainly the first attempt to create anything like the Bedford system of personal connection. York further developed the idea of military occupation by a foreign power by the anglicisation of his council in France and of civil and military administration in general.[75] It may be that York's policies worked against the developments of the previous five or six years and created some degree of tension between the conflicting elements of central control and patronage in the army. He may also have tried to loosen the control of the English council. Certainly he and the latter, still anxious to maintain such control, were out of step on several occasions. He can only have resented their continuing interference, which included criticism of his complaints of shortage of money and troops, and culminated in the sending of Somerset with an army and dubious powers in 1443.[76] The council played an active role in the recruitment and organisation of this 1443 army, and countenanced the development of the Beaufort party, which was given many rewards at this time, again reminiscent of those given to the Bedford connection twenty years earlier.[77] When Edmund Beaufort became lieutenant general in 1447, the Beaufort party achieved a stranglehold over military organisation in Normandy.[78] With the re-establishment of personal connection, the Duchy had become the seed bed of faction between two conflicting groups: this demonstrates that the personal system of military organisation could only work when one person was in supreme control. Both York and the Beauforts suffered from the continuing reliance of the council on Suffolk, and from the growing gulf between the personnel of the council and the personnel of the occupation.[79] The struggle for power in England and Normandy was at the expense of discipline in the Norman garrisons, and of Norman finances: even Somerset, himself an arch-protagonist and previously a supporter of conciliar intervention admitted this in the cold light of experience.[80]

The effects of this conflict on military organisation in Normandy were disastrous indeed. Overall confusion as to who controlled the army led to no control at all. Towards the end of the war, payments of wages to captains and their troops, always a problem, became increasingly irregular: this suggests the final breakdown of the bureaucratic system.[81] Captains could continue to impose loyalty by other means, and indeed had probably increased their personal hold over troops in the last years of the occupation in order to fill the vacuum left by the lack of effective central control in Normandy.[82] The government, no matter how large and strong the clientele of its lieutenant governor nor the degree of its centralising efforts,

208

could only control the army, in the last resort, by financial remuneration. When this failed, then the whole system fell into jeopardy. In the last years of the war, there was less opportunity for plunder and legitimate gains of war and so proportionately more need for the regular payment of wages. The lack of central military control was significant in the reconquest. Indeed, it can be seen that the final defeat was due rather to disorganisation than to shortage of manpower. Royal garrisons, now the only effective military force in the Duchy, were left to work out their own action, under the command of their captains, with little, if any, central directive. Hence some fortresses held out longer than others, even after Somerset's own surrender at Rouen. Defeat, like the initial conquest, was conducted in purely personal terms.

A study of the army in Lancastrian Normandy reveals the inability of the fifteenth-century English mind to conceive of anything other than a personal system. The failure to establish a professional and bureaucratically controlled army, at a time which afforded a good opportunity to do so, illustrates the final victory of patronage. The Wars of the Roses were fought by armies recruited in the traditional manner: the expedition to France in 1475 was with an army raised and organised along personal lines.[83] Indeed, English military organisation lagged behind that of the rest of Europe in the later fifteenth and sixteenth centuries. Whereas France, Italy and Spain established state controlled armies, efficiently run and of high military calibre, the English continued to maintain a 'medieval' system which proved inadequate for the demands of 'modern' warfare.

Notes

1. This paper, originally a communication presented at the Bristol colloquium, provides some initial conclusions of research carried out during my tenure of a research assistantship at Teesside Polytechnic. I am grateful to Dr. A.J. Pollard of the Polytechnic and to Dr. C.T. Allmand of the University of Liverpool both for their comments on this paper and for their overall guidance and support in my research.
2. *Cambridge Medieval History*, Vol. 8, ed. C.W. Previté-Orton and Z.N. Brooke, (1969), Chapter 21.
    C.W. Oman, *A History of the Art of War in the Middle Ages, II, 1278-1485*, (London, 1924, reissued 1959).
    F. Lot, *L'art militaire et les armées au moyen âge, en Europe et dans le Proche Orient*, 2 vols., (Paris, 1946).
3. P. Contmine, *Guerre, Etat et Société à la Fin du Moyen Age, Etudes sur les Armés des Rois de France, 1337-1494*, (Paris, 1972). The lack of secondary material on English military organisation in the medieval period is revealed in R. Higham, *A Guide to the Sources of Military History*, (Berkeley, 1971), pp. 43-64.
4. For instance, see M. Powicke, *Military Obligation in Medieval England*, (Oxford, 1962).
5. See the works of H.J. Hewitt, A.E. Prince and J.W. Sherborne, mentioned in the bibliography of C.T. Allamand, *Society at War*, (Edinburgh, 1973), pp. 201-202.
6. The most important works are Newhall's *The English Conquest of Normandy, 1416-1424*, (Newhaven and London, 1924), henceforward referred to as *Conquest*, and *Muster and Review*, (Harvard, 1940), henceforward referred to by its title. There are four unpublished theses which contain valuable work on certain aspects of the army:
    B.J.H. Rowe, *John Duke of Bedford as regent of France, his policy and administration in the North*, (Oxford B. Litt, 1928) (Rowe), E.M. Burney, *The English Rule in Normandy, 1435-1450*, (Oxford B. Litt, 1958) *(Burney)*, A.E. Marshall, *The role of English war captains in England and Normandy, 1436-1461*, (Wales, M.A. 1975) *(Marshall)*, and A.J. Pollard, *The family of Talbot, Lords Talbot and Earls of Shrewsbury in the fifteenth century*, (Bristol Ph.D. 1968) *(Pollard)*. Another most important work is C.T. Allmand, 'The Lancastrian Land Settlement in Normandy, 1417-1450', *Economic History Review*, 2nd series, vol. 21, (1968) *(Allmand)*.
7. See R.A. Newhall, 'Henry V's policy of conciliation in Normandy', in *Anniversary Essays in Medieval History by students of C.H. Haskins*, (Boston, 1929).
8. For the fourteenth century see in particular J.W. Sherborne, 'Indentured retinues and the English expeditions to France, 1368-1380', *English Historical Review*, vol. 79, (1964).
9. Newhall's *Muster and Review* is particularly weak on the period after 1435.
10. See below p. 197.
11. S. Andreski, *Military Organization and Society*, (London, 1954, 2nd edition 1968), pp. 30, 34.
12. M. Weber, *The Theory of Social and Economic Organization*, (London, 1947, English translation) and also ed. D.S. Pugh, *Organization Theory*, (London, 1971), and *Writers on Organizations*, (London, 1962).

210

13. D. Hay, 'The division of spoils of war in fourteenth century England', *Transactions of the Royal Historical Society*, 5th series, vol. 4, (1954). Edward III issued some disciplinary ordinances but these were limited to the non-violation of churches and the like. H.J. Hewitt, *The Organization of War under Edward III, 1338-1362*, (Manchester and New York, 1966), p. 97, n. 1.

14. M. Powicke, *op.cit.* p. 186.

15. *Conquest*, ch. 5. Sir John Gray of Ruthin was appointed during royal pleasure to the captaincy of Gournay, but the relevant indenture, dated 23 December, 1420, did not lay down any regulations for the size of his garrison. ed. L. Puisieux, 'Roles normands et français et autres pièces tirées des archives de Londres par Bréquigny en 1764, 1765, 1766', *Mémoires de la Société des Antiquaires de Normandie*, vol. 23, (1858), (Bréquigny), pièce no. 889.

16. *Muster and Review*, p. 4, n. 1.

17. These powers are detailed in the appointment of Richard Woodville dated 18 January 1421. *Bréquigny*, pièce no. 924.

18. For a list of the printed editions of these 1419 ordinances see F.P. Barnard (ed.) *The Essential Portions of Nicholas Upton's De Studio Militari before 1446*, (Oxford, 1931), p. 60. 37.

19. *Bréquigny*, pièce no. 995 (1421). The solution to the problem of men who were, for one reason or another, of no retinue was their forcible reattachment to a captain. *Bréquigny*, pièce no. 1039.

20. See the ordinances made by the Earl of Salisbury. N.H. Nicolas, *History of the Battle of Agincourt*, (London, 1827), Appendix, p. 41.

21. N.H. Nicolas, *op.cit.* p. 333-364, 373-389. J.W. Sherborne, *op.cit.* p. 720. J. Lander, *Crown and Nobility, 1450-1509*, (London, 1976), p. 238 and Appendix E.

22. *Rot.Parl.* vol. 4, p. 171. *P.O.P.C.* vol. 3, p. 247. See below p. 204.

23. In general, see *Muster and Review*, p. 28. A. Burne, *The Agincourt War*, (London, 1956), p. 219, postulates that there was a complete standstill in the war when Bedford was in England from Dec. 1425 to April 1427. Military appointments made by Warwick, Salisbury and Suffolk during this absence were only provisional and needed confirmation by Bedford. (Archives Nationales Xia 8603 f. 90, *Rowe*, p. 87.) The minority of Henry VI required many of those previously active in France under Henry V to remain in England. Warwick, for instance, was tutor to the king and compelled to remain about his person. (*P.O.P.C.* vol. 3, pp. 294, 296, 300. *Marshall*, p. 24 sq.). Lord Hungerford agreed to go to France with Exeter in 1423, but needed first to be discharged from the duties imposed upon him by the terms of the late king's will. (*P.O.P.C.* vol. 3, p. 37). He remained titular captain of Cherbourg, but remained in England as a regular councillor. When there was a threat to Cherbourg in 1427 he again needed the council's permission to proceed there. (*P.O.P.C.* vol. 3, p. 230).

24. His household was, to some extent, a military establishment. J. Stevenson, *Letters and Papers Illustrative of the Wars of the English in France during the Reign of Henry VI*, (Stevenson), Rolls Series, (London, 1861-4), vol. 2 pt. 2, p. 540, 560. The members of his household and their captaincies are listed in *Stevenson*, vol. 2 pt. 2, p. 434 sq. although it is difficult to distinguish between those who were actually 'nobles of the household and retynew in fees, wages and

pencions' and those who were not. Certainly more research on the Bedford 'connection' would be most useful; it may well be that Bedford fits in with Holmes' and McFarlane's picture of the use of private indentures of retainer as the basis of contract armies. (*Pollard*, 251). To quote but a few random examples, Thomas Maistresson, his esquire, was also bailli of Caux and was involved in arrangements for the Duke's marriage in 1423. (B.L. Additional Charters, (Add.Ch.) 11,599, 7,933). John Fastolf, grand master of his household, was also governor of Anjou and Maine (*Rowe*, p. 50), 'governeur et supervéeur de toutes les villes, chasteaulx, forteresses, et pays subgiez au roy es bailliages de Rouen', in 1424, (Bibliothèque Nationale, manuscrits français (ms. fr.) 26047/200) and held several important garrisons and field commands.

25. *Rowe*, p. 83, 83a.

26. The Bedford 'group' was — not surprisingly considering Bedford's own territorial possessions — prominent in the Maine campaigns, (*Stevenson*, vol. 2, pt. 2, p. 553) as was the personal retinue of the Earl of Salisbury, (B.L. Add.Ch. 94).

27. See *Allmand*, p. 466 and *Stevenson*, vol. 2 pt. 2, pp. 550-1, for grants of land made after Verneuil. The Bedford connection figure prominently in the recipients. (Archives Nationales, Collection Dom Lenoir, vol. 21 passim). Indeed, his household were granted many valuable fiefs. Thomas Maistresson held lands in the baillliages of Rouen, Caux, Gisors, Mantes and Vexin. (Dom Lenoir, vol. 42, f. 415). Thomas Repston, Bedford's third chamberlain, held the seigneuries of Ventes and Bellencombre, (B.L., Egerton Charter, 166). Rempston received further favour by virtue of his connection in negotiations for his release from French captivity, (*P.O.P.C.* vol. 4, p. 109 sq.).

28. This can be seen in the cases of Rouen and Caen where local tabellionage records exist, and is the subject of further research. (Archives Départementales de la Seine Maritime, Rouen, and Archives Départementales du Calvados, Caen, Serie 7E).

29. In general, see *Allmand*, p. 461-5, and *Burney*, p. 220 sq. The Greys were granted the comté of Tancarville and were thus responsible for the defence of the castle of Tancarville and for the payment of its captain and garrison. (Archives Départementales de la Seine Maritime, Série E, unclassified). John Popham, granted the fortress and seigneurie of Thorigny, had to provide one man at arms and three archers to ride with the king in wartime at his own costs, and was also responsible for defence of the castle of Caen. (Dom Lenoir, vol. 74, f. 393). Many grants made to men at arms and archers were small and piecemeal, (e.g. houses in Caen, Harfleur, Honfleur and Cherbourg — possibly the *maisons fortes* of Add.Ch. 12,649), and were intended to be lived in. Restrictions were indeed placed upon return to England for those holding lands; the defensive system demanded residence. (*Bréquigny*, pièce 1052, November 1421, and, for a specific example, Dom Lenoir vol. 42, f. 417). See below n. 33.

30. This obligation was enforced early in the occupation. e.g. letter from the bailli of Rouen to those responsible for the watch at the chateau of Courtonne, 1422, ed. Lechaudé d'Anisy, *Extraits de chartes etc. qui se trouvent dans les archives du Calvados*, (Caen, 1834), vol. 2, p. 2. See below n. 37.

31. See below p. 8. For the obligation placed upon such armies to return home at the end of their contract, see the indenture in *Stevenson*, vol. 1, pp. 405 sq.

32. See *Stevenson*, vol. 2, pp. 24-28.
33. Walter Hungerford's absence from his captaincy has already been noted. See above no. 23. He had also been granted the seigneurie of Bréauté, the fortress of Neuvill and a house in Rouen, and was to provide 15 soldiers in wartime and to guard the castle of Rouen as required. (Dom Lenoir vol. 74, f. 339). His absence would make this difficult. *Burney*, p. 254 notes increasing absences in the later years of the war.
34. *P.O.P.C.*, vol. 3, p. 349.
35. For instance, fifty of Somerset's garrison of Avranches were called out for field service in June 1442, but only fifteen turned out. (B.L. Birch Ms. 4101, f. 50).
36. *Allmand*, pp. 471, 473.
37. The parties mentioned above (n.30) as responsible for the watch at the Chateau of Courtonne were, in 1448, refusing to fulfil their obligation. (Lechaudé d'Anisy, *op.cit.* p. 22). In 1438 retinues of Treasury officials were used to reinforce the watch at Rouen. (Archives Nationales, Série K, 64/23/3). The obligation was frequently commuted for a money payment. R.A. Newhall, 'Bedford's ordinance on the watch of September 1428', *English Historical Review*, vol. 50, (1935).
38. *Muster and Review*, p. 114.
39. *Burney*, p. 86.
40. *Pollard*, pp. 262-3, 265, 273. *Burney*, p. 193.
41. See below n. 58.
42. *Burney*, pp. 193-4.
43. L. Jarry, *Le compte de l'armée anglaise au siège d'Orléans, 1428-1429*, (Orleans, 1892), pp. 172-193.
44. *Stevenson*, vol. 2, pt. 1, p. 40. For the siege of Tancarville, the Duke of York had to call out 300 lances and 900 archers from the garrisons: it is difficult to see how they could provide such a number without weakening the defensive structure. (B.L. Add. Ch. 1176, *Muster and Review*, p. 143-144.).
45, *Muster and Review*, p. 111, 127.
46. The conclusion on indentures of captains is based upon a study of these documents in the Additional Charters. For the turnover rate in the ranks of Talbot's troops, see *Pollard*, p. 279. I am investigating the question of turnover in several other retinues and garrisons.
47. *Bréquigny*, pièce no. 1039. Bibliothèque Nationale, quittances et pièces diverses, ms. fr. 26052/1130. Archives Départementales de la Seine Maritime, Fonds Danquin, 11/87,88.
48. The relevant ordinances have been studied most adequately in the works of B.J.H. Rowe. *Rowe*, ch. 6, and 'Discipline in the Norman Garrisons under the Duke of Bedford', *English Historical Review*, vol. 46, (1932). See also R.A. Newhall, 'Bedford's ordinance on the watch of September 1428', *English Historical Review*, vol. 50, (1935).
49. For instance, the system of mustering, *Muster and Review*, p. 45-6, the introduction of the commissioned rather than indentured controller, *Ibid*, pp. 55-63. After Orleans, the government took up the right to determine the size of the garrison, *Ibid.* p. 65, and could order the captain to increase or decrease the size of his retinue, *Ibid.* p. 129. On the period after 1435, *Ibid.* pp. 133 sq. although more work is certainly needed on the later years.

50. *Rowe*, ch. 6. *Muster and Review*, passim. This is also the subject of future study.
51. *Muster and Review*, pp. 114-5.
52. See, for instance, the petition of Stephen Drop, a barber, who had been serving as an archer in the garrison of Rouen, protesting against non-payment of wages. Archives Départementales de la Seine Maritime, Fonds Danquin, 9/D(1447-1448).
53. *F.P. Barnard, op.cit;* Nicholas Upton writes 'furthermore men of war be in such a restraint that they ought not to meddle with tilling or ploughing of lands nor keeping of beasts, nor occupying of merchandise, or other man's business. Also they ought to buy no lands for the time that they use war, neither in their own name, neither in any other man's: nor yet to be bound to any business of the cities they be of, and if they buy any lands at that time, they shall be forfeit to the king's behove'. (p. 4.).
54. *Muster and Review*, pp. 119-120.
55. Bibliothèque Nationale, quittances et pièces diverses, ms. fr. 26053/1395.
56. *Muster and Review*, p. 120.
57. *Muster and Review*, p. 131 (Scales), Dom Lenoir vol. 26, f. 193-4 (Talbot). Compare the activities of Woodville and Scales as seneschals: Scales is never seen as a musterer (*Muster and Review*, p. 132, *Stevenson*, vol. 2, pt. 1, pp. lv-lviii). Dr Pollard has communicated the conclusion on Talbot's marshalcy.
58. For example, Archives Nationales, K 67/1/32, 68/12/1, Dom Lenoir, vol. 74, f. 179. Those who have arrived recently from England and who are now living off the land are specifically mentioned. In the years of the truce of Tours, the threefold remedy of prison, transportation back to England and forcible re-recruitment was used. Bibliothèque Nationale, quittances et pièces diverses, ms. fr. 26074/5299.
59. Jarry, *op.cit.* p. 77. *P.O.P.C.* vol. 3, p. 322. *Rot.Parl.* vol. 4, p. 419.
60. B.J.H. Rowe, 'The Grand Conseil under the Duke of Bedford', in *Essays presented to H.E. Salter*, (Oxford, 1934), pp. 224 sq.
61. For instance, Cardinal Beaufort replaced Richard Woodville as captain of Caen and Sir John Fastolf as captain of Honfleur. (*Marshall*, pp. 235-6, 256). The latter also lost the captaincy of Verneuil to Humphrey, Earl of Stafford. (*Ibid*. pp. 274-5). There are several other examples.
62. *P.O.P.C.*, vol. 4, pp. 91 sq. The Council's discussions even threatened Bedford's patrimony of Anjou and Maine. *Ibid*. p. 37.
63. Bibliothèque Nationale, quittances et pièces diverses, ms. fr. 26054/1523. (March, 14231).
64. B.J.H. Rowe, 'The Grand Conseil etc.', p. 225.
65. For instance, indentures after 1435 were made between the King and captain directly, not with the lieutenant-governor. See also *Marshall*, pp. 42 sq. on the situation at Bedford's death.
66. *Stevenson*, vol. 2, pt. 2, pp. 575 sq.
67. *P.O.P.C.* vol. 5, p. 6, *Marshall*, p. 13 (York). *Stevenson*, vol. 2, pt. 1, pp. lxvi sq. (Warwick).
68. For instance, the visits of John Popham. (*P.O.P.C.* vol. 5, pp. 70, 74, 86, 89). The involvement of the Council was formalised in a statement made in 1440. *Stevenson*, vol. 2, pt. 2, p. 455. See also Burney, p. 167, and *Muster and Review*, p. 148.

214

69. *P.O.P.C.* vol. 5, pp. 6, 26.
70. For instance, a council of the Earls of Somerset (lieutenant général sur le fait de la guerre), Dorset, and the Lords Fauconberg and Talbot planned the siege of Dieppe, July, 1440 (Archives Nationales, K 66/1/26).
71. *Rot.Parl.* vol. 5, pp. 32-33.
72. *Muster and Review,* pp. 152-154.
73. *Stevenson,* vol. 2, pt. 2, pp. 585-91.
74. For instance, William Minors was in Bedford's household until the latter's death (Dom Lenoir, vol. 21, f. 275), in limbo from 1435 to 1441, then in the York connection henceforward. (*Marshall,* ch. 3, passim). Significantly York was eager to ensure that he alone had the power to appoint to captaincies. (*Stevenson,* vol. 2, pt. 2, p. 591).
75. C.T. Allmand, *The Relations between the English Government, the Higher Clergy and the Papacy in Normandy, 1417-1450,* (unpub. D.Phil, Oxford, 1962), pp. 164, 170. Louis of Luxembourg as Chancellor of France had pursued a similar policy after the death of Bedford.
76. *P.O.P.C.* vol. 5, pp. 226, 230 sq.
77. *Ibid.* p. 251.
78. *Marshall,* pp. 106, 119, 122. This was also true of the 1450 army. *Ibid.* p. 150.
79. Thomas Hoo, a nominee of the Earl of Suffolk, was Chancellor of France from October, 1444, and was also captain of the key garrison of Mantes. *Burney,* p. 140. It must be remembered, too, that many of the Council were of the younger generation of peers who had never served in the wars.
80. *Rot.Parl.* vol. 5, pp. 147-148. Mention can be made of another quarrel between the Duke of Gloucester and John Talbot over the marshalcy, which Dr. Pollard is studying.
81. For instance, see B.L., Birch Ms. 4101, f. 37-56, and compare with the payment of wages during Bedford's rule in *Rowe,* p. 197.
82. Upton's work on military theory, possibly written shortly before 1446, emphasises the power of the captain over his men. (F.P. Barnard, *op.cit.* pp. 4, 7). François Surienne could not keep in his service the troop with which he had taken Fougères 'as the men-at-arms who were with me were under divers captains of Normandy who each day required them to return to them in their places'. (*Stevenson,* vol. 1, p. 291).
83. J. Lander, 'The Hundred Years War and Edward IV's 1475 campaign in France', in *Crown and Nobility,* (London, 1976). C. Ross, *The Wars of the Roses: a Concise History,* (London, 1976), ch. 4. For comparative studies of European armies in the early modern period, see C. Barnett, *Britain and Her Army, 1509-1970,* (London, 1970), pt. 1.

Index

Kings, queens and princes have been indexed by their Christian names, noblemen by their titles, and bishops by their sees. Many place-names referred to only incidentally have been omitted.

Abergavenny; George Nevill, Lord, (d 1492) 120
Agincourt, campaign 196
Akamatsu, family 147, 152, 161
Akamatsu Mitsusuke 147, 148, 152
Albret, Sire d', Alain le Grand 79
Allington, Sir William 79
Annales of William of Worcester 67
Anthony, Bastard of Burgundy 71
Antigone, dau. Humphrey of Gloucester 17
Arblaster, James 103
Arthur, Prince of Wales (1486-1502) 113, 116, 125
Arthur, Son of Humphrey of Gloucester 17
Arundel, Earls of:
    William FitzAlan (d 1487) 68
    Thomas FitzAlan (d 1524) 66, 68
Arundel, Margaret Wydeville, Countess of 68
Ashikaga, family 145, 146, 147, 148, 160, 161, 162
Ashikaga Takauji 145
Aske, family 47, 48
Aske, Roger 49, 50
Audley, Lords:
    John Tuchet (d 1491) 120
    James Tuchet (d 1497) 120, 123
Ayala, Pedro 128

Babthorpe, family 51
Bacon, Francis 134
Barnard Castle 55, 56
Barnet, Battle of 42
Bath and Wells: Bishops of
    Oliver King 128
    Adriano de Castello 112
Baugé, Battle of 17
Beauchamp, Sir Walter 95, 97, 104
Beaufort, Cardinal, see Winchester, Bishops of
Beaufort, family 19, 20, 22, 24, 25
    see also Somerset
Beaufort, Margaret, see Derby, Margaret Countess of
Beaumont, William Viscount 69
Beckwith, family 51
Bede, prophecies 178
Bedford, Dukes of:
    John (d 1435) 16, 17, 18, 22, 24, 26, 62, 64, 101, 194, 196-208 passim
    Jasper Tudor (d 1495) 65, 113, 116, 121, 122
Bedford, Duchesses of:
    Anne of Burgundy 17
    Jacquetta of Luxemburg 17, 60, 62-64, 66, 67, 68, 71
Berkeley estates 89
Berkeley, James 90
Berners: John Bourchier, Lord (d 1474) 70

216

Bingo Province, Japan 161
Bizen Province, Japan 147, 148, 161
Blore Heath, Battle of 28, 30
Bosworth, Battle of 126: compared with Battle of Sekigahara, 162
Bourchier family 72
Bourchier, Lords:
High Stafford (d 1420) 99
Lewis Robessart (d 1431) 100
Bourchier, Sir Humphrey 70
Bourchier, William Viscount (d 1471) 66, 67
Bourchier, Anne Wydeville, Lady 67
Boynton, Christopher, of Sadbury 48, 49
Brandon, Sir William 87, 88
Bray, Sir Reginald, 101-102, 116, 120, 123, 125, 128, 131
Brian, Richard 43
Broke, Lord, see Willoughby de Brooke
Brompton on Swale 43
Browne, Anthony 103
Brutus 176, 177, 178-179
Buckingham, Dukes of:
Humphrey Stafford (d 1460) 20, 21, 23, 24, 30
Henry Stafford (d 1483) 66, 68, 70, 78, 80, 81, 126
Edward Stafford (d 1521) 91, 99, 100, 101, 104, 105, 114, 120-121
Buckingham, Anne Nevill, Duchess of 21
Burgh family 47, 48
Burgh, John 203
Burgh, Wiliam 43, 45, 47, 49, 50, 53
Burgh, William (the second) 54
Burgundy, Philip Duke of 17
Burgundy, Margaret, Duchess of

Cade, Thomas 104-105

Cadwaladr 176, 177, 178-179, 182, 183, 187
Caister Castle 89
Calais 29, 121
Calthorp, William 95
Cambridge, Richard Earl of (d 1415) 172
Cambridge, Anne Mortimer, Countess of 172
Canterbury, Archbishops of:
Cardinal John Morton (formerly Bishop of Ely) 111, 128
Henry Deane 111
William Warham 111
Catterick family 47
Catterick, John 50
Chancery, Court of 92, 93
Charles VI, King of France 16, as Dauphin 31
Charles VII, King of France 23, 24, 198
Chester 29, 30
Chester, County of 65, 76
Chetwynd, Sir Philip 94
Cheyne, Sir Hugh 100-101
Chronicle of the Lincolnshire Rebellion 41, 42
Chronicle of Onin 149-150, 153, 156-157
Clarence, Dukes of:
Lionel (d 1368) 13, 16, 19, 20, 25, 30, 172
Thomas (d 1421) 16, 17, 102
George (d 1478) 41, 66, 69, 72, 74, 80, 81
Claxton, Lionel 54
Claxton of Claxton, family 48
Clerionet, William 45
Clervaux family 47, 48, 50
Clervaux, Marmaduke 55
Clervaux, Sir Richard, of Croft 45, 48, 49, 50, 51, 52, 54-55, 56

Cleseby, Elizabeth 48
Cleseby family 48
Clifford, Henry Lord (d 1523) 132
Clifton, Sir Gervaise 70
Colville family 45
Common Pleas, Court of 91, 119, 132
Commynes, Philippe de 98
Compendium Historiae in Genealogia Christi 173
Conyers, Christopher 48, 49
Conyers family, 48, 51, 53, 56; of Hornby 44, 47; of Wynyard 48
Conyers, Sir John 41, 42, 48, 49, 50 53, 54, 56
Conyers, Sir Richard 43, 53, 56
Conyers, Richard 53
Conyers, Roger 48, 53
Conyers, Sir William 37, 41, 48
Conyers, William, 48, 53; son of Sir John 56; of Wynyard 48
Cornwall, Duchy of 65, 73
Council, Royal 128-134
Councillors, remuneration 102-103
Coverham Abbey 46
Croft, Sir Richard 78
Cromwell, Ralph Lord (d 1455) 104
Croyland, Chronicler 126

Dacre of the North, Thomas Lord (d 1525), 118-119, 133
Dacre of the South, Richard Fiennes, Lord (d 1484) 76, 77, 79
Danby, Sir Robert 49, 51
Darcy, Thomas Lord (d 1538) 48
Daubeney, Giles Lord (d 1508) 115, 121, 128, 131
De la Pole family 21
Deepham, Manor of 104
Derby, Thomas Stanley, Earl of (d 1504) 114, 121
Derby, Margaret Beaufort, Countess of 19, 21, 22, 101, 114, 126, 128

De Vere estates 94
De Vere family 103
Devereux, Sir Walter 101
Devon, Edward Courtenay, Earl of (d 1509) 112, 123
Doget, John 132
Donne family 71
Dorset, Marquesses of:
Thomas Grey (d. 1501) 60, 66, 68, 73, 79, 80, 114
Thomas Grey, 2nd Marquess (d 1530) 74
see also Somerset, Dukes of
Dorset, Cecily Bonvile, Lady 73
Dudley, Edward Lord (d 1531)
Dudley, Edmund 121, 123, 128, 130
Dunster, Lord, see Pembroke, Earls of
Durham, Bishop of 92
Durham, Thomas Ruthall, Bishop of 128
Dynham, John Lord (d 1508) 123, 125
Dyve, John 70

Edgecote, Battle of 41
Edward I, King of England 177, 184; parallels with mediaeval Japan 144, 145, 146
Edward II, King of England, parallels with mediaeval Japan 146
Edward III, King of England 13, 172, 176-177, 179, 180, 186, 187, 188, 193; parallels with mediaeval Japan 146
Edward IV, King of England 26, 41, 42, 64-78 passim, 81, 82, 83, 87, 90, 98, 109, 110, 113, 115, 120, 121, 126, 130, 172, 174, 176, 177, 179-185 passim; as Earl of March, 23, 29, 171; parallels with mediaeval Japan 160

Edward V, (Prince of Wales 1471-1483) King of England, 75-76, 77, 78, 79, 80, 81

Edward Prince of Wales, Son of Edward III (1330-1376) 90, 180, 182, 187

Edward Prince of Wales, Son of Henry VI (1453-1471) 16, 26, 27, 31

Elizabeth Wydeville, Queen of England 63, 64, 65, 68, 71, 72, 73, 74, 77, 79, 99-100, 114

Elizabeth of York, Queen of England 114

Ely, Bishops of:
John Alcock (formerly Bishop of Worcester) 75, 77, 78, 81
James Stanley 114

Empson, Sir Richard   129, 130

England, throne of 15; claim to 20; law of succession to 19

Englefield, Thomas   128

Essex, Henry Bourchier, Earl of (d 1483) 90, 94

Exeter, Dukes of:
John Holand (d 1400) 92
Thomas Beaufort (d 1426) 19, 102
John Holand (d 1447) 20, 21, 104
Henry Holand (d 1475), 20, 21, 24, 27, 28, 68

Exeter, Anne of York, Duchess of 19, 68

Exchequer, Court of   93, 119

Fairfax, Sir Guy   50

Fastolf, Sir John 62, 101, 102, 204-205

Fauconberg, William Nevill, Lord (d 1462) 48

Ferrers, Eleanor Lady   94

Ferrers of Charley, Walter

Devereux, Lord (d 1485) 78, 81

Ferrers of Groby, Edward Grey, Lord (d 1457) 63

Ferrers of Groby, Elizabeth, Lady 63

Fitton, Thomas, of Cawarden   50

FitzHenry family   48

FitzHenry, John   55

FitzHugh, Henry, Lord (d 1472) 42, 44, 45

FitzRandall family   44, 48

FitzRandall, Ralph   54

FitzWalter, John, Lord (d 1496) 132

FitzWilliam of Sprotburgh, family 48

Fogge family   71

Fogge, Sir John   77

Fortescue, Sir John   87, 112, 160

Fountains Abbey   46

Framlinghams, ducal council at 89

Frank family   48

Frank, Thomas   50

Frowyk, Thomas   126

Fulthorpe, Alan   49, 50

Garter King of Arms   45

Gascoigne family   51

Gascoigne, William   52

Gate, Sir Geoffrey   66, 74

Geoffrey of Monmouth 175-176, 177, 178, 179, 182, 183, 184

Gildas prophecies   178, 183

Gloucester, Dukes of:
Thomas of Woodstock (d 1397) 20, 92, 97
Humphrey (d 1447), 16, 17, 18, 19, 21, 24, 26, 27, 102
Richard, see under *Richard III*

Gloucester, Duchesses of:
Jacqueline of Hainault 17
Eleanor Cobham 17, 18

Glyndwr, Owain   177, 185

Gower, Thomas   203

Grafton, Richard 13
Green, Godfrey 52
Grey, John, of Groby 63
Grey of Powis, Edward Lord (d 1544) 133
Grey of Ruthin, Lord, see *Kent, Earls of*
Grey, Richard 60, 73, 74, 80
Greystoke, Ralph Lord (d 1487) 44
Guildford, Sir John 75
Guildford, Sir Richard 131
Gwynedd, House of 176
Gwladys Ddn 176

Hall, Edward 13; work compared with *Chronicle of Onin* 147
Hamerton family 51
Hastings family 71
Hastings, Sir John 119
Hastings, Lords:
William (d 1483) 52, 65, 69, 73, 80, 82, 103
Edward (d 1506) 133
Hastings, William 91
Hatakeyama family 155
Hante family 71
Hante, Jacques 70
Henry II, King of England, parallels with mediaeval Japan 144
Henry IV, King of England 15, 16, 19, 179, 181, 185, 188; parallels with mediaeval Japan 148
Henry V (Prince of Wales 1399-1413) King of England, 15, 16, 26, 183, 195, 196, 199, 202; parallels with mediaeval Japan 146-147
Henry VI, King of England 13-30 passim, 62, 64, 65, 104, 109, 110, 126, 171, 172, 173, 179, 181, 184; parallels with mediaeval Japan 144, 147, 149, 150-156 passim

Henry VII, King of England, 14, 22, 37, 56, 91, 105, 109-134 passim; parallels with mediaeval Japan 161, 162
Henry VIII, Prince of Wales (1504-1509), King of England 113, 114, 117, 120
Herbert, Lord, see *Pembroke, Earl of*
Herbert, William 81
Hereford, Thomas Millyng, Bishop of (formerly Abbot of Westminster) 76, 77, 81
Heydon, John 95
Historia Regum Britanniae 176, 179, 184
Historie of the Arrivall 42
Hulyard of Holderness 42
Hobart, James 125
Holand estates 81
Holand family 20, 24, 25
Hornby family 47
Hosokawa family 151, 152, 155
Hosokawa Katsumoto 152, 155, 156-8
Household, Royal 126-127
Howard, John Lord, see *Norfolk, Dukes of*
Hundred Years War 193
Hunt, Roger 95, 97
Huntingdon, William Herbert, Earl of (d 1491) 66, 69, 78, 80-81
Huntingdon, Anne Holand, Countess of 66, 68, 73
Huntingdon, Mary Wydeville, Countess of, 81
Hussey family 47

Ingleby family 44, 48, 49, 51
Ingleby, William 54
Ise Sadachika 153
Isham, Robert 70

220

James II, King of Scots 28
Jeanne of France 23
Jervaulx Abbey 46
Jinson, Abbot 159-160
John, King of England 185; parallel with mediaeval Japan 145
John of Bridlington, prophecy 180-182

Kamakura Shogunate 144-145
Kantō Provinces, Japan 148
Katherine of Valois, Queen of England 27
Kent, Earls of:
Edmund Grey (d 1490) 66, 68, 81, 95
George Grey (d 1503) 66, 68
Richard Grey (d 1523) 120, 123
Killinghall, John 50
Kings Bench, Court of 91, 132
Kings Lynn 79
Knaresborough, Honour of 51
Kyoto, Japan 145, 150, 153, 155, 156, 157, 158, 159, 160-161, 162

Lancaster, Duchy of, 65, 76, 91, 102, 105
Lancaster, House of, 14, 15, 16, 17, 19-20, 171, 176, 180, 182; parallels with mediaeval Japan 151, 152
Lancaster, John of Gaunt, Duke of (d 1399) 16, 19, 20, 172
Lancaster, Thomas, Earl of (d 1322), parallels with mediaeval Japan 146
Langton of Wynyard, family 48
Langton, Sybil 48
Lascelles family 44, 47, 48, 53
Latimer, George Nevill, Lord (d 1469) 41, 44, 49
Laton family 44, 48

Laybourne, Roger 131
Lewis, Sir Henry 75
Lincoln, Bishops of:
Richard Fleming 90
William Smith 111, 116
William Atwater 111
Lincolnshire County of 47
Lisle, John Grey, Viscount (d 1504) 123-124
Lisle, Muriel Howard, Lady 123-124
Llywelyn the Great 176
Llywelyn the Last 177
Lockwood family 45
Longworth, Maykin 203
Losecoat Field 41
Louis XI, King of France 98; as Dauphin 23, 24
Lovell, Francis Viscount (d 1487) 56
Lovell, Sir Thomas 128, 130, 131
Lovell of Bedale 44
Lucas, Thomas 113
Ludford Bridge, Battle of 28, 30
Ludlow Castle 76
Lumley family 47
Luxembourg, Louis of 205

Madeleine of France 23
Maldon, Bailiff of 103
Maltravers, Thomas FitzAlan, Lord (d 1524) 78, 81
Mancini, Dominic 83
March, Roger Mortimer, Earl of (d 1398) 94, 100-101
March, Earldom of 76
March, East, towards Scotland 118-119
March, West, towards Scotland 118-119
Marches, Council of 75-79, 80
Marches, Welsh 93
Margaret of Anjou, Queen of England 19, 22, 23, 26, 27, 31,

171; parallels with mediaeval Japan 156, 159

Margaret of Scotland, Dauphiness France 23

Markenfield family 44, 48

Markenfield, Thomas 54, 56

Marie, dau. of John Duke of Bedford 17

Masham, Presbendary of 46

Matsuda family 147, 161

Metcalfe, Thomas 43

Merlin, prophecies 178, 182, 187

Metcalfe family 53

Metham family 44

Middleham, Lords of 44, 45, 53, 54, 55, 56

Middleham, Lordship of 37, 42, 53

Mill, Thomas 97

Montague, John Nevill, Marquis of (d 1471) 41

Mortimer, Anne, see under *Cambridge, Anne Countess of*

Mortimer family 176, 188

Mortimer, Ralph 176

Mountjoy, William Blount, Lord (d 1534), 66, 97

Mount Grace Priory 50

Mountfords of Hackforths family 44, 48

Mountford, Thomas 49, 50, 54, 56

Mowbray, Anne 79

Mowbray estates, 81-82

Nedeham, John 50

Nevill family 42, 44, 47, 52, 53, 56, 65, 66, 68, 69, 72, 82; parallels with mediaeval Japan, 148, 152. See also *Warwick & Salisbury*

Nevill, Sir Henry 41

Nevill, Thomas, Bastard of Fauconberg, parallels with mediaeval Japan 159

Nicholson, Richard of Hornby 41

Norfolk, Dukes of:
John Mowbray, 2nd Duke (d 1432) 95
John Mowbray, 3rd Duke (d 1461) 20, 87, 88, 102
John Howard (d 1485) 82
Thomas Howard (d 1524) 97, 117

Norfolk, Katherine, Dowager Duchess of 66, 68, 69

Northampton, Battle of 30, 31

Northumberland, Earls of:
Henry Percy, 4th Earl (d 1489) 52, 82, 99, 116
Henry Percy, 5th Earl (d 1527) 100, 103, 116, 117, 118, 119, 120, 122, 127

Norton family 44, 53

Norwich, Robert 95

Oda Nobunaga 162

Ogard, Sir Arthur 101

Oldhall, Sir William 97-98, 101, 102

Onin War 148-163 passim

Orleans, siege of 198, 200, 201, 202, 202-203, 204

Ormond, Thomas Butler, Earl of (d 1515) 90, 123, see also *Wiltshire, Earls of*

Otter, Thomas 45

Oxford, Earls of 92, 94:
John de Vere, 13th Earl (d 1513) 96, 121
John de Vere, 15th Earl (d 1540) 103

Paston, Sir John 42, 70, 87, 89, 96, 97, 103-104

Peerage under Henry VII 112-115, 123

Pembroke, William Herbert, Earl of (d 1469) 65, 68, 72 see also *Bedford, Dukes of*

Percy Council 103
Percy family 44, 52, 118, 185; parallels with mediaeval Japan 148, 152. See also *Northumberland*
Peter of Poitiers 173
Pickering family 48
Pigot family 44, 51
Pigot, John 49
Pigot, Randolph 49, 54
Pigot, Richard 49, 50, 51
Place family 48
Place, Roland 51, 55
Plantagenet, Henry 19
Plantagenet, Ursula 19
Plumpton papers 43, 51, 52
Plumpton, Sir William 52
Powtrell, Thomas 97
Poynings, Sir Edward 131
Protectorate of England 26-28
Pudsey family 48
Pudsey, Roland 53
Pudsey, William 50

Ratcliffe, Sir Richard 55
Recognisances 121-122
Retaining, policy of Henry VII 115
Richard II, King of England 13, 179, 181, 185, 187, 188; parallels with mediaeval Japan 146
Richard III, King of England, Duke of Gloucester 26, 43, 50, 52, 53, 54, 55, 56, 80, 82, 83, 120, 121
Richard, Duke of York, brother of Edward V 79
Richard, son of John Duke of Bedford 17
Richmond, Edmund Tudor, Earl of 22, 65
Richmond, Honour of 37, 44, 52, 53
Richmondshire, Archdeaconry of 37, 46, 50

Risely, Sir John 131
Rivers, Earls
    Richard Wydeville (d 1469) 60, 62, 63-64, 66, 67, 68, 71, 72
    Anthony Wydeville (d 1483) 63, 64, 66, 69, 70, 73, 74, 75, 77, 78, 79, 80, 82, 83, 100
Rivers, Countesses
    Elizabeth Scales 70, 74
    Mary Lewis 74
Robin of Redesdale 37, 41
Robinson, John 53
Roche Fen, Norfolk 75
Rochester, Bishop of see *Ely, Bishop of*
Roger of St Albans 173, 174
Romagière, Charles de la 93
Roos, Thomas, Lord (d 1464) 74
Roos, Philippa, Lady 74-75
Roses, Wars of the 14, 15, 23, 208; parallels with the Onin War 151-155 passim, 159-163 passim

St Agatha, Easby, Abbey of 43, 46, 50
St Albans, Abbey of 92
St Albans, 1st Battle of 30
St Albans, 2nd Battle of 171
St Asaph, Richard Redman, Bishop of 111-112
St Davids, Richard Martin, Bishop of 81
St Mary's Abbey, York 46, 49, 50
Salisbury, Richard Nevill, Earl of (d 1460) 28, 45, 49, 52, 53, 54, 171, 204
Saltmarsh family 44, 47
Say, William Fiennes, Lord (d 1471) 68
Scales family 75
Scales, Lady, see under *Rivers, Elizabeth, Countess of*

Scales, Thomas, Lord (d 1460) 203
Scrope of Bolton, Lords:
    Henry, (d 1458) 43, 44
    John, (d 1498) 48, 49
Scrope of Bolton, Mary, Lady 48
Scrope of Masham, Thomas, Lord
    (d 1575) 41, 42, 44
Sekigahara, Battle of 162
Sever, William 117
Shaa, John 127
Shakespeare, William, *Henry VI* 22, 23
Sheffield, Sir Robert 127
Sheriff, Office of 125-126
Shiba family 155
Shrewsbury, John Talbot, Earl of
    (d 1453) 78, 203
Simeon, Geoffrey 111
Somerset, Dukes of:
    John Beaufort (d 1444) 20, 21,
    64, 102, 207
    Edmund Beaufort (d 1455) 21,
    24, 27, 75, 207; parallels with
    mediaeval Japan 155
Somerset, John Beaufort, Earl of
    (d 1410) 19
South Cowton, Manor of 45, 55,
    56
Southwell, Robert 131
Spylleman, Henry 95
Stafford Council 97
Stafford, Earls of:
    Thomas (d 1392) 97
    Humphrey (d 1458) 21, 22
    see also *Gloucester, Thomas
    Duke of*, and *Buckingham,
    Dukes of*
Stafford, Margaret Beaufort,
    Countess of 21
Stafford family 20, 22, 25, 102
Stafford, Henry 22
Stafford, Sir Humphrey 90
Stanley, Lord, see *Derby, Earl of*

Stanley, Edward 114-115
Stanley family 78, 79, 114, 120
Stanley, George 78
Stanley, Sir William 78, 114
Stapleton, Anthony 103
Star Chamber, Court of 132
Stockdale, John 45
Stockdale, Thomas 45
Stockdale, William 45
Stonor, William 97
Strange of Knockin, John, Lord
    (d 1477) 63, 78, 81
Strange of Knockin, Jacquette
    Wydeville, Lady 63
Strangways family 44, 48, 51
Strangways, Sir James 47, 49, 50
Strangways, Sir James junior 49, 54
Succession to English throne, law
    of 19
Suffolk, Dukes of:
    William de la Pole (d 1450) 20,
    28, 64, 207
    John de la Pole (d 1492) 21, 133
Suffolk, Edmund de la Pole, Earl of
    (d 1513) 120
Surrey, Thomas Holand, Duke of
    (d 1400) 92
Surrey, Thomas Howard, Earl of
    see *Norfolk, Dukes of*
Surtees, Thomas 49
Swaldale family 45
Swaldale, Thomas 43

Talbot, Lord see *Shrewsbury, Earl of*
Testamenta Eboracensia 43
Tewkesbury, Battle of 42
Thomson, John 45
Thomson, John of Bedale 50
Throckmorton, John 96
Tokugawa Ieyasu 162
Tomiko, Lady 155, 156-157
Toyotomi Hideyoshi 162

Troyes, Treaty of   31, 194
Tudor, House of   14, 105
Tunstall, Sir Richard   54
Tunstall, Thomas   54
Tynemouth, Prior of   103

Urakami family   147, 161

Vaughan, Thomas   76, 77, 78
Vavasour family of Haslewood 47,
    51
Vergil, Polydore 13, 14, 15, 37, 56,
    122
Vincent family   45
Vincent, Roger   49

Wakefield, Battle of   171
Wales, Principality of   76, 93
Wales, Tudor policy towards 116
Wandesford family   44, 49
Wandesford, John   49
Warbeck, Perkin   112
Warkworth, John   37, 41, 160
Warwick, Earls of:
    ThomasBeauchamp (d 1401) 92
    Richard Beauchamp (d 1439)
    89, 90, 95, 96, 104, 201, 205
    Richard Nevill (d 1471) 29, 30,
    41, 42, 52, 53, 54, 55, 56, 66,
    72, 98, 171
    Edward Plantagenet (d 1499) 74
Welles, John Viscount   112, 113
Weltden, Christopher   45
Weltden family   47
Weltden, John   45
Wenlock, John, Lord (d 1471)   98
Westminster Abbots of see Here-
    ford, Bishop of
Westmorland, Earls of:
    Ralph Nevill, 1st Earl (d 1425)
    21
    Ralph Nevill, 2nd Earl (d 1484)
    44

Ralph Nevill, 3rd Earl (d 1499)
    91, 118
Westmorland,   Joan   Beaufort,
    Countess of   19, 21
Whitgreve, Robert   94
Willoughby de Broke, Lords:
    Robert (d 1502) 115
    Robert (d 1521) 120
Willoughby de Broke, Maud, Lady
    69, 75
Wiltshire, Earls of:
    James Butler (d 1461) 90
    Henry Stafford (d 1523) 101
Winchester, Bishops of:
    Henry, Cardinal Beaufort 19,
    20, 204
    Richard Fox 111, 112, 117, 128
Witham, Thomas   49
Worcester, Bishops of:
    Giovanni de Gigli (d 1498) 112
    see also Ely, Bishop of
Worcester, John Tiptoft, Earl of 66
Worcestre, pseudo William of   67
Wycliffe family   48
Wycliffe, John   50
Wycliffe, Robert   53
Wydeville, Sir Edward   73, 75
Wydeville family 60, 63-73 passim
    75, 77, 78, 80, 83 see also
    Elizabeth Wydeville and Rivers
Wydeville, Sir John   66, 68, 69, 70
Wydeville, Richard   60, 62
Wydeville, Sir Richard   69, 70, 73
Wydeville, Thomas

Yamana family 151, 152, 155, 161
Yamana Sōzen   152, 155, 157-158
Yonge, Thomas   25
Yoritomo   144
York, Archbishops of:
    Thomas Savage 117-118, 128
    Thomas, Cardinal Wolsey 91
York, Dukes of:

Edmund of Langley (d 1402) 172

Richard Plantagenet (d 1460) 13, 14, 15, 19, 20, 21, 23, 24, 25, 27, 28, 29, 20, 31, 97, 98, 101, 102, 171, 172, 187, 188, 205, 206; parallels with mediaeval Japan 153, 155, 156 see also *Richard (d 1483)*

York, Cecily Nevill, Duchess of 19, 114

York, City of 37, 41, 56

York, House of 14, 171, 176, 179, 180; parallels with mediaeval Japan 151, 152

Yoshihisa 156, 160

Yoshimasa 144, 149-156 passim 160

Yoshimi 156-157, 158

Yoshimitsu 144, 146, 147

Yoshimochi 147

Yoshinori 147, 148, 152, 153